Mary Queen of Scots
and the Casket Letters

For our grandchildren,
Elizabeth, Thomas and Iona

Mary Queen of Scots and the Casket Letters

AE MacRobert

I.B. Tauris *Publishers*
LONDON • NEW YORK

Published in 2002 by I.B.Tauris & Co Ltd
6 Salem Road, London W2 4BU
175 Fifth Avenue, New York NY 10010
www.ibtauris.com

In the United States of America and in Canada distributed by
Palgrave Macmillan, a division of St Martins Press,
175 Fifth Avenue, New York NY 10010

ISBN 1-86064-829-0

A full CIP record for this book is available from the British Library
A full CIP record for this book is available from the Library of Congress

Library of Congress catalog card: available

Project management by Steve Tribe, London
Printed and bound in Great Britain by MPG Books Ltd, Bodmin

CONTENTS

ILLUSTRATIONS

PREFACE AND ACKNOWLEDGEMENTS

Mary Queen of Scots and the Casket Letters investigates the most controversial and misunderstood passage in Scottish History. The aim is to unravel what actually happened during the years 1567–68 from the myths and lies and misconceptions which have persisted for over four centuries. The original evidence has been re-examined rigorously and many new questions have been raised and probed. There is a detailed analysis of the events and the Casket Letters. The result is a much-needed measure of historical revision.

Quotations from documents have in some cases been given in modern English to facilitate understanding, but even that does not always bridge the gap between sixteenth-century and present-day minds. It should nevertheless be appreciated that what may seem stilted or obscure today may have been very clear over 400 years ago, especially to the recipient. No alterations, however, have been made to the texts of the Casket Letters.

In references to the Casket Letters, the Letters are spelt with a capital L to distinguish them from other correspondence. The famous Casket is also shown with a capital C. Readers who have not previously seen the Casket Letters may wish to have a quick perusal of them in the Appendices before reading Chapter 5.

Sources have been quoted especially for those documents which may otherwise be difficult to trace. In some books there is confusion whether references to documents in the Calendars of State Papers are to the pages or the item numbers. In this book the references are to the item numbers in the Calendars, unless otherwise stated.

I wish to record my appreciation of assistance from Glasgow University Library, the National Library of Scotland, the Scottish Record Office, the Public Record Office in London, the British Library, Hatfield House Library, the Mitchell Library in Glasgow, the National Museums of Scotland and the Royal Commission on Historical Manuscripts; information from the Department of Midwifery in Glasgow University; advice and encouragement from Dr Lester Crook; the conversion of the manuscript into a typescript by Allander Office Services, Milngavie and Southpark Secretarial Services, Springholm, and for the scanning of the text by Southwest Business Services, Dumfries; and assistance from Alison Walker.

The author and publishers wish to thank the following for supplying illustrations and for their permissions to reproduce them in this book: Glasgow Museums (nos 1, 5 and 6); Mr John F Walker (2); Historic Scotland (3); Glasgow City Libraries (4); Scottish National Portrait Gallery (7, 8, 9, 10); Public Record Office, Kew (14); National Portrait Gallery, London (15); by courtesy of the Marquess of Salisbury (16).

1. INTRODUCTION

THE CASKET LETTERS WERE the documents allegedly contained in a Casket belonging to James Hepburn, Earl of Bothwell, the third husband of Mary Queen of Scots. The Casket was seized in June 1567 by Mary's opponents, who claimed that the contents proved that she and Bothwell conspired to murder her second husband Henry Stuart, Lord Darnley, at Kirk o'Field in Edinburgh early on 10 February 1567.

The documents, which were eventually displayed for scrutiny at Westminster in December 1568, comprised eight Letters and twelve Sonnets, all originally written in French, and two Marriage Contracts between Mary and Bothwell. It was asserted that Mary had written the Letters to Bothwell and that she had composed the Sonnets for him. The Letters are usually numbered from I to VIII but the actual sequence shown by historians should be checked.

For over 400 years there has been a lively and often acrimonious debate among historians over the questions of Mary's involvement in the murder and the authenticity of the Casket Letters. One of the main reasons why the debate has continued is that the original documents disappeared about 1584. Arguments and theories have therefore been based on what can be gleaned from the copies and translations made in 1568. It is unlikely that any further evidence of much significance will be found.

There are three main reasons for producing now another book on the Casket Letters. First, the starting-point for this book was interest in the arguments over the authenticity of the Casket Letters. Their evaluation requires a detailed study of the documents. Although copies of the full set of the Casket Letters are available in several books, these are relatively old and not very accessible. It is therefore opportune to provide a new set.

Secondly, the Casket Letters cannot just be pushed to one side and ignored. These Letters comprised the core of the evidence against Mary for complicity in the murder of Darnley. They provided the excuse for Elizabeth to keep her as a prisoner in England, and they stained her reputation across western Europe. If they were completely genuine, they prove her guilt. If they are shown to be false evidence, they not merely go far to exonerate Mary but also cast grave doubts on the integrity of

1

her opponents and the critical faculties of contemporaries and historians who accepted them as genuine. They are documents of great historical importance.

Thirdly, historians should always aim at presenting an accurate and balanced account of the past. This obligation is particularly important for the sequence of events in 1567. What happened had profound consequences for the future development of Scotland and England and the rest of western Europe. Yet there is no agreed version or interpretation of these events. Many accounts of the crisis, moreover, are inaccurate and very misleading.

As a result of the drastic re-evaluation in this book, several new lines of enquiry have been started. What happened was probably much more complicated than is shown in most standard histories. It is therefore essential to appreciate that the contemporary sources for the study of this period in Scottish history are very limited. The most useful are the Calendars of State Papers held in London. They contain mainly correspondence involving the English government, such as despatches from the English ambassadors in Edinburgh. These State Papers do not necessarily disclose the full or the correct facts and it is also important to allow for bias. It is very regrettable that there may be significant gaps in the surviving Scottish Records. Cromwell's army in 1651 seized most of the Scottish Records and sent them to London. In 1660 a ship bringing back many of the Records encountered a gale and foundered. There are also several valuable collections of letters and documents, such as those of James Anderson (1727) and Robert Keith (1734), followed in the mid-nineteenth century by those of Prince Labanoff and Alexandre Teulet.

There are two important Memoirs – those of Sir James Melville and Lord Herries – but they were written at much later dates and may have been influenced by hindsight or other writings. Melville was a well-known courtier in Mary's reign, but it is probable that he wrote his Memoirs in the early years of the seventeenth century. The Herries Memoirs[1] were almost certainly not written by the fourth Lord Herries who accompanied Mary across the Solway in May 1568, but possibly they may contain information from him or his heir. The Memoirs may not have been compiled until the mid-seventeenth century. A more suitable title for them would be 'An Abridgement of the Scottish History by Lord Herries'. This was the title given to them by the person with the initials JP, who wrote a transcript of part of the Abridgement in the mid-eighteenth century. That is the only surviving portion.

A Memoir in French entitled *Les affaires du Comte de Boduel* (Bothwell) has survived.[2] Apparently Bothwell wrote it in Copenhagen in January 1568 after escaping from Scotland. The authenticity of this

Memoir has not been established, but it has been assumed that Bothwell at least supplied the details. Many important events are omitted or avoided. The original of an alleged Testament by Bothwell before his death in 1578 has disappeared, but the internal evidence from copies casts doubt on its authenticity.[3]

Three diaries include brief references to the events of 1567–68. The author of the *Diurnal of Remarkable Occurrents* is unknown but he was an Edinburgh citizen who did not have access to inside information.[4] The *Diary* of Robert Birrel covers the wide span from 1532 to 1605.[5] Nothing is known of him except that he was also an Edinburgh citizen. His diary is a simple terse record of events and has long gaps. A diary of events leading to the murder of Darnley and continuing as far as the Battle of Langside in 1568 was produced by the Earl of Moray at Westminster in 1568 for the benefit of the English Commissioners examining the Casket Letters. It is referred to as Moray's or Cecil's *Diary* or *Journal*.[6] The actual compiler is not known.

John Knox did not finish his *History of the Reformation in Scotland*, and his text reached only 1564. A book written by an anonymous Continuator extended Knox's *History* to 1567.[7] This additional book was first published in 1644. It is not known when it was written, but it may contain material which Knox intended to use. Knox's *History* must be regarded as a partisan version of events. Likewise, George Buchanan's *Summary* in Latin (*De Maria Scotorum Regina*) of Mary's alleged misdeeds and his *History of Scotland* (1582) have to be read with caution. Buchanan was unscrupulous.[8] Darnley's father, the Earl of Lennox, wrote an account of the events prior to the death of his son.[9] This *First Narrative*, or draft *Bill of Supplication to Queen Elizabeth*, is a complete distortion of his son's disreputable record. In the late autumn of 1568 Lennox's material was combined with the *Indictment*[10] – a loose translation of Buchanan's *Summary* – to form the *Book of Articles*. No copy of the *Book of Articles* has survived, but a manuscript found in the collection of the Earl of Hopetoun is probably very similar to the final version.[11] A translation of Buchanan's Latin *Summary* was published in 1571 and is known as the *Detection*.[12] An anonymous tract known as the *Oration* (*Actio Contra Mariam*) was included in the same volume.

There were few contemporary documents defending Mary. John Leslie wrote 'A defence of the Honour of Mary Queen of Scotland' in 1569, but it contained few facts. Her own recollections are almost certainly contained in the 'Memorials of Mary Stewart'.[13] These were written by her secretary, Claude Nau, who was in her service between 1575 and 1586, but they have to be read with caution.

In the crisis of 1567 there were great issues at stake. Many of the leading persons were prepared to resort to intrigue, deceit, forgery and even murder to achieve their goals. A strong impression from the contemporary evidence is that facts are remarkably elusive. It is therefore essential to establish what are the undisputed facts so that everything else can be re-examined.

Part 1

The Crisis of 1567–68

2. FACT

MARY'S REIGN FROM 1542 TO 1565

MARY WAS BORN IN December 1542 just a few days before the death of her father James V, and she succeeded him on the throne. The English attempted by diplomacy and then by ferocious invasions to obtain Mary as a bride for Edward, the son of Henry VIII, so that England would gain control of Scotland. In order to protect Mary, the Scots sent her to France in 1548. In 1558 she was married to the Dauphin, Francis, who was a year younger and of poor physique. In 1559 Francis became King of France but died in December 1560. Meanwhile Mary's French mother, Mary of Guise, had acted as her Regent in Scotland from 1554 until her death in 1560. With help from French soldiers she had tried to maintain the Catholic religion in Scotland, but with English support the Protestants had prevailed. Mary decided to go back to Scotland and arrived by sea at Leith in August 1561. She returned to a country which was under Protestant control and had also been in turmoil for much of the preceding two decades.

Despite all the difficulties confronting Mary on her return to Scotland she was remarkably successful in giving stability to the country for the next four years. During this period she relied to a considerable extent on advice from her eldest surviving half-brother, Lord James Stewart, who was an illegitimate son of James V and a leader of the Scottish Protestants. In January 1562 Mary created him Earl of Moray. He was an able and astute man who followed three main interests: the protection of the Protestant religion, the maintenance of good relations with Protestant England, and the advancement of his own position. Mary retained the Protestant settlement but insisted on practising her own faith.

A surprising degree of religious toleration for those times was maintained after the heat of the religious turmoil in 1558–60. The only serious opposition to Mary's authority came – unexpectedly – from the Catholic 4th Earl of Huntly, who in 1562 opposed her progress (visit) to Inverness. Huntly was probably jealous of Moray's growing prominence and power. Royal authority was asserted against 'an overmighty subject', even though Huntly was a Catholic.

Mary's own interests during those four years concentrated on trying to establish a friendship with Queen Elizabeth in the hope of being recognised as her heir, and also on looking for a husband of appropriate rank. It was important for Mary to remarry again and produce an heir, as otherwise she would have no clear successor and there would be civil war after her death. It was, however, very difficult to find a suitable husband among the princes of Europe. Her choice of husband was her first major mistake and proved to be a blunder of considerable magnitude. Lord Darnley, son of the Earl of Lennox, returned from England in February 1565. He possessed both Stewart and Tudor royal blood and was a tall, handsome young man, three years younger than Mary. Although he had attended Protestant services in England, his mother was a Catholic and he was regarded by many as a Catholic. Mary was attracted to him and before discovering his many weaknesses she married him in July 1565. Mary gave Darnley the title of King but not the crown matrimonial, which would have given him the right to succeed her if she died without an heir. Moray and some of the other Protestant nobles feared that the marriage would lead to an attack on the Protestant religion and started a rebellion. They did not, however, obtain widespread approval, and the Queen, with substantial support from both Protestants and Catholics, was able to force Moray and his supporters to seek refuge in England in what was called the Chaseabout Raid.

THE DANGER TO MARY FROM DARNLEY

Before the end of 1565 Mary began to realise the extent of Darnley's faults and vices: his neglect of official business, his drunkenness and wantonness. Her own position was becoming too isolated with the defection of Moray and her growing disdain for Darnley. Increasingly she relied on her secretary for French correspondence, David Riccio, who was an Italian, to conduct her business. Riccio, however, became unpopular as a foreigner of relatively humble origins; as a suspected Papal agent (but there is no proof of that); and on account of his growing arrogance. At the same time Darnley became jealous of Riccio's influence and resentful of Mary's refusal to give more authority to himself. His jealousy was stimulated by false insinuations that Riccio had become his wife's lover.

Although Darnley lacked the ability to apply himself to work, he was ambitious and was aiming at supplanting Mary as the monarch. The result was a conspiracy between Darnley and a group of Protestant nobles including Morton, Ruthven, Lindsay and Moray. The nobles promised to grant the crown matrimonial to Darnley and to support him in his claim to the crown if Mary died without issue, while Darnley promised to obtain their remissions and not allow any forfeitures or diminutions of their estates. Implicit in their agreements was the intention to get rid of Riccio.[1] This led to the murder of Riccio on the evening of 9 March 1566 while attending a small dinner-party given by Mary in the Palace of Holyrood. Mary was heavily pregnant at the time, and the murder could have led to a miscarriage and also her own death.

Late on the following day Moray arrived from England. Meanwhile Mary had persuaded Darnley to abandon the other conspirators, and in the early hours of 12 March she and Darnley escaped to Dunbar. Mary with the help of the Earl of Bothwell was able to raise a substantial force and she quickly regained control of Edinburgh from the conspirators. Some of her opponents, including Morton, Lindsay and Ruthven, fled to England. Mary split her opponents by offering pardons to those, such as Moray, who had taken part in the Chaseabout Raid but had not been present at Riccio's murder.

The Queen's position, despite her successful return, had become even more isolated. Now there were very few of the nobles whom she could trust. One of the few was Bothwell. He had led her forces in routing Moray in 1565 and he had again proved his loyalty at the time of Riccio's murder. Mary turned more and more to Bothwell for advice. At the same time her dislike for Darnley had turned into loathing for his part in the murder of Riccio and the threat to her own life. The birth of Prince James in June did not mend the breakdown between Mary and Darnley.

Although Darnley had failed to seize power in March 1566, he continued to plot against Mary. He began to seek support from Catholics in England and on the continent for a Catholic coup in Scotland which would allow him to supplant Mary as monarch. On 30 September 1566 the Queen asked Darnley in front of her councillors and the French Ambassador about a letter she had received from his father stating that Darnley was proposing to go overseas and had a ship ready. Darnley had nothing to say and departed rudely without bowing to the Queen. He assured her that she would not see him for a long time. He did not, however, go abroad. The Queen's anxiety about his plans led to discussions at Craigmillar near Edinburgh early in December 1566 with Moray, Bothwell, Argyll, Huntly and Lethington about possible steps, such as a divorce, to solve the problem.

On 17 December there was a great state occasion at Stirling when the infant Prince James was baptised. Mary was determined to make the ceremony as memorable and spectacular as possible. Darnley, however, sulked and refused to attend the baptism. At the end of December he went to Glasgow where he was ill for some weeks with either smallpox or the effects of syphilis.

9

By this time Darnley had many enemies. His fellow conspirators in the murder of Riccio were furious with him for deserting them after the murder. These included Morton and the Douglas faction. The Hamiltons were the hereditary foes of his family and also cherished their claim to the succession to the crown. Both Moray and Bothwell had their own ambitions, and Darnley also lay in their paths.

Just after the baptism the Queen announced several important measures. A grant of £10,000 in cash was to be given to the Protestant Church. This was a substantial sum at that time. The Catholic Archbishop of St Andrews was restored to his consistorial jurisdiction, though this was reported by Bedford to have been revoked early in January 1567.[2] If, however, he retained this power, it would allow him to pronounce null the Queen's marriage with Darnley and also that between Bothwell and his wife. Pardons were granted to Morton and his associates who had been involved in the murder of Riccio.

THE MURDER OF DARNLEY

On Monday 20 January or Tuesday 21 January 1567 Mary left Edinburgh to visit Darnley in Glasgow. Bothwell accompanied her as far as Callendar House near Falkirk (not to be confused with the town of Callander at one of the entrances to the Highlands). He then went to Liddesdale in the Borders for a foray against the Elliots. Mary arrived in Glasgow on the 21st or 22nd or 23rd. She stayed there for about five days before bringing Darnley back to Edinburgh in a litter. Darnley arrived in Edinburgh on or about 31 January to complete his recuperation in the Old Provost's Lodging at Kirk o'Field in what was regarded as a healthy part of the town.

It must be clarified that Darnley was lodged in a house near the Church of St Mary-in-the-Fields called Kirk o'Field, not in a house called Kirk o'Field. References to Kirk o'Field in this book therefore allude to the locality, not the house. His lodging was one of a group of buildings forming a quadrangle just inside the town wall and near a gate in the wall. These buildings were close to the Church of St Mary-in-the-Fields and Hamilton House, the lodging of the Duke of Chatelherault, the Head of the House of Hamilton. (James Hamilton, Earl of Arran, had been rewarded by the French in 1549 with this Dukedom.) The Old Provost's Lodging formed the southern side of the quadrangle. The ground sloped steeply at that time down to the east. At the west end of the house was a *salle* (reception room) and at the east end two chambers (bedrooms), one above the other. The upper bedroom (where Darnley slept) had a small gallery which projected to the town wall. Vaults ran below the house: they were very low under the west end of the house but higher at the east end. In the south-west corner of the quadrangle was the New Provost's Lodging, and this house was very close to the western end of Darnley's lodging. The site is now the south-east corner of the Old College of Edinburgh University.[3] Both the Old Provost's Lodging and the New Provost's Lodging had been granted on 9 December 1566 under the Privy Seal[4] to Robert Balfour, a brother of Sir James Balfour who held high legal office and was a privy councillor. The Old Provost's Lodging had been lying unoccupied but it was quickly refurbished with furniture and furnishings brought from the Palace.[5] Darnley had several servants with him including his valet, William Taylor. Mary stayed in the house on two nights (probably Wednesday 5 and Friday 7 February), sleeping in the room below Darnley's bedroom.

There are very few firm facts concerning what took place at Kirk o'Field on the night of the murder. There is conflicting evidence or interpretation of the evidence on almost every detail. On the evening of 9 February Mary and a party of nobles (including Argyll, Bothwell, Cassilis and the 5th Earl of Huntly) were visiting Darnley. The Queen suddenly recollected or was reminded that she would have to return to the Palace to keep a promise to attend the wedding dance of her servants Bastien Pages and Christina Hogg. So she and the nobles left the house.

Early in the morning of 10 February a little after 2am the people of Edinburgh heard a loud explosion. The Old Provost's Lodging had been blown up with great force and was a complete ruin. The letter from Mary to the Archbishop of Glasgow on 10 February[6] stated that the explosion was of such vehemence that of 'the whole lodging, walls, and other, there is nothing remained, no, not a stone above another, but all carried far away or dashed in stone dross to the very ground'. There is, however, no evidence of the full extent of damage to the adjacent pro- perties or of any injuries to their occupants.[7] A few hours later the bodies of Darnley and William Taylor, clad in their night-gowns, were found in a garden nearby but on the other side of the town wall. As shown on the contemporary sketch-plan of the site sent to Sir William Cecil, near the bodies lay a belt with a dagger, a chair, a dressing-gown and another garment, which was probably a cloak or a quilt rather than a coil of rope. Darnley was barefoot and his valet wore only one slipper. Their bodies were unmarked by the explosion. The sketch-plan is confusing in its design as it does not show accurately the line of the town wall and the position of the Kirk.[8] At least two other servants died in the explosion, but Thomas Nelson, who was sleeping in the gallery, survived. Rumour soon pointed to Bothwell as the murderer.

MARY AND BOTHWELL

On 16 February Mary went to Seton near Edinburgh to recuperate. A reward of £2,000 and other inducements were offered for information on the crime. Darnley's father, the Earl of Lennox, accused Bothwell of being the murderer but provided no evidence. On 9 April Moray left for London and France. The trial of Bothwell was held on 12 April in Edinburgh. Lennox and his supporters did not attend. Bothwell brought large numbers of his followers to Edinburgh. He was acquitted by the jury as no evidence was brought against him.

On 19 April Bothwell held a supper party. At it he obtained the signatures of eight earls and 11 barons (including Argyll, Cassillis, Glencairn, Herries, Huntly, Morton, Rothes and Seton) to a document which recommended that Mary should marry him. According to Buchanan's *History*, eight bishops signed their names on the following day. Unfortunately there is no trace of the original document, and the available lists of the signatories were compiled from memory. Bothwell went to see the Queen at Seton on the 20th.

On 21 April Mary travelled to Stirling to visit her infant son. Buchanan stated in his *History* that Mary left Stirling on 23 April and stopped for the night at Linlithgow due to ill-health but this lacks corroboration. On the 24th the Queen proceeded towards Edinburgh. According to the author of the Diurnal the Queen was accompanied 'with ane few number'. Her escort included Huntly, Lethington and Sir James Melville. Somewhere between Linlithgow and Edinburgh – there is controversy over the exact location, but probably at a bridge over the River Almond[9] – they were stopped by Bothwell with a great company of his followers. Bothwell led the Queen's party past Edinburgh to his Castle at Dunbar. Mary stayed there until early May when Bothwell brought her back to Edinburgh.

Arrangements were expedited to annul the marriage between Bothwell and his wife Lady Jane Gordon, sister of the 5th Earl of Huntly. On 12 May the Queen in the presence of the Chancellor and the Lords of Session officially forgave Bothwell and his accomplices for her detention at Dunbar contrary to her will. Then on 15 May the Queen and Bothwell were married according to the Protestant form. The marriage aroused strong opposition as public opinion viewed with disfavour the marriage of the Queen to the man widely regarded as the murderer of her late husband. Her marriage to a Protestant further diminished her reputation in Catholic courts.

A group of rebel nobles (known as the Confederates), including Morton, Mar, Lindsay and Ruthven, gathered forces at Stirling, and in June they moved to Edinburgh. Sir James Balfour, the Captain of

Edinburgh Castle, joined them. Their aims were to free the Queen, preserve Prince James and pursue those who had murdered Darnley. Meanwhile the Queen and Bothwell had moved to Borthwick Castle (south-east of Edinburgh). The rebel lords surrounded the Castle but Bothwell escaped. On the night of 12/13 June the Queen, dressed in male attire, escaped, and Bothwell met or found her about a mile away. They proceeded to Dunbar.[10] From there they advanced with Bothwell's followers towards Edinburgh without waiting for support from other parts of Scotland. On 15 June they confronted the rebel lords at Carberry Hill a few miles to the east of Edinburgh. There was no battle but during prolonged negotiations Bothwell's forces began to drift away. Eventually the Queen agreed to go back to Edinburgh with the rebel lords provided Bothwell was given a safe-conduct to depart. Bothwell escaped to Dunbar and subsequently to the north of Scotland and then Norway. Mary was escorted back to Edinburgh in humiliation as a prisoner. On the evening of 16 June she was forced to leave the Palace and was taken to Lochleven Castle. There she remained a prisoner. While she was very ill after a miscarriage, she was browbeaten into abdicating the crown to her infant son in July 1567. Moray returned to Scotland in August 1567 and was appointed Regent. Meanwhile the rebel lords had started to arrest some of Bothwell's followers for the murder of Darnley.

THE ACCUSED

A few days after Carberry, the rebel lords began to apprehend Bothwell's followers. William Blackadder was hanged in June and his brother in September. Powrie, Dalgleish, Hay and Hepburn were hanged in January 1568. According to the depositions taken from those four,[11] the gunpowder was brought from Dunbar and stored in Bothwell's lodging in the Palace. Late on the evening of 9 February Powrie and another man brought the powder in trunks on horseback from the Palace through the streets of Edinburgh to Kirk o'Field. The powder was taken into the house (while the Queen, Bothwell and several other nobles were with Darnley) and placed on the floor of the Queen's room, which was below Darnley's room. Hay and Hepburn remained in the house until 2am, when they lit the fuse.

In June 1569 Bothwell's servant, nicknamed French Paris, made two depositions.[12] In the first he placed the guilt for Darnley's murder on Bothwell and said nothing to implicate Mary. This was rectified in the second deposition, though not convincingly. Paris was executed in August 1569. Another of Bothwell's followers, Black Ormiston, made a confession in December 1573[13] and was then executed.

In these depositions and confessions there was no attempt to explain why Darnley's servants and the attendants of the Queen's party neither saw nor heard Bothwell's servants bringing in the gunpowder and trying to get a barrel into the house. There is also no explanation for why there was apparently a delay of at least three-quarters of an hour after the sound of the explosion before Bothwell was informed in his lodging about 'the crack'.

For many years accusations of complicity in the murder became a useful way to try to eliminate political opponents. These included Lethington, Balfour, James Hamilton (the Catholic Archbishop of St Andrews), Morton and Archibald Douglas, but no proper evidence of their guilt was produced.[14]

The genuineness of the depositions and confessions must be questioned, and even if they were reliable evidence they did very little to incriminate the Queen. Her opponents tried to provide further proof through the Casket Letters.

THE CASKET LETTERS

In December 1568 Morton claimed that on 21 June 1567 he had announced to a group of nobles that on the previous day he had obtained a Casket which Bothwell had left in Edinburgh Castle. He said that the Casket had been forced open in their presence. Morton alleged that they had found incriminating letters from Mary to Bothwell about the murder of Darnley. Morton retained the Casket and its contents but no inventory was taken of the contents. The existence of the Casket Letters was not divulged in public until the meeting of the Scottish Parliament in December 1567,[15] but rumours had meanwhile spread about the discovery of incriminating letters.

On 2 May 1568 Mary escaped from Lochleven. Although her reputation and popularity had been at a very low level for much of 1567, about 6,000 men joined her within a few days of her escape. Despite numerical advantage over the Regent Moray's forces her badly-led army was quickly routed at Langside on 13 May. Mary escaped to Galloway and crossed the Solway on 16 May to seek shelter and help from Queen Elizabeth. To her dismay she soon found herself a virtual prisoner in England.

Queen Elizabeth held that Mary's conduct had been reprehensible and that Mary would have to clear herself of the accusations against her before she herself could meet Mary. This led to a conference at York in October to discuss the charges and counter-charges made by Mary and her opponents over her deposition. Elizabeth appointed the Duke of

Norfolk, the Earl of Sussex and Sir Ralph Sadler as her Commissioners. Moray was accompanied by four other Commissioners (Morton, Lindsay, Bishop Adam Bothwell, who was not a relative of the Earl of Bothwell, and Robert Pitcairn, a Senator of the College of Justice) and also by Lethington, George Buchanan and the lawyers James McGill and Henry Balnaves. Mary appointed Bishop Leslie, Herries, Livingstone, Boyd, Gavin Hamilton (the Commendator of Kilwinning Abbey), Sir John Gordon of Lochinvar and Sir James Cockburn of Skirling (near Biggar). It may be surprising to later generations that Mary chose a predominantly Protestant group.[16] At York, Moray did not formally accuse Mary of being involved in the murder of Darnley but tried to justify the action taken in deposing her. Copies of some of the Casket Letters were nevertheless shown secretly to the English Commissioners. On 16 October Norfolk and Lethington had a long meeting, but it is not certain that they discussed the Casket Letters.

In November, Elizabeth decided that the proceedings should be transferred to Westminster. On 26 November, Moray openly and formally accused Mary in an Eik (an additional charge) of foreknowledge of the murder and intent to murder her son.[17] No evidence was ever brought forward to support the second charge. Mary denied both charges strongly and indignantly. After Mary's Commissioners withdrew from the conference on 6 December, the Casket Letters were formally produced on 7 December, but neither Mary nor her Commissioners were shown them. Mary was not allowed to attend any of the proceedings at York and Westminster, and during that time she was kept in confinement far away at Bolton Castle in Wensleydale, North Yorkshire.

The enquiry came to a standstill because of a procedural impasse. Elizabeth would not show Mary the originals or even copies of the Casket Letters unless Mary agreed to answer the charges against her, and subsequently Mary would be pronounced either innocent or guilty. Mary, as an independent sovereign, refused to accept these stipulations and demanded to appear in person before Elizabeth, her nobles and all the foreign ambassadors in London. Eventually on 10 January 1569 the English government intimated:

> Whereas the Earl of Moray and his adherents come into this realm, at the desire of the Queen's Majesty of England, to answer to such things as the Queen their sovereign objected against them, and their allegiances; for so much as there has been nothing deduced against them, as yet, that may impair their honour or allegiances; and, on the other part, there had been nothing sufficiently produced nor shown by them against the Queen, their sovereign, whereby the Queen of England should conceive or take any evil opinion of the Queen, her good sister,

for anything yet seen; and there being alleged by the Earl of
Moray the unquiet state and disorder of the realm of Scotland,
now in his absence, her Majesty thinketh meet not to restrain any
farther the said Earl and his adherents' liberty; but suffer him
and them at their pleasure to depart relinquishing them in the
same estate in the which they were of before their coming within
this realm, till she hear farther of their Queen of Scotland's
answer, to such things as have been alleged against her.[18]

This statement virtually ended the proceedings, leaving Moray able
to return to Scotland as Regent while Mary was detained as a prisoner
in England with her reputation besmirched.

This chapter has attempted to present some of the main indisputable
facts relevant to an account of the murder of Darnley and the question
of Mary's complicity. These facts provide the basis for closer examination
of many significant and controversial events.

3. CONJECTURE

IT IS REMARKABLE THAT there is so much doubt over what actually took place in so many of the key events of 1567. It is therefore important to point out the main areas where there is no agreement on the facts.

MARY'S RELATIONSHIP WITH BOTHWELL

One of the most controversial issues has been the nature of the relationship between Mary and Bothwell. In recent decades Bothwell has not lacked defenders. He was undoubtedly brave, intelligent and well-educated. It is also clear that he was brash and brutal in behaviour, coarse in speech and immoral in conduct. It is nevertheless not impossible that Mary became attracted to Bothwell during the course of 1566. He was certainly a virile contrast to her first husband, the young and sickly Francis, and to the sulky, sottish, immature and cowardly Darnley. There is, however, no evidence of a passionate attachment to Bothwell either prior to or after the murder of Darnley. Mary's enemies had to rely on crude libels on her conduct concocted by George Buchanan. They were unable to produce any reputable, substantial evidence against her. Categoric statements by historians that she was falling in love with him are mere conjecture and rank about the level of romantic fiction. The long-held assumption that there was an illicit relationship between them can be a major obstacle to elucidating the truth.

What is clear is that from the autumn of 1565 Mary relied increasingly on support from Bothwell as so many of the other nobles had been involved in plots against her. That, however, did not necessarily mean an emotional involvement with him. If there had been any impropriety between the Queen and Bothwell, Mary's many detractors would have avidly and immediately published it. Her good reputation towards the end of 1566 – at least in Catholic circles – is shown in the despatch dated 6 November from the Venetian Ambassador in France to the Signory in Venice on the recovery of Mary from a very serious illness:

> Let God be ever praised for preserving this most virtuous
> Princess, who is worthy to live not only the ordinary term of
> life, but for a far more lengthened period.[1]

In late 1566 Mary's chief concerns were making the arrangements for the baptism, pressing her claim to succeed Elizabeth and thwarting the machinations of Darnley. On 2 December 1566 Du Croc wrote from Edinburgh to the Archbishop of Glasgow in Paris that the Queen was at Craigmillar but was not well and wished to be dead.[2] He believed that the principal cause of her illness was her deep grief and sorrow, implying that Darnley's conduct was the real problem. Her state of mind was at complete variance with the notion that she was becoming passionately in love with Bothwell. She was far from being radiantly happy.

After the murder of Darnley her authentic statements in the first half of 1567 and what she relayed to Nau about ten years later contain no indication of any passionate love for Bothwell nor even affection for him. She had, however, become even more dependent on his support due to her political isolation at home and abroad. It is nevertheless significant that Mary did not accord Bothwell the title of King after their marriage and that the marriage contract provided that her signature was required for any official correspondence and any gifts, dispositions and privileges.

There is no sound evidence that after the summer of 1567 Mary showed any anxiety for Bothwell's safety. As a result of her miscarriage in July 1567 there was no longer the bond that Bothwell was the father of the baby or twins she had been carrying. On the other hand there is the assertion by Lady Lennox in a letter to Cecil on 3 October 1568 that Mary after her escape from Lochleven gave the Laird of Riccarton letters for Bothwell[3] and on 9 October Lennox wrote to Cecil stating that when Mary wrote to Denmark in favour of freeing Bothwell, Riccarton received the letters and 'was of mind to pass therewith'.[4] At that time, however, Lennox and his wife were trying to besmirch Mary and their statements must be considered with caution. (By November 1575 the Countess of Lennox had changed her opinion of Mary and was on cordial terms with her.)

By the autumn of 1568 Mary was contemplating the ending of her marriage ties to Bothwell. In October 1568 she instructed her Commissioners at York that if her marriage to Bothwell and its unlawfulness were raised at the Conference, they were to reply that she was content to use the appropriate laws to arrange a separation from him.[5] By 1569, or even as early as the autumn of 1568, she was interested in the possibility of marriage with the Duke of Norfolk. In July 1569 Lord Boyd tried unsuccessfully to obtain from the Regent's Council approval of a procuratory subscribed by Mary to pursue an action of divorce against Bothwell.[6] Mary's statement was based on the assertion that her marriage was unlawful and did not mention her abduction. In March 1571, however, when Mary was trying to obtain a decision on her marriage from the Pope, she emphasised the force used by Bothwell in his abduction of her and requested without success that the marriage which she had been forced to contract with him should be annulled.[7] It is clear that Mary had no deep-seated infatuation for Bothwell nor any lasting loyalty to him.

On Bothwell's side there is no evidence that he ever held any real affection for Mary. During 1566 it is conceivable that he was becoming interested in the possibility of marriage with the Queen, not for her female attractions but as a way to achieve power and wealth for himself. As Sir James Melville wrote in his *Memoirs*: 'The Earl Bothwell had a mark of his own that he shot at'. There is nevertheless no definite evidence that Bothwell, up to the time of the murder of Darnley, was aspiring to marry the Queen. Knowledge of Bothwell's subsequent actions – especially in April 1567 – do not provide retroactive proof of his designs prior to Darnley's death. His lack of real concern for Mary may be evident in his departure from Carberry in June 1567 and abandonment of her to their enemies.

Bothwell's conduct of his own personal life in 1566 certainly does not indicate any growing passion for Mary, as his love-life seems to have been very complicated. In February 1566 Bothwell, with the Queen's approval, married Lady Jane Gordon.[8] It was almost certainly not a genuine love-match. Just over a year later his wife began proceedings to dissolve the marriage on the grounds of Bothwell's adultery in 1566 with her serving-maid. Most historians assume that pressure was put on Lady Jane to take this action in order to facilitate a marriage between Bothwell and Mary, but Lady Bothwell was probably glad to part from him. Lady Jane, however, never publicly revealed her own version of the events in 1567.[9]

It is remarkable that in the divorce proceedings there was no mention of the mysterious lady who seems to have been kept in seclusion in Scotland in about 1565–66 by Bothwell and was almost certainly the author of several of the Casket Letters and also the Sonnets. One possibility is that she was Anna Throndssen, the daughter of a Norwegian admiral. Bothwell met Anna in Copenhagen in 1560 and later that year she accompanied him to Flanders. She was probably with him in Scotland from February 1561 until 1563 when she received a passport to return to Norway.[10] There is no proof of her presence in Scotland after 1563. It is also questionable if Anna remained on good terms with Bothwell. Randolph referred in June 1563 to a northern gentlewoman (presumably Anna) who had sent Bothwell just a Portuguese coin when he was detained in England and in financial need.[11] The intense jealousy shown against Lady Jane in the Sonnets proves that the Sonnets were written in 1566, and it is most unlikely that Anna was in Scotland in that year. The style of Anna's handwriting, moreover, was very different from that of Mary.[12] So the originals of Anna's letters could not have been shown as the originals of the Casket Letters.

It seems much more probable that the author was a well-educated but not very wealthy French lady brought by Bothwell from France in 1565 and kept in seclusion, perhaps in his remote Hermitage Castle in Liddesdale. This lady was very jealous of Bothwell's marriage to Lady Jane and wrote in disparaging terms of her. It is not known if the Queen was aware of her presence in Scotland. The evidence for the existence of the French lady is very slight apart from what can be assumed from the contents of some of the Casket Letters.[13] James Maitland, the son of Secretary Lethington, wrote an *Apology* (Justification) for his father about 1610.[14] He stated that Bothwell in April 1567 had three wives: the Earl of Huntly's sister in Scotland, a gentlewoman in Norway and 'ane uther' in France. As James Maitland was only five years old when his father died in 1573, he cannot have had any personal knowledge about events in 1567. On the other hand, it is unlikely that he simply invented his assertion. It should be noted that he clearly distinguished Anna Throndssen from the wife in France. There is no information on what eventually happened to the French lady. Probably she returned to France, leaving a son with Bothwell's mother. To a large extent the presence of the French lady in Scotland can only be inferred from the Casket Letters, but otherwise some of them are incomprehensible.

MARY'S VISIT TO DARNLEY AT GLASGOW

Various explanations can be advanced for Mary's decision to go to Glasgow and bring Darnley back to Edinburgh in late January 1567. At the same time it is necessary to consider Darnley's own motive for agreeing to the move.

In recent decades it has been asserted that by January 1567 Mary knew she was pregnant by Bothwell and that she had to restore marital relationships quickly with Darnley to avoid a public scandal over such a pregnancy. There is, however, no substantial evidence that she was pregnant at that time. The state of her health would have been known to her personal attendants. A pregnancy would have become common gossip – especially when it was widely known that she and Darnley were not sleeping together. The news would have been promptly relayed to foreign courts. Such a rumour would have been spread eagerly at a time when so many people were looking for faults in her conduct.

It is significant that there are three passages in the long Glasgow Letter (one of the Casket Letters) in which Darnley insisted that after his convalescence he and Mary must again be 'at bed and board' together. Yet according to the Letter the Queen 'feigned' agreement to his demand. It appears that Darnley, not Mary, was the spouse who was anxious to resume marital relationships as soon as possible. These passages would seem to contradict the assertion that Mary was desperate in January 1567 to readmit Darnley as a husband.

Another point to refute such a conjecture is that if Mary had been pregnant she would have taken steps to safeguard Darnley's life at least until he had completed his convalescence and she had resumed marital relationships with him at the Palace on the night of 10 February. The death of Darnley on the night of 9 February would have been a major disaster for Mary if she had been pregnant. She could not have sanctioned his murder at Kirk o'Field, and she would have displayed far more agitation over his death and the consequential ruin of her reputation. It is also impossible to reconcile a pregnancy at that time with George Buchanan's allegations of her placid attitude and social activities after the murder. Mary's detractors tend to entangle themselves.

The traditional explanation of the visit to Glasgow is that Mary was playing her part in a plot to murder Darnley, so that she could marry Bothwell. This is the implication which we are expected to accept from the Casket Letters, especially the long Glasgow Letter. Mary was supposed to have lured Darnley to Edinburgh where he could be murdered. This explanation depends very largely on the acceptance of the Casket Letters as genuine. Yet even if the authenticity of the Casket Letters is questioned or rejected, the circumstantial evidence is still sufficiently strong in the opinion of some historians to leave no doubt of Mary's complicity in the murder plot. Such a judgment depends on a particular interpretation of various events and decisions both before and after the murder. Other reasons can be given to account for Mary's conduct during these months.

Another explanation is that Mary brought Darnley to Edinburgh not to kill him but to keep him in ward (under guard) until such time as her marriage could be honourably ended without prejudice to the legitimacy of Prince James. There is no definite evidence to prove this conjecture but it remains a possibility. It would be in line with the tone of discussions at Craigmillar in December 1566 and the rumours circulating that Darnley was to be placed in ward.[15] It is simply not known what would have happened to Darnley if he had survived his stay at Kirk o'Field.

A fourth explanation would be that Mary had decided to keep Darnley at court under her surveillance to stop him from plotting against her or from leaving Scotland and so causing grave embarrassment to her. Again there is no evidence to prove such an explanation, but the Queen could not have allowed Darnley's machinations to continue. It is clear that Mary by this time was deeply suspicious of Darnley. The French Ambassador in Scotland wrote to the Archbishop of Glasgow on 2 December 1566 that Mary could not perceive any nobleman conversing with Darnley without suspecting some contrivance between them.[16] Darnley was not 'an innocent lamb' as his father asserted. He had become a danger to herself, her son, her reputation abroad, and the peace of Scotland. It must also be stressed that Darnley was a menace to the power and influence of the leading nobles who at that time helped Mary to govern Scotland. Darnley was creating not only personal problems for Mary but was also arousing fears of a profound political unheaval.

Darnley's conduct was especially embarrassing at a time when Queen Elizabeth was indicating deceitfully – perhaps to prevent Mary conspiring against her with Catholic Ambassadors at the baptism – that she might recognise Mary as her successor. Mary's great goal seemed to be in sight. On 7 November 1566 Elizabeth had instructed Bedford to state that she would never suffer anything prejudicial to Mary's right and that Mary might well assure herself of Elizabeth's friendship.[17] Mary's reluctant consent late in December 1566 to the return of Morton and his supporters from England should be linked with her wish to keep on good terms with Elizabeth, whose government was pressing for their pardons. Then on 3 January 1567 Mary wrote to thank Elizabeth for her opinion of the equity of her cause and to tell her that she would send some of her Council to treat and confer with Elizabeth and her Council.[18] In the early weeks of 1567 Mary must have wished to avoid at all costs any scandal or major catastrophe such as being accused of complicity in the murder of her husband. It is most unlikely that Mary would have risked being detected in a murder plot, as that would have ruined her great expectation of succeeding to the throne of England.

All these possibilities involve a considerable degree of duplicity on Mary's part. The long Glasgow Letter, provided certain passages are genuine, emphasises her dislike of being deceitful. It is certainly indisputable that Mary brought Darnley to Edinburgh at least to keep an eye on his activities. It might also be held that she knew that she was placing Darnley in a position where his life would be in peril. He had, however, been in great danger since deserting the other murderers of Riccio in March 1566, and it is highly probable that his numerous enemies would eventually have killed him. Mary was well aware of the hatred which Darnley had incurred, but the move to Edinburgh did not necessarily make Mary a party to his murder.

There is also the intriguing question of why Darnley agreed to accompany Mary, as it seems that he went willingly and not as a prisoner. Perhaps he was lured by her promises and signs of renewed affection.

Mary had shown her influence over Darnley immediately after the murder of Riccio, and it seems that in Glasgow she was again successful in wheedling or browbeating him to do what she wanted. On the other hand, Darnley may have realised that he would be safer near her than away from the court. He may also have been deceiving Mary by agreeing to go with her in order to implement his own ambitious schemes.

Another point on which there can be only conjecture is precisely when did Mary decide to move Darnley to Edinburgh. Had she determined to do so before setting out from Edinburgh or did she take her decision after reaching Glasgow? According to the long Glasgow Letter the Queen brought a litter to Glasgow, but this is not necessarily true. Historians have tended to assume that she went to Glasgow not just to visit her sick husband but also to take him to Edinburgh. Yet there is no firm evidence on this point. There was, moreover, no possibility of arresting Darnley in Glasgow and taking him as a prisoner to Edinburgh. The Queen did not have enough armed support in Glasgow to do so.

There can be no doubt on one point: Mary's decision to go to Glasgow showed once more her courage and resourcefulness. She was placing herself in a hazardous position in a Lennox stronghold, even though she was escorted by a party of Hamiltons who would not have sided with the Lennox faction.

It is not known where Mary resided in Glasgow, nor where Lennox and Darnley were living in Glasgow during her visit. Mary may have stayed in the Archbishop's Castle (or Palace). This building was very close to the western end of the Cathedral, as shown in old prints. At that time it would have been in the centre of what was still a very small town. By the late seventeenth century it was becoming ruinous and it is no longer visible.

There is also an old local tradition that the Queen resided in Provand's Lordship. This was the manse of the Prebendary of Provan and at that time it seems to have been held by William Baillie, known as Lord Provand. He was a Senator of the College of Justice, and in January 1567 occupied the chair of the Lord President of the College of Justice. The house was close to the Castle and to the west of the Cathedral. It is the only house in Glasgow which has survived since the time of Mary and it can be visited. In 1567 it must have been rated as substantial and prestigious, though its appearance now is not imposing. The building is three storeys in height. The older, front portion was built in 1471 and the extension at the back in 1670.

According to the *Diurnal of Remarkable Occurrents* for 14 January, Darnley was lying sick in the Castle of Glasgow 'in the polkis' (with smallpox). If this statement is correct, it would mean that Mary did not stay in the Archbishop's Castle and would point to her residing in

Provand's Lordship. Darnley and Lennox, however, may have been in the Lennox town-house. This was at the Place of Stable-Green, which was west of the Cathedral and just north of Provand's Lordship. There used to be a small building called Darnley's cottage in the vicinity of the modern Cathedral Square. It was of no great antiquity and it is unlikely that it was there in 1567. The cottage, which no longer exists, occupied for many years part of the site of the former manse of the parson of Erskine. If Darnley was in neither the Castle nor the town-house, he may have been in that manse, but it is more likely that he was lying in the Castle.

What is reasonably certain is that the Queen stayed a very short distance away from Lennox and Darnley in the area to the west of the Cathedral.[19]

WAS MARY RECONCILED TO DARNLEY?

According to Nau's *Memorials*, Darnley sent several times for Mary during his illness at Glasgow, but she was unable to visit him until she had recovered from a fall from her horse at Seton. The dates of these letters are not known, nor is the date of Mary's accident. These messages may indicate there had been a change of mood on Darnley's part, or perhaps he was fearful of some action to be taken against him as there had been some leak of the Craigmillar discussions. Bishop Leslie asserted in 1569 that Mary went to Glasgow because she had heard that Darnley was repentant and sorrowful. Leslie claimed that it irked and grieved Mary's enemies (Moray and his associates) to the very heart to hear of the reconciliation.[20] If Leslie's statements were true, they imply that the reconciliation was widely accepted as genuine and also that the Queen had no intention of destroying Darnley.

It is not impossible that the Queen may have been willing to give Darnley a further opportunity to mend his ways. It is difficult to know how prone Mary was to harbour resentment. One of her weaknesses as a ruler was to be too forgiving. Her deep and bitter hatred of Moray, Morton and Lethington seems to have developed during her traumatic experiences in the summer of 1567. The story of a reconciliation is supported in Nau's *Memorials*. He stated that while Darnley was at Kirk o'Field he was often visited by Mary with whom he was perfectly reconciled. There is certainly no sound evidence of a further quarrel between them during Darnley's stay at Kirk o'Field.

It seems that, in addition to the evening of Sunday 9 February, the Queen stayed at Kirk o'Field on the nights of Wednesday 5 and Friday 7 February. Possibly she may also have visited Darnley during daytime and between 1 and 4 February. Insufficient consideration has been given to her reasons for visiting Darnley at Kirk o'Field. It could be held that she was trying to allay Darnley's suspicions prior to the murder. Darnley, however, did not seem to be perturbed about his security, and apparently did not even have a night-watchman on duty. On the other hand, her visits may merely have been a well-intentioned attempt to look after Darnley and develop their reconciliation. Perhaps the most likely explanation is that it was part of her plan to keep Darnley under surveillance and try to end his wild plotting against her.

According to Nau, during Mary's visits to Kirk o'Field Darnley promised to give her much information of the utmost importance to the life and quiet of both of them. He warned Mary that certain persons (whose names he said he would reveal) had advised him to make an attempt on her life. He also warned her more particularly to be on her guard against Lethington who was planning the ruin of the one by the means of the other and meant in the end to ruin both of them. As with so much of the evidence this account of their conversation is brief, tantalising and obscure. It is difficult to be convinced that such a conversation did take place, as it is surprising that Mary did not manage to wheedle more information out of Darnley, who was garrulous and indiscreet. There must also be doubts over Darnley's sincerity and veracity.

Lennox alleged that he and his son had been deceived by the sweet but crafty words of Mary. In his *First Narrative* he stated that when Mary and Darnley set out for Edinburgh he had believed 'all controversies past between them were clean forgotten and buried'. According to a letter which Darnley was alleged to have sent to his father on 7 February, Darnley also believed he was again on good terms with Mary. This letter is included in the *First Lennox Narrative*, but the original was not preserved and cannot be checked. Darnley wrote that his love the Queen did use herself like a natural and loving wife, and he added that he hoped God would lighten their hearts with joy that had so long been afflicted with trouble. This short letter may be genuine, but perhaps it is too effusive in tone and too opportune in timing to be accepted as a true indication of Darnley's feelings and as an authentic letter from him. It should be perceived that it contains no information of a more general nature. The narrow content of the letter suggests that it was drafted specifically to show that Mary had been deceiving Darnley. There is no reference to Darnley's letter in either the *Detection* or the *Indictment* or the *Hopetoun Manuscript*.

Although it is possible that Mary did recover some of her affection for Darnley, it is difficult to accept that such a remarkable change in her attitude occurred so quickly. During 1566 Mary had despised and perhaps even loathed Darnley. Nau related that she had discovered both inconstancy and treachery in his character. He had put her life and that of their unborn child at grave risk during the murder of Riccio – probably deliberately so. Her attitude to him at the time of her departure to visit him in Glasgow is shown in her letter dated 20 January 1567 to Archbishop Beaton in Paris:

> As for the king our husband, God knows always our part towards him; and his behaviour and the thankfulness to us is equally well known to God and the world, especially our own indifferent [impartial] subjects see it, and in their hearts, we doubt not, condemn the same.[21]

Mary's subsequent assertion of a reconciliation may have been part of her defence against any accusations of complicity in the murder of Darnley. It is also possible that the apparent reconciliation was superb acting on Mary's part to lure Darnley into custody or to his death. There can be no certainty of a genuine and mutual reconciliation. It is difficult to detect any expression of sorrow for Darnley in Mary's statements after his death. Her attitude seems to have been a polite reticence except in her conversations with Nau.

It is a serious error to underestimate the problems created by Darnley's behaviour during 1566. It is regrettable that the alleged romance between the Queen and Bothwell and the events of Kirk o'Field have overshadowed for so long the perception of the reality of the situation confronting Mary in January 1567.

THE CHOICE OF KIRK O'FIELD

It is not clear why, when and by whom Kirk o'Field was chosen for Darnley's recuperation. Apparently the original plan was that he should stay at Craigmillar Castle near Edinburgh. According to Nau, the King chose Kirk o'Field on the report of James Balfour and some others.[22] This was against the wishes of the Queen who had proposed Craigmillar as he could not stay in the Palace in case he gave the infection to the Prince. If Nau's statement is true, it probably implies that while Darnley was still in Glasgow he was in contact with Balfour and that in turn might raise further questions about the purpose of their discussions.

Darnley's servant, Thomas Nelson, stated in December 1568 that the original intention was that Darnley should go to Craigmillar but as he had no will thereof it was concluded that he should lie beside the Kirk o'Field.[23] Nelson did not state when this decision was taken nor why Darnley did not want to go to Craigmillar. Darnley's father claimed in the *Lennox Narrative* that his son would have preferred to stay in the Hamiltons' house at Kirk o'Field as it seemed fairer in his sight, but the Queen dissuaded him. It should be added that Nelson (according to his deposition) believed that Darnley wished to stay at the Duke's house. It is, however, astonishing that Darnley would have expressed a desire to stay in the house of the enemies of his family. Lennox's version seems an attempt to incriminate the Queen over the choice of the residence. There must also be doubt over Nelson's integrity. Contemporaries who heard these assertions should have known their improbability.

Presumably before Mary and Darnley reached Edinburgh she sent instructions to prepare the house at Kirk o'Field. It should be appreciated that there was nothing inevitably sinister about lodging Darnley at Kirk o'Field. The Old Provost's Lodging was certainly not a lonely, ruinous building suitable for the commission of a dire deed. Darnley could just as easily have been eliminated at Craigmillar or Holyrood by poison or dagger. There was no need to choose a house which could be easily blown up just to kill one person. There was also nothing sinister about the grant of the house and the adjacent house to Robert Balfour on 9 December 1566, as at that time Darnley's illness could not have been foreseen. The choice of Kirk o'Field (apparently by Darnley himself) may have been related to one of the conspiracies being hatched early in 1567, or it may have been selected just for its healthy and convenient location. There is certainly no proof that Mary went to Glasgow to lure Darnley specifically to the house at Kirk o'Field. If there were any conclusive evidence on its selection, that would be a most important clue to the solution of the entire mystery.

THE USE OF GUNPOWDER

The decision to use gunpowder is astonishing. Gunpowder was a clumsy and uncertain way to murder just one particular person. The procurement of a considerable amount of gunpowder and its conveyance to Kirk o'Field were bound to involve various people and jeopardise the secrecy of the conspiracy. Gunpowder, moreover, was dangerous to handle. The reason for using gunpowder is not clear. It is very unlikely that the purpose was just to obliterate any evidence of the intended murder. The purpose may have been either to kill Mary and the lords accompanying her while they were all at Kirk o'Field or to kill both Mary and Darnley during the night. If the conspirators were aiming just at Darnley, presumably they considered that it was easier to kill him at Kirk o'Field by a mysterious explosion than by stabbing him in the Palace and risk being identified. Perhaps the murderers of Darnley intended to give the impression that the explosion was aimed at blowing up both Mary and Darnley and so leave the Queen clear from any accusations, but such a plan seems too devious. Possibly the decision to stage a big bang was to create an atmosphere of fear and intimidation in Edinburgh as part of a dramatic coup.

There is uncertainty when, where and by whom the gunpowder was placed in the house. According to the depositions of the alleged accomplices of Bothwell and the statements in the *Book of Articles* and Buchanan's *History*, some of Bothwell's men placed it in the Queen's chamber on the night of the murder. This version incriminated Mary and very probably was intended to do so. It is, however, surprising that Bothwell, in his *Memoir*, also stated that it was put under Darnley's bed (presumably in the Queen's room and directly below Darnley's bed).

It is most unlikely that the gunpowder was placed in the Queen's room. Several authoritative contemporary statements on the extent of the damage caused by the explosion indicate that almost certainly the gunpowder was put in the vaults. Experts in modern times on the use of explosives have usually endorsed this view about the explosion at Kirk o'Field.[24] It is also supported by the allegation in the *First Lennox Narrative* that when Darnley arrived at the house, it was already prepared with under-mines and trains of powder. Further corroboration is given by the Spanish Ambassador in London in a despatch to Philip II dated 21 April 1567.[25] He stated that Moray had told him that the house had been entirely under-mined. It certainly took time for Mary's enemies to co-ordinate the statements intended to incriminate Mary!

The assertion that Bothwell and his accomplices brought gunpowder into the house and put it in the Queen's chamber while 'the Queen with the greater part of the nobility and the gentry at present in her suite'[26] were in the building is not credible. The traditional version implies that Darnley's own servants and the numerous followers of the Queen and her attendant lords neither heard nor saw the persons who allegedly brought and stored the gunpowder in the house while the Queen was there. It also implies that Mary was willing to be present in the house while gunpowder was being stored below her. It is difficult to imagine that she would have risked her life as an accident with the gunpowder could easily have occurred. It is highly unlikely that the Queen would ever have visited the house if she had known it had already been under-mined. Furthermore, if Bothwell was hoping to marry the Queen and knew that the house was already prepared with gunpowder, it is very improbable that he would have allowed her to stay there overnight on 5 and 7 February and also to visit the house on 9 February. Bothwell's ambitions and his own security depended on keeping Mary alive and in power. In the event of the deaths of the Queen and Darnley political power would have passed to enemies such as Moray and Morton or the Hamiltons, and his own position would have been in great jeopardy. There must be very strong doubts that Mary and Bothwell knew that the building had been mined with gunpowder.

There seems to be only one credible explanation of how the gunpowder was placed in the house. This would involve the presence or the mining of a connecting underground passage from the adjacent New Provost's Lodging. That emphasises the complicity of the Balfours in the plot and the significance of the choice of the Old Provost's Lodging for Darnley's recuperation. According to the alleged confession of the Laird of Ormiston in December 1573, James Balfour had advised using gunpowder.[27] If a passage through the vaults was already in existence that could explain why Darnley's servants seem to have been unaware of a plot to use gunpowder. It should also be added that there is no record that the explosion exposed any link between the two buildings. There is, however, in Drury's letter of 28 February 1567 to Cecil[28] a pointer to a possible 'cover-up'. He reported that a proclamation had been made in Edinburgh forbidding people to raise any of the stones or timber at the house where Darnley was murdered. It is not known what was found when the debris was cleared.

The amount of gunpowder brought to Kirk o'Field is not known. Calculations made on the basis of the story contained in the depositions of Bothwell's followers that Powrie and Wilson brought the gunpowder on horseback on two journeys from the Palace to Kirk o'Field may be ill-founded. The story in the depositions may or may not be true.

It has always been assumed that it was intended to ignite the gunpowder on that night. Yet the decision to use gunpowder was so peculiar that all conjectures must be considered. One possibility is that the gunpowder was just being stored at Kirk o'Field for use elsewhere in one of Darnley's wild schemes. Another is that the gunpowder had been placed there so that it would be discovered and adduced as evidence to support a charge of treason against Darnley. He would have been apprehended in the house with the gunpowder still intact. It is also not impossible that it was exploded accidentally, especially considering the condition of gunpowder in those times. If the gunpowder was to have been ignited, the most probable target would have been the Queen and her attendants.

KEYS AND BEDS

The traditional version of the murder implied that Bothwell and his companions possessed at least some of the external and internal keys of

29

the house or copies of them. Again there was a failure to co-ordinate the statements intended to incriminate Mary and Bothwell. The *First Lennox Narrative* alleged that the locks and double keys of all the gates and doors were in the Queen's custody. Buchanan in the *Indictment*, written a few weeks later, stated that French Paris had the keys of both the fore and back doors of the house, and that Darnley's servants had the whole remaining keys of the lodging, but in his *History* he stated that Darnley's servants could not get possession of the keys from those who had prepared the lodging. It is, however, inconceivable that Darnley's servants had no keys for the main doors of the house.

In the deposition of John Hepburn in December 1567 it was stated that 14 false keys were made to open all the doors. There was a slight variation in Ormiston's confession in December 1573 as he referred to 13 keys. It is improbable that any duplicate keys would have been required if, as alleged by Lennox, the Queen had custody of all the keys and was involved in the plot.

Another point of confusion is why Darnley's rich bed was removed from the house. According to the *First Lennox Narrative*, on 9 February the Queen substituted a meaner bed. Mary's explanation was said to be that they would both be in the other bed in the Palace on the night of the 10th. Lennox claimed that her real reason was to save it from the explosion. In contrast, Darnley's servant Nelson asserted that it had been taken away several days previously to avoid it being spoilt when Darnley had his purifying bath.

These inconsistencies on points of detail indicate the unscrupulous ways in which evidence was concocted or twisted in order to incriminate the Queen. Perhaps those preparing the case against Mary showed excessive interest over the possession of the keys and the removal of the bed in their zeal to try to incriminate her.

FRENCH PARIS' ROLE

A Frenchman, Nicholas Hubert, had been in Bothwell's service for some years. In January 1567 when Mary was at Callendar House on her way to Glasgow he may have transferred to her service. The reason for this move is not known. He was a Parisian nicknamed 'French Paris' but was often referred to just as 'Paris'. Mary's opponents asserted that Paris gave her the signal that the storage of the gunpowder in her bedroom had been completed and she could return to the Palace.

One of the most intriguing passages in Nau's *Memorials* is the following:

> That very night, as Her Majesty was about to leave the King,
> she met Paris, Lord Bothwell's valet-de-chambre, and noticing
> that his face was all blackened with gun-powder, she exclaimed
> in the hearing of many of the lords, just as she was mounting
> her horse, 'Jesu, Paris, how begrimed you are!' At this, he
> turned very red.

It is likely, though not certain, that Nau obtained this information from Mary herself, as during Mary's captivity his opportunities to obtain such information from other sources must have been very limited. The paragraph stands as a potentially very incriminating account if it means that Mary identified the grime as gunpowder. If Mary did not realise at the time that the grime was gunpowder, her remark could be interpreted as exonerating her from fore-knowledge of the gunpowder plot. The inclusion of the comment in Nau's *Memorials* may also signify that Mary by that time was willing to advance evidence which would put the blame on Bothwell. It is, however, a story that needs to be regarded with caution. The grime was not necessarily gunpowder. It is also not clear exactly where and in what kind of light the Queen saw Paris, observed the grime on his face and then noticed his face turning very red.

Mary's encounter with Paris on her departure seems to have been common knowledge or gossip. It was mentioned by Adam Blackwood in his *Mary Queen of Scots* (1587).[29] Blackwood was a lawyer who lived in France and was a friend of the Archbishop of Glasgow. He was a very partisan supporter of Mary, and his book is not a balanced version of events. His inclusion of the story is nevertheless interesting, though certainly not conclusive confirmation of its authenticity. He stated that:

> the Queen going forth of the lodging to go to her palace, she
> did meet Paris, the Earl of Bothwell's servant whom she asked
> whence he came, he smelled so of gunpowder.

Despite the apparent currency of the story it is curious that in the depositions allegedly taken from French Paris in August 1569 there is no mention of this encounter with the Queen.

Another version of Paris' movements is contained in Buchanan's *Indictment*. He asserted that as soon as Mary saw French Paris coming into the room she knew that the powder had been laid and it was time to depart. In contrast, it should be recollected that the Queen, according to Nau, met Paris outside the house. It is difficult, moreover, to believe that an experienced servant such as Paris would have entered the King's chamber in the presence of the Queen and several nobles in a grimy condition.

It may have been too readily accepted by historians that Paris was at Kirk o'Field for some nefarious purpose connected to the murder plot. Unless his depositions made in 1569 after his arrest are accepted as proper evidence, it is not known why he was there, who sent him or what he was doing. There is, however, the possibility that while exploring the grimy vaults for some reason he had discovered the gunpowder. Perhaps Bothwell had received a tip-off and had told Paris to investigate.

MARY'S RETURN TO THE PALACE

Towards midnight on the Sunday night Mary and her party of nobles left Kirk o'Field to return to the Palace. It is not certain whether she herself recollected her commitment to attend a masque there or someone reminded her. There is also the allegation that such a reminder was a signal that the gunpowder had been placed in position and her presence as a distraction was no longer needed. Lennox, in his *First Narrative*, provided another (and innocent) explanation for her departure: Bothwell reminded her that she had arranged to ride in the morning to Seton (about nine miles to the east).

Darnley's reactions to her decision to return to the Palace are not known, and there is uncertainty whether she intended to return to Kirk o'Field after the masque. There is no indication in Nau's account about her intentions, but Lennox's *First Narrative* gives the impression she was not proposing to return. It is possible that originally she had intended to stay the night at Kirk o'Field. In her letter to the Archbishop of Glasgow in Paris immediately after the murder she said that it was by very chance she tarried not all night in the house due to the masque. Furthermore, Darnley's servant, Thomas Nelson, stated in the evidence he gave to the English Commissioners at Westminster that the Queen had promised to stay at Kirk o'Field on the Sunday night. Yet if Darnley and his servants had expected the Queen to return, it is very remarkable that apparently all of them went to bed. A return journey from the Palace in the middle of a February night would have been most unlikely. On balance it is very improbable that she was expected to return to Kirk o'Field.

On her arrival at the Palace the Queen – according to Buchanan – retired to her chamber and had a long talk with Bothwell. The only other man present was the Captain of the Guard, John Stewart of Traquair.[30] As Buchanan was so unreliable, it is not possible to be certain that such a conversation did take place. It was not mentioned by Nau nor in the depositions taken from Bothwell's followers. There can only be speculation about what may have been discussed. It should not be assumed from our knowledge of what happened about two hours later that the subject must have been the murder of Darnley. They may have discussed important matters unrelated to him. Another possibility is that Bothwell received information (initially from Darnley's servant, Sandy Durham, with confirmation from French Paris' investigations in the vaults) about the presence of gunpowder in the Old Provost's Lodging, and that he discussed the ramifications of this with the Queen and John Stewart. If the midnight conversation was related to the discovery of gunpowder, it could have taken Bothwell some time to convince the Queen that her husband or her half-brother Moray had been plotting to kill her.

BOTHWELL'S RETURN TO KIRK O'FIELD

There is conflicting evidence in the depositions whether Bothwell left the Queen with the intention of returning to Kirk o'Field. In the confession of Bothwell's servant, George Dalgleish, before his execution in January 1568, he stated that Bothwell was going to his bed and had taken off his hose. Then Paris came and whispered to Bothwell who put on other clothes and left the Palace. Dalgleish's statement is interesting but it lacks confirmation. It also conflicts with the depositions of Powrie and Paris himself as these do not suggest that Bothwell was getting ready to go to bed. Perhaps whoever recorded Dalgleish's confession did not realise there was such a significant contradiction. Possibly Bothwell did not hear what Paris had discovered in the vaults until after his conversation with the Queen.

If Bothwell did return to Kirk o'Field, it may be significant that apparently he went with some of his own trusted followers and not with men from the Queen's Guard. There could be either an innocent or an incriminating explanation of his choice.

The standard account of subsequent events based on the depositions of Bothwell's followers indicates that he made little effort to conceal both his return after midnight to Kirk o'Field and his subsequent journey back to the Palace a little after 2am. Yet he could possibly have approached the house from outside the town wall. According to the depositions both times he went through the town and did not use 'the secret way' which Mary followed to visit Darnley.[31] It can be assumed that her route avoided using the main streets and gates. In the depositions it was stated that Bothwell's party on their way to Kirk o'Field proceeded up the Canongate (which further west becomes the High Street), through the town wall at the Netherbow Port (Gate), and up the High Street before turning south into lanes and through the grounds of the Black

Friars Monastery to reach the house. If this version is correct, it would indicate that he was either brash and brazen and heedless of any retribution in the knowledge he had the support of the Queen and some of the most important nobles in disposing of Darnley; or he was proceeding innocently to investigate the reported presence of gunpowder in the house.

Several questions arise over what happened when Bothwell and his men approached the house. Did they arrive before Darnley and Taylor were strangled in the garden? From the depositions of Bothwell's men it is clear that they did not know that Darnley had fled from the house and had been murdered outside. It seems that Bothwell and his followers were also not aware of the presence of any other conspirators. Possibly, however, some of the other conspirators saw Bothwell and his men, or perhaps they had already fled after strangling Darnley and Taylor. It is also necessary to question whether Bothwell arrived before or after the explosion. Historians have assumed too readily from the questionable evidence in the depositions that Bothwell's men ignited the gunpowder. The very dubious story in the depositions is that two of his followers – Hay and Hepburn – had apparently remained in the Queen's chamber with the gunpowder until 2am, when Bothwell arrived in the back yard. They then lit the fuse and left the house, locking the doors. There is, however, some confirmation of Bothwell's involvement with the explosion through the evidence given in Paris in 1575 by Cuthbert Ramsay, brother of Lord Dalhousie, during a judicial process to try to end Mary's marriage to Bothwell.[32] He stated that John Hepburn had told him that Bothwell had become impatient over the slow-burning fuse and had approached the house, but the train suddenly emitted fire and Hepburn pushed the Earl back from the house. A caveat is that Ramsay could have been considered a hostile witness in respect of Bothwell's involvement in the murder of Darnley.

According to the depositions, Bothwell and his band on their return journey to the Palace went to the Cowgate and then the High Street. They had intended to leap over the town wall at the Leith Wynd, but Bothwell thought it was too high. So they again went through the Netherbow Port. By that time the people of Edinburgh had been wakened by the explosion and were in a state of alarm. It is very curious that Bothwell escaped through the centre of the town instead of returning to the Palace outside the town wall. The accounts of his escape given in the depositions of his followers should therefore be considered with caution. It should be noted, moreover, that the details of the return journey given in the depositions of Powrie, Dalgleish, Hay and John Hepburn are very similar. This suggests that the same person wrote or edited their depositions. It should also be appreciated that apart from depositions given almost certainly under the threat of torture, there is very little evidence that Bothwell did return to Kirk o'Field.

THE DATE AND TIMING OF THE EXPLOSION

The decision to stage a coup with an explosion was probably accelerated by the fear that Mary's apparent reconciliation with Darnley might lead to his return to power. Darnley had been staying at Kirk o'Field for about ten days, and he was due to leave the house early on 10 February. It is surprising that the conspirators delayed their action and risked the chance of some last-minute hitch. The murder took place just a few hours before Darnley was expected to depart. Those intending to kill him might have found that by 2am on the 10th he had already left. Those planning to kill the Queen at the same time cannot have been certain that she would stay in the house on the night of the 9th. Opportunities to blow up the Queen and probably some of her leading supporters had already been missed on 5 and 7 February when she slept in the house.

Two obvious explanations of the delay would have been problems in obtaining the gunpowder and in arranging access to the vaults. According to the deposition of Bothwell's follower John Hepburn, the powder was brought from Dunbar (where Bothwell was Governor of the Castle) some days before the 10th. An alternative version was that James Balfour had purchased 60 Scots pounds-worth of powder from an Edinburgh man. This was mentioned by Drury in his letter of 28 February 1567 to Cecil.[33] One of these versions may be false, but neither seems to explain fully the delay. There may also have been a delay in obtaining access to the vaults under the Salle of the Old Provost's Lodging. Possibly there may have been a connecting passage from the New Provost's Lodging; otherwise it would have been necessary to dig a short tunnel.

There are several possible explanations why the murder of Darnley took place about 2am. By that time it could be assumed that the household was asleep. The conspirators may also have had the prudence to ascertain that there was no watchman (though the apparent absence of one is almost incredible). Alternatively, if the plan depended on Bothwell's presence, time would have to be allowed to let him return from the Palace. The timing may also have depended on the arrival or departure or readiness of other parties involved in the plot. These explanations, however, may be too obvious and could obscure some other factor. Vital evidence on the date and timing must be either blurred or missing. It is also possible that the plans of at least one conspiracy went amiss that night. A further complication could be that what was originally a plot to blow up both Mary and Darnley during the night may have turned into an attempt just on Darnley's life after Mary's departure. That may have required further consultations among the conspirators.

It is not known whether Darnley died before or just after the explosion. According to Mary's letter of 10 or 11 February 1567 to the Archbishop of Glasgow, the explosion took place a little after 2am.[34] If Darnley was strangled before the explosion, the time of his death may have been any time after midnight to about 2am. If he died after the explosion there must have been a very short time-gap as many people would have been arriving on the scene. On balance it seems probable that he died just before the explosion, but the possibility of an earlier time should not be discounted.

HOW MANY CONSPIRATORS TOOK PART?

It is very probable that while Darnley and his valet were escaping from the house, they were caught and strangled not by Bothwell and his followers but by a second band of conspirators. Possibly a cordon of conspirators was placed around the house to prevent Darnley escaping before or after the gunpowder was ignited. As the town wall was so close to the house, cordons would have been needed on both sides of the wall. The evidence to support the presence of another group or even groups of conspirators is not consistent and should be scrutinised carefully. The Spanish Ambassador in London reported that Moray had told him 30 or 40 people were involved.[35] Lennox, in his *First Narrative*, stated that 50 persons environed the house. This number included Bothwell's band which was 16 strong. Buchanan, in his *History*, asserted that in addition to Bothwell and his followers two other bands of the conspirators came by different routes. Yet the depositions from Bothwell's followers do not mention any other conspirators. Their statements, however, were probably concocted to place the guilt solely on Bothwell and to avoid incriminating any other nobles. The inconsistencies in the case framed against Bothwell and his followers are not edifying.

If Moray's statement about 30 or 40 people being involved was true, it raises several questions. How did Moray obtain this information and why were so many conspirators not detected by neighbours? How long had the conspirators been in position near the house? Was there a complete cordon round the house? Did all of them know about the presence of gunpowder? If they were waiting for the explosion how near were they to the house? By what route or routes did they escape after the murder or the explosion? If there were other bands present at Kirk o'Field in addition to Bothwell and his followers, how far were all of these conspirators aware of the presence of others and what were the tasks of each group? It would be surprising if there had not been some measure of co-ordination among the conspirators for the timing of the murder. Yet it should not be assumed too readily that there was a master-plan hatched by several of the leading nobles in Scotland to murder Darnley at a prearranged time. It may have been a fortuitous coincidence that so many were at Kirk o'Field about 2am. The whole situation may have been confused and much more complicated than has hitherto been assumed.

HOW DID DARNLEY DIE?

There are wide variations in the accounts of how Darnley died. It should be appreciated that as the only witnesses were the unidentified murderers, any account of how he died is suspect. At the time many believed that he and Taylor were blown out of the house. Robert Birrel recorded that Darnley would have lived if he had not been cruelly strangled with his own garters after he had fallen out of the air. Mary wrote in her letter to the Archbishop of Glasgow that the King was lying sleeping in his bed when the explosion took place. In Nau's *Memorials* it is stated that the King's body was blown into the garden by the violence of the explosion. According to Moray's *Diary*, between two and three o'clock the King was blown in the air by the powder. This version was supported by evidence taken from Bothwell's followers that the gunpowder had been placed in the Queen's chamber, but the depositions allegedly taken from them are highly dubious.

It is very unlikely that Darnley died as a result of the explosion, as most of the evidence indicates that the two bodies were unmarked. Even Buchanan stated in his *History* that there were no fractures or wounds or bruises on Darnley's body. One report to the contrary is that from the Papal Nuncio in Paris to the Vatican on 8 March stating he had learnt from a servant of Mary that one of the King's ribs had been fractured and all the inward parts were bruised and broken in pieces.[36]

Another version is that Darnley and Taylor were strangled in the house. According to the *Diurnal*, the King and his valet were 'wyrreit' (strangled) in their beds by intruders and then taken out of the house before it was blown up. Lennox, in his *First Narrative*, also claimed that Darnley had not died in the explosion. He stated that 50 persons led by Bothwell surrounded the house. Some of the conspirators entered the house with a set of the keys and suffocated Darnley in his bed with a wet napkin steeped in vinegar. Then they took his body into the garden. Buchanan stated in his *History* that Darnley was strangled in his chamber and his corpse was taken into a nearby garden. Melville, in his *Memoirs*, asserted that Bothwell suffocated Darnley and then blew up the house. It is, however, improbable that any conspirators who knew that the house was mined would have dared to enter. It is also astonishing that apparently there was no watchman on duty and that none of the other servants wakened. By modern standards it was not a large house. The room in which Darnley was sleeping was about 170 square feet.[37] Other servants, such as Thomas Nelson, cannot have been far away from Darnley and Taylor. It would have been very difficult for a band of assassins to avoid making some noise opening doors and carrying two corpses down a spiral staircase.[38] There is no suggestion that any of the servants (including Taylor) had been drugged or were drunk. Although there is no evidence to prove or disprove this, Darnley and Taylor were not incapacitated and Nelson gave no hints of any problems. Furthermore, the motive in removing the corpses from a house which was to be blown up is very difficult to perceive. This version of Darnley's death is virtually incredible.

A third version is that Darnley escaped from the house but was caught and strangled in the garden. This assumes that Darnley and Taylor had been wakened and alarmed by noises from the conspirators; Darnley fled outside, followed by Taylor carrying the chair and at least some of the other articles found in the garden. If Darnley knew about the gunpowder in the vaults it is not surprising that he had stayed awake. If he then heard alarming noises, it is also not surprising that he rushed out of the house in his night-gown without calling to his servants for help. There is some confirmation of this version in a statement from M de Moretta, who was the representative of the Duke of Savoy and was in Edinburgh on 10 February.[39] The information came from certain women who lived in the neighbourhood. Towards midnight Darnley had heard a great disturbance. There were many armed men around the house. So he let himself down from a window on the garden side of the house. There are, however, some flaws in this story. It is unlikely that it was about midnight. If there had been a great disturbance, the other servants would have woken. It is also not clear how the women knew what Darnley did.

A variation of this version is that Darnley and Taylor awoke from the smell of the burning fuse.[40] Darnley immediately realised the implications and hurried outside. As Taylor was not aware of the presence of gunpowder, he took time to collect a chair and a few articles for the comfort of Darnley while he was waiting outside on a cold February night until the fire was extinguished. This would be a plausible explanation if the fuse had been burning near Darnley's chamber, but it was far below in the vaults at the other end of the house. It is difficult to be convinced that the smell could have been detected. It is most unlikely that the door and windows of Darnley's chamber would have been open on a February night. A further flaw is that if Taylor had smelt burning, he would surely have woken the other servants – unless he was an accomplice to the gunpowder plot in which case he would not have wasted any time carrying a chair and clothing.

There is also the possibility that Darnley left the house as part of his plot to kill Mary and seize power. This would assume that he mistook the approach of Bothwell and his followers for the return of the Queen, as, according to the *Lennox Narrative*, Bothwell and his followers came along the Queen's 'secret way'.[41] Darnley then lit the fuse. There are considerable difficulties in accepting such an explanation. It would involve believing that Bothwell and his men on foot could have been mistaken in the darkness for the Queen's party which would have been much larger. Some would have been mounted and attendants would have carried torches. The presence of any cloud cover is not known, but in any case there would have been no bright moonlight on that night. Furthermore, if Darnley lit the fuse, there is the question how close to the house was Bothwell's party at the time of the explosion. They must still have been at some distance as apparently none of them was injured. The major flaw in the theory that Darnley lit the fuse is the lack of firm evidence that Mary intended to return. The available evidence indicates that Darnley's servants were not expecting her to return and had gone to bed.

It is very surprising that the conspirators made enough noise to waken Darnley. The original plan was probably to kill him by the explosion but to have a cordon around the house in case he escaped. Such a plan would not have involved any attempt to break into the house, as access to the gunpowder would have been through the vaults. The most probable explanation of what happened is nevertheless that Darnley and Taylor were aroused by some noise. It should not be assumed that the noises were made by Bothwell's group. Others may have been responsible. Possibly Darnley's horses (if they were stabled nearby) were disturbed by the presence of conspirators, and their neighing awoke him or Taylor. They left in a panic without carrying anything or wakening the others. Then they were murdered in the garden. About the same time someone lit the fuse, unaware of what had happened to Darnley.

When Darnley left the house he could have run in various directions such as west towards the church or east to Black Friars. He decided to escape southward through the nearby gate in the town wall which (unless he had a key) must have been unlocked. Presumably this seemed the least hazardous route. He may also have hoped to find the articles which had been left for him in the garden.

It should be noted that Darnley died from strangulation; not from the stroke of a sword or from a dagger. This may have been fortuitous or to avoid excessive noise. On the other hand it is possible that the conspirators had previously decided for some reason that if Darnley escaped from the house before the explosion, he would be strangled to try to give the impression that he had been killed in the explosion.

Unless Darnley was strangled just as he left the house and his corpse was then taken into the garden, it should be realised that he might have escaped in the darkness. If the house was in fact surrounded by 30 to 50 men (as indicated by Moray and Lennox), his chance of escape to safety was slight. It is, however, possible that the number of conspirators was much smaller and that Darnley was unlucky to encounter any of them. On the other hand, perhaps his assassins knew exactly where he would go.

THE ARTICLES IN THE GARDEN

One of the most remarkable features of the murders was the assortment of articles (see page 11) found near the bodies of Darnley and Taylor as shown in the contemporary sketch. The person who drew the sketch for Cecil showed the articles very conspicuously. He must have known that Cecil would notice the articles and draw certain conclusions from their presence. The only recorded identification of any of the articles is contained in the *First Lennox Narrative*, which stated that the night-gown found beside Darnley was his night-gown of purple velvet furred with sables. This reference helps to corroborate what was shown in the sketch.

There are several possible explanations why these articles were found in the garden. It can be ruled out that they were blown from the house by the explosion and landed neatly beside the bodies. It has been suggested that the chair was dropped out of the house to facilitate Darnley's descent. It would, however, have been much safer and quicker to jump to the ground than to throw down a chair and try to land on it. The ground below the window, moreover, may not have been flat as the house had been built on sloping ground. In any case, Darnley was, according to Queen Elizabeth, 'a long lad' and he may not have needed a chair. Furthermore, if he thought that escape by the stair and one of the doors was too dangerous, it is surprising that he risked drawing attention by dropping a chair from a window. Escape from a window would also clash with Hay's deposition which (if true) implies that he and Hepburn were watching for the arrival of Bothwell in the back-yard before lighting the fuse. It has also been suggested that one of the articles in the garden was not a cloak or a quilt but a coil of rope, and that the rope was used to lower the chair, but this assumes that Darnley and Taylor were able to find a long rope without any delay, and also have time to untie the rope after lowering the chair. There is also the question why they carried the chair and rope into the garden instead of escaping as quickly as possible. It is a little more plausible that Taylor took the chair for Darnley's comfort, and that the rope was a cloak or quilt to keep him warm. That, however, would imply that he followed Darnley down the spiral stairs, burdened with a chair, a dressing-gown, a cloak or quilt and perhaps also a dagger and belt. It must be asked in what conceivable circumstances Taylor would have followed Darnley carrying so much. If Taylor was fleeing from assassins, it is implausible that he encumbered himself with a chair in addition to various bulky garments, especially as he had to descend a spiral staircase or jump down to the ground. It is very difficult to accept any of these reconstructions as realistic.

A much more likely possibility is that an accomplice of Darnley placed at least some of the articles in the garden earlier that night in the expectation that the intended victim – the Queen – would be sleeping in the house. Buchanan stated in his *History* that the clothes lying near the corpses were not burnt or marked with the explosion and seemed to have been put there by hand, not by force or chance. Perhaps the accomplice had deluded Darnley into believing that he would be safe if he escaped into the garden while the fuse was lit to blow up the Queen and her retinue. He would have pretended to have had a miraculous escape and then proceeded to the Palace to seize power. Darnley knew exactly where the articles would be, and on fleeing from the house he headed straight towards the garden. In the garden, however, Darnley encountered the assassins who had double-crossed him.

It should be noted that the accounts of the murder produced by Mary's opponents asserted that Darnley was either killed by the explosion or strangled inside the house. Both versions avoided mentioning the presence of another party of conspirators lurking in the garden, and focused attention on the alleged involvement of Bothwell's party and the complicity of the Queen. Their accounts also avoided any discussion of the evidence of the assortment of articles in the garden. Yet it is impossible to reconcile the presence of these articles near the bodies with the accounts that Darnley and Taylor were blown out of the house or were strangled in the house.

None of the theories on how Darnley died can be proved convincingly, and none of them can explain all the circumstances surrounding the murder and the explosion, but any credible account of how Darnley died must explain who placed the various articles in the garden and their reasons for leaving them there.

THE HORSEMEN IN THE SKETCH

The sketch of the scene sent to Cecil showed two groups of horsemen not far from the corpses. It is not clear whether they were portrayed as some of the conspirators or as spectators on the following morning. It is not inconceivable that they were meant to represent Darnley's friends waiting to escort him to wherever he planned to go. Alternatively one of the groups may have included Andrew Ker of Fawdonside who would have been hostile to both Mary and Darnley. Ker had threatened Mary with his pistol in the wild scene at the murder of Riccio. Subsequently he had been in exile in England. Nau related that about the time of Mary's illness at Jedburgh in October 1566 Ker had returned to Scotland. 'He boasted that within fifteen days there would be a great change in the Court; that he would soon be in greater credit than ever, and then he would boldly enquire how their Queen was.' His remarks may or may not have been accurately recorded but they indicate his attitude. Although Drury's information was often inaccurate, it is worth noting that in his letter to Cecil dated 13 May 1567 he stated that Ker and others were on horseback near to Kirk o'Field on the night of the murder to help, if necessary, with the deed.[42] The danger waiting for Mary that night should not be discounted.

DARNLEY'S SERVANTS

Perhaps historians have given too much attention to Darnley's own death and have neglected what happened to his servants at Kirk o'Field. A detailed examination of the evidence concerning his servants can assist in providing a more complete reconstruction. There may have been only six servants staying overnight in the house: Taylor, Nelson, Symonds, Taylor's boy (ie apprentice), MacCaig and Glen. One servant, Sandy Durham, had already left, and it is not clear if Bonkle the cook was in the house.

According to Nelson, who claimed to have had a miraculous escape, he and Symonds and Taylor's boy were sleeping in a little gallery off the King's chamber. It is not clear whether Symonds and the boy survived, but MacCaig, Glen and Taylor died. There is no information on where MacCaig and Glen slept: they may have been in the Salle directly above the gunpowder. The death of MacCaig is mentioned in various contemporary legal documents, but there is no information on where his body was found. In 1586 when a jury acquitted Archibald Douglas of Darnley's murder they mentioned William Glen as well as Taylor and MacCaig,[43] but it is curious that Glen's name was not included in the indictments 20 years earlier. Some other contemporary reports provide a little more information. The Register of the Privy Council for 12 February 1567 referred to the deaths of Darnley and a servant and added that some others through the ruin of the house were oppressed and some at God's pleasure preserved. A report from a French envoy, M de Clernault (who left Edinburgh on 11 February) stated that Darnley's body had been found 60 or 80 paces from the house lying in a garden, as were also a valet-de-chambre and a young page.[44] According to a letter from the Spanish Ambassador in London to Philip II dated 22 February 1567, a servant had been found dead in the ruins of the house but five others had escaped.[45]

The scanty evidence about Darnley's servants has usually been accepted and repeated without further consideration. First it is necessary to question the overall veracity of Nelson's deposition. It should be appreciated that his statement was part of the package presented at Westminster to incriminate the Queen. It was not necessarily what he stated when he was examined immediately after the murders. There is at least one improbable story in his account: the assertion that the Queen and Lady Reres went into the garden at night to sing – in early February in Scotland! His statement that Darnley had expected to stay in the Duke's house at Kirk o'Field is also suspect. Nelson's account may have been drafted for him in order to support the evidence in the depositions from Bothwell's followers. Their statements, and that from Nelson, implied that Darnley had been killed in the explosion which Bothwell had prepared. Nelson said nothing about where the bodies of Darnley and Taylor had been found nor anything about the articles in the garden. Another significant gap in his evidence is that he made no reference to what actually happened to Symonds and Taylor's boy, who were sleeping beside him. That is a remarkable omission. His own story about being found on the nearby town wall after the explosion has been accepted much too readily. It is curious that apparently Nelson was not questioned at Westminster on any points. Perhaps the English Commissioners did not wish to probe too deeply into the evidence; possibly any questions were simply not recorded. It should also be noted that no evidence has survived on precisely where the bodies of MacCaig and Glen were found and what marks, if any, were shown on their bodies. It may therefore be unwise to assume that MacCaig and Glen died in the explosion. Possibly they were strangled or stabbed by the conspirators. Perhaps any watchman suffered the same fate. It would be unwise to accept too readily the scenario presented by Mary's opponents.

It is surprising that apparently Darnley did not have a larger retinue of servants at Kirk o'Field. He was a king and that night he had been entertaining the Queen and some of the leading nobles. The house, however, was not very large, and Darnley was due to leave it in a few hours. Possibly he had given leave of absence to some of his servants. The small number of servants staying overnight suggests that he was not planning a coup, but perhaps he retained only those whom he could trust.

An alternative but probably impossible explanation of the small retinue is contained in the tract known as the *Oration*, published with the *Detection* in late 1571.[46] It was asserted that most of Darnley's few servants were spies carrying news to the Queen and that they were withdrawn until only Alexander Durham was left. When he could find no reasonable excuse to depart, the Queen herself thrust him out. These assertions are vague, especially on points such as how many servants were spies and exactly how and when they were withdrawn without arousing Darnley's suspicions. Perhaps the assertion was made to hide Darnley's own dismissal of servants who might have betrayed his plans.

It is surprising that Darnley apparently did not alert his father and his friends to the possibility of an attack on him. There is the curious story related by Buchanan in his *History* that Lord Robert Stewart (the Queen's half-brother) warned Darnley at Kirk o'Field about an attempt on his life.[47] Darnley told Mary, but Lord Robert denied that he had given such a warning. It is difficult to believe that Darnley did not realise he was in danger from his many enemies, and it is also difficult to accept that he was not taking measures to protect himself and possibly also to dispose of his enemies. Yet the surviving evidence does not mention the presence of any of Darnley's friends and supporters during the time he was at Kirk o'Field. That, of course does not preclude the possibility of contact with them, at least for his own protection. It should also be kept in mind that Darnley himself chose to reside at Kirk o'Field, and presumably he therefore did not consider it a particularly dangerous place.

WILLIAM TAYLOR

The role of Darnley's valet, William Taylor, must be considered carefully in more depth. Very little is known about him. According to Nau, he was English and slept in Darnley's room at Kirk o'Field. There are at least two possible explanations why Taylor fled from the house: he may have been an accomplice in any plot being hatched by Darnley; or he may have been disturbed by the conspirators, or by Darnley, and simply have followed Darnley from the house. Whatever Taylor's motives in following Darnley were, it is remarkable that apparently he did not stop to alert his fellow-servants who were nearby. It is very improbable that

Taylor carried all the articles found in the garden. It can, however, be assumed that Taylor followed closely behind Darnley as their bodies were found together in the garden.

There are some further ramifications to consider. Did any of Darnley's servants know about the gunpowder? Taylor was Darnley's closest servant and it would be astonishing if he had been unaware of any plot being hatched by his master. It would also be surprising if the articles placed in the garden could have been taken in advance out of the house without Taylor either knowing about the arrangements or becoming very curious over their disappearance. It is difficult to avoid the conclusion that Taylor must have been involved in any plot being hatched by Darnley.

It is curious that Darnley's other servants such as Thomas Nelson were not brought into any plot being hatched by Darnley. They seem to have fallen asleep unaware of the presence of gunpowder in the vaults of the house. It should be noted that ostensibly at least five servants were not wakened by whatever disturbed Darnley and Taylor. Yet there is no certainty that all these servants were asleep. It is simply not known what was happening in the house. The whole scenario from the evidence available is bizarre.

SANDY DURHAM

Durham was another of Darnley's servants at Kirk o'Field. There is little information about him. He may have been the son of Alexander Durham, the Queen's silversmith and pursemaster,[48] as sometimes he was referred to as Young Sandy. References in indexes should therefore be carefully checked to avoid confusion.

There is an interesting mention of Sandy Durham in Paris' *Second Deposition*. (This deposition, however, was probably produced through leading questions and worse treatment and is very dubious testimony). Paris asserted that in January 1567 when the Queen was on her way back to Edinburgh from Glasgow she wished to replace Durham in Darnley's service with Gilbert Curle, as she did not trust Durham. According to one version of the deposition of another of Bothwell's followers, John Hepburn of Bolton, Bothwell told him a night or two before the murder of Darnley that Sandy Durham was a good fellow and he wished that he were out of the King's service.[49] The motives for including these comments about Durham can be only a matter for conjecture, but the conflicting opinions on Durham may indicate a lapse in the careful editing of the depositions.

In the tract known as the *Oration*, it was asserted that Durham spied on Darnley.[50] He therefore had to find an excuse for leaving Darnley before the night of the murder. First he set fire to his own bed-straw, but Darnley entreated him not to leave that night. Then Durham pretended to be ill and claimed in the presence of the Queen that he would have to sleep in the town in order to get treatment. Darnley again would not get rid of him. The Queen, however, rebuked Darnley and told Durham to go where was best for him. So Durham went his way. The story that Durham had to seek excuses to leave Kirk o'Field is almost farcical and can be discounted. He probably just departed. It is not clear precisely when Durham left Darnley's service and possibly gave information to Bothwell.

Whatever Durham had overheard or discovered at Kirk o'Field must have involved both Darnley and some of the Protestant nobles, as he would not stay any longer with Darnley and was subsequently vilified as a spy by Moray's associates. Their wrath against him points to their own guilty consciences. The other servants must have been curious about his departure. If he told them what he had discovered, they either knew already or were not worried. This might suggest that he had found not the gunpowder (otherwise the servants would not have slept at Kirk o'Field), but information about some other preparations.

Although the account in the *Oration* is garbled or embellished, what is very clear from the vituperative tone is that Mary's enemies had some strong reason to be furious with Durham. The repeated accusations that he was a spy simply suggest that there was something at Kirk o'Field to be kept hidden. It could be surmised that Durham had discovered some suspicious activity in the vaults of the adjacent New Provost's Lodging and had informed Bothwell, who then told French Paris to investigate the vaults while the Queen was at Kirk o'Field on the evening of 9 February. That was how Paris became grimy.

Melville recorded in his *Memoirs* that on the next morning after the murder, he went to see Darnley's body: 'he was laid within a chamber, and kept by one Sandy Durham'. This may have been in the New Provost's Lodging. Then on 15 February 1567 Durham was made Master of the Prince's Wardrobe with remuneration of £100 per annum.[51] This was a substantial salary at that time but scarcely at the level of 'hush-money'. It could be contrasted with the sum of £2,000 offered three days earlier for information on the death of Darnley. The appointment, however, could relate to a reward for information against Darnley, or perhaps it was just an act of kindness by Mary to one of Darnley's servants.

It is not known precisely when Mary's foes either discovered that Durham had been a spy or decided to allege that he had been spying. In April 1567 Durham's name was included on a placard giving the names of the alleged devisers of Darnley's murder.[52] Then in

September 1567 he was placed in irons in the Tolbooth by Mary's foes.[53] It is also not known when and why he was released. By 1570 he was a soldier in Denmark.[54]

DARNLEY'S LAST MOMENTS AND
HIS KINSMEN

There is very little evidence about the final minutes of Darnley's life, and what is available lacks not only corroboration but probably also credibility. Moretta (the representative of the Duke of Savoy) asserted that after Darnley had let himself down from a window he had not proceeded far before he was surrounded by certain persons who strangled him with the sleeves of his own shirt under the very window from which he had descended.[55] One of his chamberlains followed him and was heard to say: 'The King is dead, oh, luckless night'. On 13 May 1567 Drury reported to Cecil that Darnley was long of dying, and to his strength made debate for his life.[56] According to a letter written by the Papal Nuncio in France to Cardinal Alessandrino in Rome on 16 March 1567, some women in nearby houses heard Darnley in the garden pleading: 'My brothers have pity on me for the love of Jesus Christ who pitied all the world.'[57] All these accounts of Darnley's death should be treated with great caution. It is not clear how it was known that Darnley escaped from a window, why the women were awake, how near were their houses and how they managed to hear his plea, especially if he was being strangled, as well as Taylor's exclamation. Possibly some of the conspirators had disturbed these neighbours. If the shouts of Darnley and Taylor were heard by neighbours, it is surprising that the noise did not waken Nelson and the other servants in the gallery. There must also be doubt over how Darnley recognised in the darkness his assassins as his kinsmen. The whole story of what the women heard seems more like an edifying tale than hard evidence. Yet the reference to kinsmen is unlikely to have been concocted. The story has been accepted by many historians, who have interpreted Darnley's reference to his brothers as meaning his Douglas relatives, thus incriminating the Earl of Morton and Archibald Douglas. This may be too narrow an interpretation.

Darnley had an intriguing assortment of relatives. His main source of support came from the Lennox through his father, and presumably the Lennox men did not murder him. He had royal Stewart blood as his Lennox great-grandfather had married a granddaughter of James II, and he was therefore related to Moray and Lord Robert Stewart, the illegitimate sons of James V. Darnley also had royal Tudor blood through his grandmother Margaret, the daughter of Henry VII. He had Douglas kinsmen through his maternal grandfather, the Earl of Angus, who was a Douglas. His Douglas kinsmen included others in addition to Morton and Archibald Douglas. French Paris mentioned that Ruthven and Lindsay together with Lethington, Argyll, Huntly and Morton knew about the intended deed. Lord Ruthven (who had been present with his father at the murder of Riccio) was a Douglas kinsman, as his mother was an illegitimate daughter of Earl of Angus. Lindsay's wife was the sister of Sir William Douglas of Lochleven. (Ruthven and Lindsay were the two nobles who browbeat Mary into abdicating at Lochleven.) The Hamiltons were also kinsfolk as the wife of his Lennox great-grandfather was the daughter of Lord Hamilton (in addition to being the grand-daughter of James II).

The kinsmen in the garden were not necessarily some of Darnley's Douglas relatives as has hitherto been assumed. Although Morton and Ruthven had returned from exile almost certainly eager for revenge on Darnley for his betrayal of the Riccio conspirators, Darnley's kinsfolk included other foes. The Hamiltons also had claims on the succession to the throne. Their Edinburgh house was very near the Old Provost's Lodging. Darnley could also have been in danger from Moray. Moray had led a rebellion to oppose Mary's marriage to Darnley and then in 1566 had been thwarted from seizing power by Darnley's desertion of Riccio's murderers. Moray himself had presumably left Edinburgh before the night of the murder, but Lord Robert was still there and allegedly there had just been a furious quarrel between him and Darnley. The whole story of Darnley's appeal to his kinsmen may have been concocted, but, if true, it could exonerate Bothwell, Huntly, Lethington and Balfour from being the murderers in the garden.

The last moments of Darnley's life remain a matter of conjecture like the rest of the events leading to his murder. There are too many missing pieces of evidence to present a complete account of the murder. Various reconstructions can be offered but all of them depend on a considerable amount of conjecture.

MARY'S REACTION TO THE MURDER

There is no evidence of the Queen's immediate reactions to the explosion and to the news of the death of Darnley, apart from the statements in the Herries *History* that she ordered an investigation of the explosion and was taken with grief when she heard what had happened, and Buchanan's claim that she went back to sleep tranquilly and with a peaceful countenance. Neither of these accounts can be verified.

Buchanan asserted in the *Detection* that she showed scant respect for the body of her dead husband; displayed little grief for him; and made no real effort to find his murderers. The first charge has been refuted in detail by historians, and there is certainly no substantiated evidence that in the next few weeks her behaviour lacked propriety. It is, however, very difficult to know what were her actual feelings. If it were true that she had just become reconciled to Darnley, her emotional feelings for him were probably not very deep. Indeed, if she had shown excessive grief, her enemies would have accused her of hypocrisy. Her main reaction to the murder seems to have been that she had also been in danger.[58] That would certainly be understandable in view of the threat to her own life at the time of the murder of Riccio less than a year before.

There is no clear evidence on the state of Mary's mind and health in the days and weeks after the murder. On the one hand there are the assertions of her unseemly attitude and behaviour contained in Buchanan's vitriolic writings. In contrast, Bishop Leslie wrote that her council, on the advice of her physicians, vehemently exhorted and persuaded her to lead a close and solitary life and to repair to some good, open and wholesome air to avoid great and imminent dangers to her health and life. It is certainly possible that Mary was on the verge of a breakdown, but some of her councillors may not have wished her to remain in Edinburgh while they failed to investigate the murder. Another opinion of her condition is contained in the report from the Venetian Ambassador in France to the Signory on 20 March 1567. He stated that M de Moretta, the Duke of Savoy's Ambassador, who had left Scotland on 11 February, told him that he had left the Queen deeply afflicted and in great fear of a worse fate.[59]

If Mary had known in advance about the plan to eliminate Darnley, it is surprising that she had not made preparations to justify his murder or to arrest scapegoats. If she had been in collusion with an audacious man like Bothwell and an astute man such as Lethington, it is even more surprising that prompt action was not taken to proclaim Darnley's treasonable plotting and besmirch his name. The only recorded expression of her disdain for Darnley after his murder is contained in Nau's account which was written about ten years later in very different circumstances. Mary's almost muted reaction to the murder immediately afterwards does not give the impression that she herself had been planning his assassination. Her conduct seems to indicate reactions of shock. In the letter which she sent to the Archbishop of Glasgow in Paris on 10 or 11 February she stated that: 'the matter is horrible and so strange as we believe the like was never heard of in any country'. These may have been her genuine reactions.

THE EXTENT OF THE INVESTIGATION

The evidence still available on the investigation carried out immediately after the murder is scanty and incomplete. On 11 February Huntly, Cassillis, Caithness, Sutherland, the Bishops of Galloway and Ross, the Comptroller, the Justice-Clerk and others took depositions from Barbara Mertine and May Crokat who lived near Kirk o'Field in the Friars Wynd and had seen men passing by after the explosion. They also took a statement from John Petcarne, a chirurgeon, but the record of what he said is brief and puzzling.[60] According to Thomas Nelson's deposition and the *Hopetoun Manuscript*, Nelson was questioned about who had the keys of the house. He replied that the keys of the Queen's chamber were in the hands of her servants. Tullibardine, the Comptroller, then said 'There is a ground' but Bothwell and others of the Council did not follow up this point. It was stated in the *Hopetoun Manuscript* that some others (in addition to Nelson) who lay in the house were questioned, but there is no record of their names or statements. Possibly the councillors took other depositions which were suppressed or lost or destroyed; for example, the examination of Powrie refers to a deposition by William Geddes. Bothwell, in his *Memoir*, stated that a barrel which had contained gunpowder had been found and put in safe keeping, after the marks on it had been noted. He claimed that he had made extensive enquiries, but several members of the Council banded together to obstruct him. His statements may or may not have been true. What is reasonably certain is that the Privy Council's investigation was brief and far from thorough.

Mary had been criticised for not acting resolutely against the murderers of Darnley in contrast to her vigorous reaction after the murder of Riccio. The circumstances, however, were not identical. The attack on Riccio took place in her presence and she knew who was guilty. Her apparent irresolution in finding the murderers of Darnley may have stemmed from one of various possible reasons. She may have been shaken by the threat to her own life. If she had not forgiven Darnley, she may have been indifferent to what had happened to him. If she knew who were responsible she may have wished to shield them (and perhaps also herself) or she may have been apprehensive about the consequences of accusing them. Although she must have realised that the person or persons mainly responsible for the murder probably came from the group present at Craigmillar in December 1566, she may not have known the actual perpetrator or perpetrators.

It is far from certain that Mary ever obtained firm evidence against anyone. Nau related that Mary told Lethington after Carberry that she believed that Morton, Balfour and he himself, more than any others, had hindered the inquiry into the murder, to which they were the consenting and guilty parties. Either Mary did not divulge or Nau did not record her evidence for this accusation. The Queen made a similar assertion in her letter issued in June 1568 to all Christian Princes.[61] Mary charged Moray with the assassination of Darnley and then laying the blame on her. She claimed that she had given Moray's accomplices express charge to inquire into the murder in order that she might discover and punish the culprits. She could not but marvel at the little diligence they used, and that they looked at one another as men who did not know what to say or do when they found themselves, with the rest of her Council, assembled for that purpose. It is certainly possible that there was confusion and uncertainty among her councillors over which of them actually ignited the gunpowder and how precisely Darnley was killed.

There is the possibility that Mary was told by Bothwell on their return to the Palace that Darnley had been planning an explosion to kill her at Kirk o'Field. Mary would have been in a quandary whether to reveal to the world that her husband had been planning to blow her up. Her own statements, however, contained no indication that she suspected Darnley was planning any coup at Kirk o'Field, and such a possibility remains conjecture. Furthermore, Mary seems to have harboured no animosity towards Darnley's friends, as she sent a letter of commendation to Sir Robert Melville, her resident at the English court, on behalf of Anthony Standen who was returning to England.[62] Standen was the younger of two Catholic brothers with the same names. He would almost certainly have been involved in any plot concocted by Darnley. Her assistance to Standen is difficult to reconcile with any disclosure to her about such a plot, but it is comprehensible if she suspected or had been told by Bothwell, that the gunpowder plot had been devised by Moray and his supporters. A curious ramification is that Standen on his way south was detained by Drury at Berwick. In June 1567 Drury released him following receipt of a letter from Cecil.[63] It is not known why he was detained.

The Queen must have been aware that popular agitation was pointing to Bothwell as the criminal. Despite the rumours he may have persuaded Mary that he had not killed Darnley, and if some of the other conspirators had strangled Darnley he could have spoken with a degree of conviction. There was no justification for arresting him as there was no evidence to prove his involvement. Mary continued to regard him as a loyal and trusted supporter.

Presumably the Queen was aware that others in addition to Bothwell were being accused. According to the *Diurnal*, it was said that many great men had consented to the deed. (This comment is included in the entry for 10 February 1567, but this entry looks as if it was made at a much later date.) M de Moretta stated in March that the principal persons of the kingdom were implicated in the act because they had been dissatisfied with Darnley.[64]

A modern police force would almost certainly have solved the murders. There can also be little doubt that even in the sixteenth century a determined investigation could have established the facts. Many people, such as the Queen's guards, the Gate-keepers, the servants in the New Provost's Lodging and people in other nearby houses could have given valuable information. Yet it should be appreciated that just a few months later no evidence was unravelled by Mary's enemies, apart from dubious confessions obtained by torture or under threat of torture and the very debatable evidence contained in the Casket Letters. Furthermore, the accounts of the murder produced by Mary's opponents were contradictory over important details. Mary was not the only person who failed, or did not wish, to unravel the whole story. The very limited and carefully chosen selection of depositions by Mary's opponents has nevertheless successfully influenced opinion for centuries against Mary and also Bothwell. It should be added that several of those who took part in carrying out the initial investigation were involved some months later in the arrests of Bothwell's followers but they were either afraid or not ready to denounce them in February 1567.

It cannot be denied that Mary did not ensure that the investigation was pursued vigorously, but her reasons for failing to do so are not known. Unfortunately for herself one of her characteristics was a lack of ruthlessness. At least she should be given the credit that she did not stoop to arrest, torture and execute innocent people simply to counter the insinuations and accusations against herself and Bothwell.

WAS THE TRIAL OF BOTHWELL RIGGED?

The rumours and placards in Edinburgh had quickly pointed to Bothwell as the murderer. It is impossible to know whether this arose from actual knowledge of what had taken place. The formal accusation against Bothwell came from Darnley's father, the Earl of Lennox. Mary's correspondence with Lennox after the murder of his son[65] has been ridiculed as insincere, but such an interpretation of her letters is unjustified and biased. At the time there was no indication that Lennox had found any positive evidence against Bothwell. In Lennox's statements written in 1568 there was still no real evidence. It has also been asserted that the trial was arranged too quickly and Lennox therefore did not have time to collect evidence. Lennox, however, should have held such evidence before accusing Bothwell.

Bothwell's trial has usually been considered a farce. Edinburgh was filled with thousands of his supporters. His accuser did not come to the court. He claimed that he had fallen sick[66] but the real reason could have been lack of evidence or fear of Bothwell. There was a report that Lennox had reached Linlithgow with 3,000 supporters but had been commanded not to come with more than six in his company and had therefore refused to attend.[67] This would have been broadly in line with an Act of 1555 which stated that the prosecuting party could have only four friends and the accused six friends at the bar. It was certainly not a full trial with witnesses producing evidence. That in turn means that Bothwell's acquittal has little validity. It is, however, possible that Bothwell wanted some form of trial leading to an acquittal in order to clear his name and so pave the way for his further advancement.

The huge following of Bothwell's supporters has to be set in the context of similar trials at that time. In the spring of 1565 the Queen had allowed Moray to charge Bothwell with several offences. Moray arrived with thousands of his friends for the day of law against Bothwell,[68] but the latter did not appear and went across to France. In 1569 Lethington avoided a trial through being accompanied by a great gathering of his supporters.

It is difficult to know if or how far there was collusion between Bothwell and the other Lords of the Council in arranging his trial. It has been assumed by some historians from the time of George Buchanan that the jury was rigged in Bothwell's favour. The Privy Council at its meeting on 28 March (which Bothwell attended) arranged for the trial to be held on 12 April,[69] but the record of the meeting neither mentions the selection of the assessors and the jury nor lists their names. Possibly the Council did choose them on 28 March, but that cannot be assumed. It seems that no record has survived showing how the jury was chosen.

Buchanan wrote in his *Detection* that the jurors were chosen not to deliberate but to acquit Bothwell. According to the Herries *History*, most of them were Bothwell's particular friends, but this assertion may not be independent of Buchanan's statement, as the compiler of the Herries *History* seems to have made some use of Buchanan's work. Yet if Lennox had appeared and produced evidence against Bothwell, it is not certain that the court would automatically have acquitted him.

It is possible that the composition of the court was intended to protect Moray and his associates from being accused of complicity in the murder or even to ensure Bothwell's acquittal as a step in a deep-laid plot against him and the Queen. It is also possible that Moray's departure from Scotland a few days before the trial indicated his apprehension that the trial would reveal some damaging information against him. Perhaps the key question on the proceedings is whether the other Craigmillar conspirators would have allowed Bothwell to be properly tried and found guilty for fear that he would have revealed their own involvement.

The trial was presided by the Earl of Argyll (Moray's brother-in-law and one of those present at Craigmillar) as Great Justiciar. The assessors (who sat with Argyll) were Lord Lindsay, Henry Balnaves, James McGill and Robert Pitcairn – all four were with Moray at York in October 1568. The chancellor of the jury was the Earl of Caithness. The other 14 members of the jury were the Earls of Cassillis and Rothes; the Lords John Hamilton, Boyd, Herries, Oliphant, Ross, Sempill and the Master of Forbes; and the following Lairds: John Mowbray of Barnbougle (West Lothian), James Sommerville of Cambusnethan (near Wishaw), James Cockburn of Langton (Berwickshire), John Gordon of Lochinvar (Galloway) and Alexander Ogilvy of Boyne (Banffshire).

In Scotland in the 1560s associations were frequently changing, and continuity in loyalty could not always be assumed. Several of those on the jury had opposed Bothwell in recent years or would do so within a few weeks, but their precise attitudes to him on 12 April 1567 are not known. Furthermore, a record of loyalty to Mary did not necessarily imply support for Bothwell. Some of the jury were certainly not his friends, and the partiality of certain others to him seems doubtful. Rothes and Boyd had joined Moray in his rebellion in 1565; Lord John was a Hamilton, and his family had no affection for Bothwell; Herries, according to Melville, tried to dissuade the Queen from marrying Bothwell; Caithness, Cassillis, Herries and Sempill subsequently joined the Confederate lords against Bothwell; the Forbeses had a long-standing family feud with the Gordons, and Huntly was Bothwell's close associate; Ogilvy was the man whom Lady Bothwell had wished to marry. Bothwell in his 'Affaires' specifically included Sempill in his list of the leaders of 'all this trouble'. Bothwell could have been apprehensive about what the court would decide, especially if he had a guilty conscience. There is confirmation of such an attitude in the confession of his follower, the Laird of Ormiston, provided it is true. When Bothwell was at the bar of the court, Ormiston told him he looked as if he were 'gangand to the deid'.[70]

DID MARY CONNIVE AT HER ABDUCTION?

Bothwell's acquittal allowed him to proceed with his plans to grasp royal power by marrying the Queen. First of all, he held a remarkable supper party for a large part of the Scottish nobility. There is uncertainty where it took place. On Cecil's copy of the Band which was signed at it, there was a note that it was commonly called in Scotland 'Aynesleyes Supper'.[71] Historians may have assumed too readily that there was an Aynesleyes

Tavern in Edinburgh and that the supper took place in it. In the *Hopetoun Manuscript*, it is stated that the supper took place within the Palace. Furthermore, Bothwell in his 'Affaires' stated that 12 earls, eight bishops, and eight lords had come of their own free accord to his place of residence, and presumably he meant his apartments at the Palace. (Holyroodhouse was extensively redesigned and rebuilt in the reign of Charles II, and the present Palace has little resemblance to that of 1567.) If this remarkable supper had taken place at a tavern, it would have attracted widespread attention and would probably have been mentioned in the *Diurnal* or by Birrel. The existence of an Aynesleyes Tavern is not known. There must be a strong presumption that the supper took place in Bothwell's quarters in the Palace.

At this party the Band recommending the Queen to marry Bothwell was signed by all present except Lord Eglinton who slipped away. It was asserted by Moray and his associates at York that as Bothwell had placed 200 *harquebusiers* (soldiers armed with muskets) in the court and about the door of the chamber where they supped, those inside had little choice other than to sign.[72] A force of 200 for this purpose within the Palace grounds seems excessive. Perhaps the number was swollen like Falstaff's men in buckram. The 200 *hagbutars* (the Scots for harquebusiers) may just have been the much smaller Queen's Guard if the party was held at the Palace. These nobles were neither cowards nor fools. The alleged intimidation may just have been an excuse given by the signatories. Mary claimed in her Instructions to the Bishop of Dunblane that Bothwell had purchased their consents by giving them to understand that she was content with the proposed marriage. Bothwell's deception was probably the key to their concurrence.

It is possible that at least some of those present knew beforehand what had been prepared. It would be very interesting to know who drafted the long and carefully worded Band. Bothwell was well-educated but he cannot have had experience of such work. Perhaps Balfour or Lethington prepared the document, but there is no evidence of their involvement. The motives of whoever helped Bothwell in this task would have to be questioned.

On the assumption that those who signed the Band were neither browbeaten nor drunk, there is the intriguing question of how many of them would have supported the actual marriage of the Queen and Bothwell if he had behaved in a more seemly manner and not abducted the Queen. Only four of them – Huntly, Sutherland, Boyd and Oliphant – attended the marriage on 15 May.

It is not known whether Mary had any foreknowledge of the Band and what were her immediate reactions to such a document. On the following day (20 April) Bothwell went to see her at Seton. According to Mary, this was the first occasion when he intimated his matrimonial intentions to her.[73] Mary claimed that she had rejected his proposal. If there was already a romance between them, it is odd that they did not agree at this meeting on the precise details of the intended abduction of Mary to be staged only a few days later but left the time and the place to be arranged by letter.

It was widely believed that Bothwell abducted Mary with her connivance. Robert Birrel recorded that she had been taken to Dunbar 'not against her own will.' Yet the traditional version that Mary had agreed in advance to Bothwell's plan to carry her off to Dunbar is almost incredible. Historians have explained her conduct by asserting that as Mary was infatuated with Bothwell she was completely irrational at this time; or by claiming that her illness after the murder had impaired her judgement. There is, however, no evidence of a passionate attachment to Bothwell, and there is also no evidence of a prolonged mental collapse.

There was no obvious advantage to Mary in consenting to such a wild plan. A contrived abduction and subsequent hasty marriage with Bothwell – a firm Protestant and a married man – would inevitably ruin her standing with Catholic supporters in Scotland and England and also the Catholic powers on the continent. Mary must also have known that Bothwell was strongly disliked at the English court and that a marriage with him would prejudice her own ambitions in England. The scandal would have wrecked her cherished hopes of being recognised by Elizabeth as her heir. If she had been infatuated with Bothwell, the path towards an early marriage with him had already been smoothed by his acquittal of the murder of Darnley and the powerful support promised to him in the Aynesleyes Supper Band. Mary may also have known that there would be no delay in arranging an early end to Bothwell's marriage.[74] An abduction seems to have been unnecessary just to give a pretext for a hasty marriage.

There seem to be just three possible explanations of the abduction, but all of them are only conjecture. The most likely is that Bothwell decided to carry her off to pressure her into accepting his proposal of marriage after the rebuff at Seton. Another possibility is that the abduction was concocted (presumably with Mary's consent) so that Bothwell could be granted a remission for this crime against the Queen and any lesser nefarious deeds (which would have included and covered the murder of Darnley). This was suggested in the letter which the English Commissioners sent to Elizabeth from York and also in the *Hopetoun Manuscript* and Buchanan's *History*. Yet Bothwell had already been tried and 'cleansed' of the murder. The third explanation would arise from the possibility that Mary in mid-April thought she was pregnant.

If Mary were pregnant she would have needed to obscure the resulting embarrassment by an immediate abduction and early marriage. This would imply her prior agreement to the abduction and probably her own suggestion of the plan. One piece of evidence for Mary being pregnant prior to her abduction might be Nau's reference to Mary's miscarriage of twins in July 1567 (see page 62). There is also the report from the Spanish Ambassador in London to Philip II on 21 June 1567 that Mary was five months pregnant.[75] That can be discounted as such a long pregnancy would have become public knowledge much sooner. A pregnancy would also be discounted if Letter VII of the Casket Letters is a genuine letter written by Mary at Stirling in April 1567. It indicated that Bothwell could aspire 'one day' to marry her. That certainly did not convey any sense of urgency. There are, however, doubts about the authenticity of that Letter. The possibility of Mary knowing by mid-April that she was pregnant must therefore remain a matter of conjecture.

It has been assumed too readily that knowledge of the intended abduction was widespread. There is certainly some evidence that the secret of Bothwell's intentions had not been kept, but it is surprising that no one warned the Queen. It is even more surprising that Lethington accompanied the Queen in such circumstances. Lethington would usually have been well-informed about any plots, and he would not have wished to endanger himself in an ambush set by Bothwell. It is also very surprising that if Mary knew about the intended abduction, she allowed Lethington and James Melville to be in her party as she could not have counted on their connivance. Unlike Huntly (who according to the Casket Letters was an accomplice of Bothwell and probably was so), they were certainly not friends of Bothwell.

It is not known what Bothwell said to the Queen when he intercepted her. Over a year later she stated that he had assured her that she was in the greatest danger.[76] She did not, however, specify the source of the danger. This is a curious and possibly significant omission. If, however, Mary was not guilty of complicity, she may at the time have recollected the rumour in July 1565 that Moray was intending to kidnap Darnley and herself at the Path of Dron on the north side of the Ochils.[77]

Perhaps Mary should have refused Bothwell's offer of an escort, but her own party was 'but 30 horse' according to Robert Melville, an older brother of James Melville.[78] Although the precise size of Bothwell's party is uncertain, it was overwhelming. The *Diurnal* mentioned 700 or 800; Nau referred to 1500; and Buchanan in his *History* just 600. James Melville, who was present, simply stated 'a great company'. Any suggestion that she should have allowed an armed combat to be staged in her presence is neither realistic nor sensible. In a despatch dated 3 May 1567, Guzman de Silva reported to Philip II that Mary had wished to avoid bloodshed.[79] According to Mary's letter sent to 'all Christian Princes' from Carlisle in June 1568, she had not wished to spill the blood of her subjects. Mary's avoidance of a struggle may have led to assertions that she went willingly to Dunbar. It can be interpreted as showing either her connivance at being abducted or her ignorance of Bothwell's intentions or her reluctance to shed blood in a hopeless situation.

It was asserted by John Cuthbert and other witnesses during the unsuccessful Divorce Proceedings instituted by Mary against Bothwell and heard in Paris in 1575 that the Queen sent James Borthwick, a squire of the royal horse, to tell the citizens of Edinburgh to get under arms and attempt to rescue her.[80] There is some confirmation of this claim in a letter from Robert Melville to Cecil on 7 May 1567 in which he stated that the Queen had commanded some of her company to go to Edinburgh and arrange for her rescue.[81] The author of the *Diurnal* recorded that the rumour of her abduction reached the Provost of Edinburgh. The Captain of the Castle at this time was Sir James Cockburn of Skirling, who was one of Mary's Commissioners at York in 1568 and presumably a loyal supporter.[82] The artillery of the Castle was fired at the passing cavalcade, but Bothwell's force was too strong to be stopped. As his followers were all mounted,[83] it was also not possible for the Edinburgh citizens to catch them. If Bothwell met the Queen very close to Edinburgh, Borthwick would have had little time to reach the Castle before Bothwell's cavalcade had passed Edinburgh. This may point to the encounter being made further west or perhaps to some delay occurring before the cavalcade moved off eastward.

The despatch of Borthwick to alert the citizens to the abduction suggests that the Queen did not believe or at least entirely believe Bothwell's assurance that some great danger had arisen. The firing of the cannon at Bothwell's force may also corroborate such a view. It is surprising that Bothwell allowed Borthwick to depart, but perhaps he calculated that his strong mounted force would be in no danger from a sally or that the Queen would become suspicious if he stopped Borthwick. On the other hand, it could be argued that Mary and Bothwell were simply playing an elaborate charade. There is nevertheless no proof that Mary connived at her abduction. Whatever was the message conveyed by Borthwick, the firing of the artillery certainly indicates that the people in Edinburgh distrusted Bothwell's intentions towards the Queen.

There is a curious lack of evidence to prove or disprove Mary's connivance at her abduction. Some of her entourage must have been well aware whether her journeys to and from Stirling had an innocent or a guilty purpose, but statements in her defence or revelations of her complicity could have led to retribution. As Edie Ochiltree, the beggar in Scott's *Antiquary*, reflected:

> The secrets of grit folk are just like the wild beasts that are
> shut up in cages. Keep them hard and fast snecked up, and it's
> a' very weel or better – but anes let them out, they will turn
> and rend you.

A detailed scrutiny of the evidence available nevertheless casts doubt on the traditional account that Mary was a willing party to her abduction.

The full facts of what happened at Dunbar between Bothwell and Mary are not known. The entire story of the abduction is omitted by Bothwell in his 'Affaires'. Melville's account is clear but very brief. He stated that at Dunbar (where he was taken with Mary) Bothwell boasted that he would marry the Queen whether she would or would not, and that the Queen could not but marry him since he had lain with her against her will. Mary's own statements about Dunbar are vague – possibly due to her embarrassment. Nau wrote:

> In answer to complaints which she made, she was reminded that
> she was in one of her own houses, that all her domestics were
> around her, that she could remain there in perfect liberty and
> freely exercise her lawful authority. Practically, however, all
> happened very differently, for the greater part of her train was
> removed, nor had she full liberty until she had consented to her
> marriage.

Mary, in her instructions to the Bishop of Dunblane in May 1567,[84] stated that she had found Bothwell's doings at Dunbar rude though his words were gentle. It is necessary to add a word of caution when studying contemporary documents as they use the word 'ravish' simply to mean 'abduct'.

While Mary was at Dunbar it seems that she did not try to escape, but it is unfair to criticise her for avoiding the further humiliation of being recaptured. Whatever actually happened at Dunbar there can be no doubt that Mary's reputation was badly tarnished by her captivity for so long under Bothwell's control. There can be hardly any doubt that Melville's account was true. Bothwell had no scruples over his conduct with females judging by his previous life, and clearly he intended to force Mary into marrying him with little delay. Mary was left with scarcely any option except to proceed to a very early marriage with Bothwell. This vital point has not been appreciated and emphasised by many historians.

Another point of controversy is over the extent of any attempts to rescue the Queen. Buchanan in his *History* asserted that the Protestant lords assembled at Stirling had sent a message to the Queen enquiring whether she was detained by force and, if so, offering to liberate her. The Queen had replied that 'she had been evil and strangely handled, but since so well used as she had no cause to complain'.[85] There is a different version in her Instructions to the Bishop of Dunblane in which she stated that she had seen no hope to be rid of Bothwell, as no man in Scotland made any move to procure her deliverance and it appeared from their own handwriting and silence that Bothwell had won them all.[86] Both versions may contain a measure of truth. One reason for the failure to rescue the Queen may have been a common belief that the abductions had been arranged with the Queen's prior consent.

MARY'S ATTITUDE TO BOTHWELL AFTER THEIR MARRIAGE

Bothwell's arrangements for his divorce seem to have been agreed both quickly and amicably with Lady Jane, and there appears to have been no hostility or hindrance from his powerful brother-in-law, the Earl of Huntly. The connivance of Huntly might have been due to his sister's disdain for Bothwell or expectations of rewards for himself if Bothwell married Mary.

There are reports that Mary was desperately unhappy after the marriage on 15 May. Melville related how he heard the Queen ask for a knife to stick herself or else she would 'fall drown' herself. The French Ambassador wrote in a despatch that Mary had told him on 15 May that she only wanted to die, and on 17 May she had been heard to cry for a knife to kill herself.[87] Mary may have been racked by the knowledge that Bothwell's divorce had involved the concealment of a valid dispensation given for his marriage to Lady Jane; mortified by the Protestant form of her own marriage to Bothwell; and shaken from the ordeal of recent weeks. On 20 May Drury informed Cecil that in the opinion of various people the Queen was the most changed woman of face that they had seen in so little time without extremity of sickness.[88] The distraught condition of Mary immediately after the marriage does not corroborate assertions that she was infatuated with Bothwell and that she had arranged her abduction to hasten their marriage.

Whatever were Mary's feelings towards Bothwell, she must have realised that she would be in some degree of peril if she fell into the control of the rebel lords. That would account for her decision not to join them when Bothwell temporarily left her at Borthwick Castle. The precise circumstances of her escape from Borthwick are nevertheless far from clear. Various questions arise, such as: was the Castle still surrounded by at least some of her enemies? Did Bothwell organise her escape? Was she hoping to meet or escape from him? The whole episode is peculiar and very difficult to interpret.[89]

At Carberry her options were much more restricted, and she had little choice except to part from Bothwell. It is difficult to know how fond or otherwise was their parting. Presumably they both thought it would be for only a short time. One account is that of a French officer who retained the courtesy title of Captain of Inchkeith from the time of the French intervention on behalf of Mary of Guise in 1559–60.[90] This officer, who was with the Queen's army at Carberry, stated that they parted with great anguish and sorrow on her part. Possibly by this time the Queen had realised that her political future was inextricably linked with Bothwell and that she was safer with him than with some of their opponents. She also knew that she was carrying his child or children. Yet a very different tone at their parting is suggested in Nau's *Memorials*. According to Nau, the Queen told Bothwell that if he were found innocent of the crime she would be a true and lawful wife, but otherwise it would be an endless source of regret that by their marriage she had ruined her good reputation and she would endeavour to free herself by every possible means.

One of the intriguing questions about Carberry is why the rebel lords allowed Bothwell to escape. They could have forced a battle and tried to kill or capture him. They made no attempt to follow him to Dunbar, although their unscrupulous treatment of the Queen immediately afterwards indicates that they would not have hesitated to break their promise of a safe-conduct. There remains an impression that some of them were content to allow him to escape. Perhaps they wished to avoid any revelations about their complicity in the plot against Darnley. In the Herries *History* it is alleged that Morton secretly passed an assurance of safety to Bothwell. No attempt was made to capture him until he was away from the mainland of Scotland.

THE MISCARRIAGE IN LOCHLEVEN CASTLE

Mary's initial weeks in captivity at Lochleven Castle were traumatic. She must have feared that she would be killed, and she was also pregnant. On 18 July Throckmorton, the English envoy, wrote to Queen Elizabeth that Mary had sent him word she would not renounce and divorce Bothwell as she was seven weeks pregnant and would not acknowledge herself to be with an illegitimate child and forfeit her honour.[91] (That calculation would make the conception soon after her marriage.) On 24 July Mary was browbeaten by Lindsay and Ruthven into abdicating. According to Nau, when they came into the Queen's chamber she was lying on her bed in a state of very great weakness, partly by reason of her extreme trouble (partly in consequence of a great flux, the result of a miscarriage of twins, her issue by Bothwell), so that she could move only with great difficulty. The words shown in brackets were added by Nau with a different ink, in a blank space a little below the rest of the sentence with a mark showing where they were be inserted. The reference to the twins and the miscarriage was therefore a deliberate addition to the text. It is impossible to judge whether this weakens or enhances the accuracy of the statement.

A miscarriage of twins resulting from a pregnancy following her marriage on 15 May could not have been apparent to her attendants. Even if she had conceived as early as her abduction on 24 April it is highly unlikely that a twin miscarriage could have been recognised in the 'great flux' reported by Nau. Perhaps an attendant made a mistake over the twins or Mary had been pregnant before her abduction.[92]

There were very few contemporary references to Mary's pregnancy and none apart from Nau's to her miscarriage. In addition to the Spanish Ambassador's letter of 21 June and Throckmorton's of 18 July (see notes 75 and 91) there seems to be only the brief statement that the Queen was with child in Bedford's letter of 15 June to Leicester.[93] It should be noted that neither Throckmorton nor Bedford added any comment which would support Guzman de Silva's assertion on 21 June that Mary was five months pregnant.

It is therefore difficult to know how widely her condition was known to contemporaries. There are no allusions to her pregnancy in Melville's *Memoirs*, Buchanan's writings or the Herries *History*. It is also difficult to understand why some historians have ignored Mary's miscarriage. One possible explanation is that it would have embarrassed supporters of the rebel lords to have admitted that Mary had been browbeaten into abdicating at a time when she was so ill. There can be little doubt that Mary did suffer a miscarriage at Lochleven in the summer of 1567, as claims that she subsequently gave birth there to a child have no sound supporting evidence. On the other hand, there is no conclusive evidence on when her pregnancy began.

It is remarkable that so many of the events during the crisis can be interpreted in opposite ways. The financial grant to the Protestant Church in December 1566 coupled with the pardon of Morton and his exiled associates can be seen as steps either to buy support for a plot to eliminate Darnley or to strengthen Mary's position against a plot engineered by Darnley. Mary could have disposed of Darnley without Morton's help, but she might have needed his support against a rebellion by Darnley and the Lennox faction. The apparent reversal on 7 January 1567 of the restoration of consistorial jurisdiction to the Archbishop of St Andrew can be viewed as a concession to the Protestants or as an indication that violence was being planned against Darnley instead of a divorce. The removal of Prince James from Stirling to Edinburgh in mid-January 1567 could have been to protect him from Darnley or from any disturbances following the murder of Darnley. The alleged reconciliation of Mary and Darnley during Mary's visit to Glasgow can be regarded as sincere or bogus on the part of one or both of them. Bothwell's abduction of Mary may or may not have been pre-arranged. There is also the mysterious background of intrigue from Darnley's threats and from warning messages to the Queen from abroad. It is very difficult to cut a clear path through such an entanglement.

Several theories have been put forward by historians to present a coherent explanation of these events. They deserve cautious examination. There must also be the proviso that what happened may have been much more complicated than can be explained by just one overall theory.

4. THEORY: POSSIBLE CONSPIRACIES

> It was said that mony greit men wes
> consentaris to this tressounable deid, quhilk
> the lyke was never hard nor sene in this realm
>
> *Diurnal*

THERE ARE SEVERAL POSSIBLE and plausible explanations of the events at Kirk o'Field. As a result of the bizarre circumstances of the murder and the explosion and the lack of well-founded evidence, various theories must be considered.

THE TRADITIONAL VERSION

Public opinion in Edinburgh very soon after the murder of Darnley pointed to Bothwell as the perpetrator and to Mary as his lover and guilty accomplice. Fortified by the publication of the Casket Letters and the *History* written by George Buchanan, this version became the standard account of what happened at Kirk o'Field. It has also been the basis for the popular romantic story of a love affair between Mary and Bothwell.

The accusations against Bothwell and Mary arose from either knowledge of what had actually happened or the effects of skilful propaganda or the obvious benefits of Darnley's death to the alleged lovers. Even by 22 February the Spanish Ambassador in London was reporting the circulation of murmurs of Mary's guilt.[1] On 21 April he relayed to Philip II a conversation with Moray.[2] Although Moray did not name any particular person, the Ambassador wrote that it was easy to understand by his discourse that he considered Bothwell to be guilty. The acceptance of Mary's complicity spread, especially when she failed to arrest the murderers. Suspicions of her guilt were reinforced by the farce of Bothwell's trial, Mary's apparent connivance at her abduction by Bothwell, and her hasty marriage to the man widely regarded as the murderer of Darnley. Her standing abroad in Catholic circles also fell as a result of her wedding according to the Protestant form. Bothwell, moreover, was known to be a resolute (though not a pious) Protestant. Mary's assertions of her innocence were regarded sceptically across western Europe.

This interpretation of events has remained the standard version despite attempts by Marian supporters to refute it. Such an interpretation has continued to colour many people's view of Mary and to influence many historians, including some who have been sympathetic to her. It is not impossible that this interpretation corresponds closely to the real facts, but a careful examination of the supporting evidence (including the Casket Letters) reveals too many flaws and lies to accept it. There are very strong reservations. A wider range of explanations must be sought and considered.

DARNLEY'S PLOT

One modern theory on the events at Kirk o'Field is that a plot hatched by Darnley to murder the Queen and seize power with Catholic support from outside Scotland backfired on him.[3] Apparently such an explanation of the events was not considered in the aftermath of his murder. Such a theory could nevertheless explain some of the evidence.

Although Darnley had been widely scorned and despised before his death, there was a very successful campaign subsequently to portray him as an innocent lamb. This was part of the plan to besmirch Mary and Bothwell. The Buchanan legacy has perpetuated the whitewashing of Darnley, and some historians have consequently paid insufficient attention to Darnley's wild machinations.

There can be no doubt about Darnley's aims and ambitions, and the Queen was an obstacle in his path. His plot against Riccio had been intended to remove Mary from power and probably also to end her life and that of their unborn child so that he would become the sole monarch. On 14 February 1566 Randolph had written to the Earl of Leicester informing him that Lennox and Darnley were plotting to obtain the Crown against Mary's will and that Riccio would have his throat cut within ten days.[4] Randolph had also heard of plans intended against the Queen's own person. As part of the agreement preceding the murder of Riccio, Darnley was to have received the crown matrimonial and succession to the throne if Mary did not leave an heir.

After the murder of Riccio there is no indication that Darnley gave up his ambition to seize power. As Darnley had lost the support of the Protestant lords following his desertion of them after the murder, he soon began to look for support outside Scotland. It can be assumed that he was keenly aware of his claim to the succession to the English throne through his Tudor grandmother and the possibility of obtaining support from some of the English Catholics. It is possible that his wild companions egged on his schemes. It seems that by the summer of 1566 Darnley was in contact with potential supporters in England. On 5 July William Rogers who had recently been in Scotland, wrote to Cecil conveying information received from Darnley's friends, the Standens, who were English Catholics.[5] Rogers referred to plans to take Scarborough with help from friends in the north of England, and also stated that gentlemen in the west country of England had sent Darnley a plan of the Scilly Isles. The accuracy of Roger's information cannot be verified, and it is possible that what he reported was incorrect. It should, however, be appreciated that the possession of the Scilly Isles and Scarborough Castle would have been of considerable strategic value to any Spanish fleet carrying an army to Scotland.

There is also some evidence that Darnley was looking for support from Catholics on the continent. Darnley had been hoping to secure Catholic backing for himself due to Mary's refusal to reinstate the Catholic Church by force. Mary's toleration of the Protestant Church in Scotland had aroused doubts on the continent about the depth of her loyalty to the Catholic faith. As early as 24 May 1566 Morton wrote to Bedford that Darnley was minded to depart to Flanders and such other places as he thought would best serve his purpose to complain about Mary.[6] According to the Continuator of John Knox's *History*, Darnley wrote to the Pope, the King of Spain and the King of France complaining of the state of the country as the Mass and Popery had not been erected again, and blamed the Queen for not managing aright the Catholic cause. The Continuator added that Mary had got copies of these letters from someone who had betrayed Darnley. These assertions receive a measure of confirmation in a letter from Guzman de Silva, the Spanish Ambassador in London, dated 13 November 1566 to Philip II. He stated that he had received a letter from Mary who 'had heard that her husband had written to your Majesty, the Pope, the King of France and Cardinal Lorraine that she was dubious in the faith'. The Ambassador added: 'it seems to me, however, difficult to believe that her husband should have taken such a course, and it must be some French device to sow discord'.[7] Then on 25 January 1567 he wrote again reporting: 'the Queen of Scotland has been written to as your Majesty commands, with regard to what she wrote to me respecting the step said to have been taken by her husband, in writing to your Majesty about her religion'.[8] It seems that Darnley had no success at least with his approach to Philip II, but nevertheless there was little goodwill at this time in Spain towards Mary.

Some Catholics on the continent might not have been averse to replacing Mary, who was regarded as lukewarm in promoting the

Counter-Reformation, by a more fervent and active Catholic. The Papal Nuncio in Paris wrote to the Vatican on 5 November 1566 that 'it may be hoped that Her Majesty after this most serious illness will embrace to more purpose and with greater zeal the most holy cause of the Catholic religion'.[9] Father Hay in his letter of 6 November 1566 to the Father General of the Society of Jesus added after reporting Mary's recovery: 'May God grant that she may lay to heart this fatherly correction, and that it may lead her to carry out with greater diligence the work which hitherto she has only begun, which all men hope and earnestly desire'.[10]

In certain Catholic circles Darnley might have been regarded as a pliant tool, just as the Scottish Protestant nobles had used him against Riccio. On 21 August 1566 the Papal Nuncio, the Bishop of Mondovi, wrote to the Vatican from Paris.[11] He suggested the murder of Moray, Argyll, Morton, Lethington, Bellenden and MacGill in order to re-establish the Catholic religion. (An interesting omission is Bothwell.) He added that although Morton, Lethington, Bellenden and MacGill were confidants of the King, the latter with his wonted levity would make no difficulty in allowing himself to be persuaded by the blandishments of the Queen to consent to their execution, which he might accomplish without the least tumult to re-establish the Catholic religion. Mary, however, rejected the proposal, and the Papal Nuncio reported her disapproval to the Vatican on 3 December.[12] A report in 1594 to the Pope from Jesuit Priests in Scotland stated that her answer had been that she could not stain her hands with the blood of her subjects.[13]

In the autumn and early winter of 1566 the danger from Darnley seemed very real to Mary. In October 1566 Du Croc, the French Ambassador, wrote to Catherine de Medici that Darnley wished to be all and to command everywhere.[14] Darnley's attitude to his wife was still sour and sulky at the time of the baptism of their son in December 1566. It is very possible that the measures announced just before Christmas 1566 were intended as safeguards against Darnley's plans rather than as paving the way for his murder. Mary's continuing anxieties about his plans are shown in the letter which she wrote from Edinburgh to the Archbishop of Glasgow, her Ambassador in Paris, on 20 January 1567.[15] (This was just before she went to visit Darnley in Glasgow.) She informed him that recently William Walker, one of the Archbishop's servants, had told her that Darnley was planning with the assistance of some nobles to take the infant Prince James and crown him and then rule in his name. Walker said that his source was William Hiegait, Town Clerk of Glasgow. Mary had then summoned Hiegait. He had denied the conversation with Walker, but he admitted that he had heard a rumour that Darnley was to be put in ward. Hiegait quoted as his source a servant of the Earl of Eglinton called Caldwell. The Queen also summoned Caldwell but he had denied the conversation with Hiegait! Mary added that her subjects would know how to judge Darnley's behaviour towards her and that she always perceived him enquiring about her doings. She nevertheless was confident that Lennox and Darnley would find very few supporters. It is a curious story indicating the extent of rumours circulating just before the events at Kirk o'Field. There are references to it in the long Glasgow Letter. The reasons for the various denials are not known, but possibly they indicate fear of retribution from the Lennox faction, which was powerful in Glasgow.

It is possible that Darnley – perhaps with encouragement from outside Scotland – had been planning another coup to kill Mary and seize power for himself. In January 1567 he may have been in collusion with James Balfour and chosen on his advice the Old Provost's Lodging. By early February Darnley was no longer a helpless invalid but a convalescent completing his recuperation. While it is not known how he occupied himself at Kirk o'Field (except when Mary was visiting him), it should be kept in mind that he was not isolated there. Those investigating the explosion should have interrogated his coterie of dissipated companions. A dramatic explosion killing the Queen and some of her leading supporters would certainly have been in Darnley's style. The array of articles found in the garden suggests that his escape from the house was pre-arranged.

There are nevertheless several obvious flaws to such a theory. Darnley and his father could have arranged the murder of Mary much more easily during her visit to Glasgow where his own support was much stronger than in Edinburgh. It is highly doubtful if his servants at Kirk o'Field would have stayed in a house which they knew had been mined (though they may not have known about the gunpowder if the plan was to bring it during the night into the vaults through a passage from the adjacent house). It is also astonishing that if Darnley was planning some mischief he did not have a watchman on duty and his friends nearby.

There are other basic weaknesses in the theory of a plot by Darnley. His many faults must have been known to the Catholic rulers on the continent, and it is unlikely that they would have placed much confidence in his leadership of an enterprise which could misfire and rebound drastically and disastrously against their cause. Darnley, moreover, had jeopardised his standing in their view by joining with the Protestant lords in the murder of Riccio. According to the Cardinal Nuncio in Spain in June 1566, Philip II had mentioned to him that Darnley was not as sound in the Catholic faith as he should have been. The Cardinal had suggested that Philip might inform Darnley either in a friendly way, or in terms of menace, as the occasion might demand, that he must either be a Catholic or count on the enmity of the Catholic King.[16] The Papal Nuncio for Scotland writing from Paris to Rome in August 1566 described Darnley as young, ambitious and unstable but aspiring to govern the realm[17] and in November 1566 he commented on Darnley's extreme youth.[18] Then on 13 February 1567 (referring to Darnley's conduct at the baptism but before receiving the news of his murder) he expressed the hope that God would deign to humble and chasten his turbulent spirit.[19] Such remarks from the Papal Nuncio confirm that Darnley's reputation did not stand high in Catholic circles. A plot hatched by the Papal Nuncio in Paris to kill Mary and replace her with Darnley seems unrealistic and very improbable. Likewise, it is very difficult to believe that the cautious Philip II would have backed Darnley in a plot against Mary.

Other underlying weaknesses were Darnley's widespread unpopularity and lack of any significant support in Scotland apart from the Lennox faction. Any coup by Darnley – even with promises of support from abroad – would have met widespread opposition from the Protestant lords and also from the many Catholics who would have stayed loyal to the Queen and her son. There was no immediate prospect of obtaining substantial military help from abroad, and furthermore the arrival of Spanish or French troops would not have been widely welcomed. Even if a coup had been temporarily successful, it is highly unlikely that Darnley's enemies would have allowed him to survive for long. Darnley, however, was sufficiently conceited and stupid to have exaggerated his potential support within Scotland and elsewhere and to have misjudged the probable outcome.

A further mystery of the night of the murders is why Darnley – according to Lennox's *First Narrative* – commanded after the Queen's departure that his great horses should be in readiness by five o'clock in the morning, for he minded to ride them at the same hour. This raises questions such as how Lennox obtained this information and how accurate it was. Possibly Thomas Nelson or one of the surviving servants informed him. There must have been stables nearby for these horses and also those of the Queen and her nobles, but it is not known where they were and what happened to Darnley's horses as a result of the explosion. It should be noted that Darnley gave the order after Mary's departure: had she told him to arrive early at the Palace or did he wish to conceal his movements from her? It is not known where Darnley intended to go. It seems a very early hour – especially in early February – to have proceeded to the Palace which was not far away. According to Lennox's *First Narrative*, Mary was intending to ride that morning to

Seton near Edinburgh. Did Darnley intend to ride to the Palace and go with Mary to Seton or perhaps arrive at Seton before her? Was his early departure linked to some scheme of his own? Was he escaping back to the relative safety of Glasgow? The answers remain elusive.

Another point of uncertainty is where Darnley's father was that night. Robert Melville wrote to Cecil on 26 February stating that Lennox had been at Linlithgow but had returned to Glasgow.[20] This letter, however, does not prove that on 10 February Lennox was at Linlithgow, ready to help Darnley in a coup. Melville's information may conflict with a report dated 27 February from the Bishop of Mondovi in Paris to Cardinal Alessandrino that on 9 February Lennox had been attacked in Glasgow by a large number of armed men and but for the bravery of Lord Sempill would have been killed.[21] The Bishop did not state the source of his information. The story may be spurious or garbled as neither Lennox nor Buchanan mentioned it.

The theory that Darnley was planning a coup cannot be completely rejected. His malevolent ambitions should not be underestimated. Perhaps Moray or Morton heard about his plans and decided to turn them to their own advantage. Darnley had the reputation of not being able to keep a secret, or an accomplice such as James Balfour may have betrayed him. It is possible that Darnley's arrangements for a dramatic explosion were used against himself. He had probably been duped into participating in the plot against Riccio, and he may have been duped again at Kirk o'Field by some of those who had been at Craigmillar. Perhaps Darnley was given the task of persuading Mary to stay overnight at Kirk o'Field, so that she could be killed in a mysterious explosion.

THE CRAIGMILLAR CONSPIRATORS

The group of nobles who had discussed the problem of Darnley when they were at Craigmillar early in December 1566 must come under suspicion: Moray, Argyll, Bothwell and Huntly, aided by Lethington and possibly also James Balfour, the talented lawyer who was prone to changing sides. Some of the most important and influential men in Scotland were in this group.

There were interesting links and animosities between the four nobles. Bothwell and Huntly were brothers-in-law, and so were Moray and Argyll. (These links may have been strained by Bothwell's infidelity to Lady Jane Gordon and by Argyll's dislike of his wife.) All of the four were Protestants though Huntly relied locally on Catholic support. Huntly and Bothwell worked closely together, but Huntly and Moray were on bad terms over the Earldom of Moray. Bothwell and Moray had been at variance for some years as Bothwell was a Borderer and opposed to Moray's pro-English policy. Bothwell must have been most unwise to have put any reliance on Moray's loyal complicity in any plot.

The motives of Moray and Bothwell in getting rid of Darnley went far further than mere dislike of him. Bothwell may have been looking beyond the disposal of Darnley to the prize of the crown matrimonial. Moray also coveted power and perhaps the crown, and presumably he regarded both Mary and Darnley as obstacles in his path. Yet for both Moray and Bothwell the death of Darnley might have led to unwanted complications. Mary could have discovered their involvement and taken action against them. She might also have decided subsequently to marry someone who would have thwarted their plans.

In addition to the four nobles there was a very devious person at Craigmillar. Lethington was nicknamed 'Mitchell Wylie', a variation of Machiavelli. It was said that he was wont to cast the stone and conceal the hand.[22] John Knox described him as a man of good learning and of sharp wit and reasoning. Lethington tended to switch sides. Any guiding principles – apart from preserving his own life and trying to promote the union of Scotland and England – are difficult to discern during the years 1566–69. His record of loyalty to Mary in those years is very questionable. Bothwell and Lethington were on bad terms and according to Melville early in June 1567 Mary had to intervene to stop Bothwell from attacking Lethington. The author of the *Diurnal* recorded that on 5 June 1567 Lethington left the court as he suspected that his life was in danger. It is therefore clear that there were several potential rifts between those present at Craigmillar, and it would have been astonishing if such a group had maintained a solid cohesion for more than a brief time.

There was some confusion among contemporaries between the Band which was allegedly signed at Craigmillar and the Band which had previously been signed in Edinburgh early in October 1566. The latter, according to Moray's declaration on 19 January 1569, was signed by Huntly, Argyll, Bothwell and himself, and it recognised their reconciliation. According to Archibald Douglas in a letter written in 1583 to Mary, it bound them not to obey Darnley's commands.[23] Although this earlier Band was not a commitment to murder Darnley, that would have been the implicit outcome.

Mary's version of what was discussed at Craigmillar is contained in a statement which she sent to Huntly and Argyll to sign at the time of the proceedings at Westminster.[24] Cecil intercepted the statement, and it is therefore not certain that the two nobles would have endorsed it. The document asserted that in return for pardoning the murderers of

Riccio the nobles had proposed to find means to arrange a divorce between the Queen and Darnley. It should be appreciated that a divorce would have eliminated Prince James from the succession, and that the motives for suggesting this could be suspect. Mary had replied that such a divorce must be made lawfully and not prejudice her son. She had added: 'I will that ye do nothing through which any spot may be laid upon my honour or conscience, and therefore I pray you, rather let the matter be in the condition that it is, abiding till God of His goodness put remedy thereto; lest you believing that you are doing me a service, may possibly turn to my hurt and displeasure'. Lethington replied: 'Let us guide the matter among us, and your Grace shall see nothing but good, and approved by Parliament'. Mary's statement ended by asserting that Moray and Lethington were the devisers of the murder. If the proposed 'Protestation' by Huntly and Argyll is an accurate account of what was discussed over two years previously at Craigmillar, it can be interpreted as exonerating Mary. A substantial confirmation of Mary's refusal at Craigmillar to despatch Darnley is contained in the Instructions given by Argyll, Huntly and other Scottish nobles in September (1568) to the Queen's commissioners.[25] They stated that the Queen had refused 'as is manifestly known' the proposals that Darnley should be despatched. There is further confirmation of the accuracy of the Protestation in a despatch dated 18 January 1567 from the Spanish Ambassador in London to Philip II: 'The displeasure of the Queen of Scotland with her husband is carried so far, that she was approached by some who wanted to induce her to allow a plot to be formed against him which she refused, but she nevertheless shows him no affection'.[26] On the other hand, Lethington and the others may have assumed she was really turning a blind eye to what they were intending to do. It could be held that it would be naive to suppose that Mary did not know that they would murder Darnley, but her connivance cannot just be presumed and her refusal discounted.

There has been an assumption that Mary knew about the murder plot from what is contained in the letter which Archibald Douglas sent to her in 1583.[27] He claimed that while Morton was at Whittingehame (south-west of Dunbar) in mid-January 1567 with Bothwell and Lethington, he was sent to ask the Queen for a warrant to kill Darnley, but she refused to give him such a warrant. Douglas, however, stated clearly that Bothwell and Lethington, who accompanied him to Edinburgh, gave him the Queen's answer. He was therefore not a witness to what, if anything, was discussed with the Queen about Darnley. It is possible that Bothwell and Lethington may just have been reporting to the Queen on the likelihood of Morton continuing to be a danger to herself. Mary must have had considerable misgivings over allowing

72

Morton to return from England. In any case, Archibald Douglas was one of the greatest rogues of that time, and his testimony has to be treated with great caution. There is no sound evidence that the Queen knew about a specific plan to murder Darnley. It is also most improbable that she would have associated herself in such a conspiracy with Morton, her own enemy and the friend of the English government. There should be a presumption that she was not aware of such a plot.

It is possible, though not certain, that the nobles at Craigmillar signed a Band setting out their intentions about Darnley. Some indication of this quickly became known to Lennox. According to his *First Narrative*, Lennox learnt that his son was to be put in ward after the baptism of Prince James and the departure of the ambassadors. He warned Darnley who would have escaped from Scotland by ship if he had not fallen ill.

If a Band was signed at Craigmillar, it is not known what happened to the original and any copies. According to Nau, before Bothwell left Mary at Carberry he gave her his copy, showing her the signatures of Morton, Lethington, James Balfour and some others who in June 1567 were opposing them. Bothwell told her to take good care of the paper. This seems a dubious or garbled story, as either the Band should have shown Bothwell's signature or he should have explained how he obtained it. Nau did not relate what Mary did with the copy. It is scarcely conceivable that Mary managed to retain it during the turmoils of the next 12 months and that this was the evidence she intended to produce against her enemies. Yet Mr John Wood (Moray's emissary) wrote on 12 June 1568 from Greenwich to Lethington, telling him that he had been surely informed that Mary had accused Lethington and Morton as being privy to Darnley's murder and she had also affirmed she had both their handwritings to testify the same.[28] There are also various accounts of what happened to the original. According to the Herries *History*, the Band was in the Casket entrusted by Bothwell to Balfour. On 28 October 1567 Sir William Drury informed Cecil that the writing with the names and consents of the chief conspirators was turned into ashes, but Drury quoted no source for his statement.[29] Then on 15 October 1570 Randolph wrote to Cecil, relating that after Carberry the Murder Band was now denied and that another Band had been produced.[30] It had been signed by several noblemen including Moray a long time before the Band for the murder of Darnley.

It is possible that the Craigmillar group after subscribing to their Band early in December 1566 continued to plan the elimination of Darnley and that they were joined by Morton on his return from exile in January 1567. According to Morton's confession in 1581, Bothwell had tried to involve him in the conspiracy. Morton claimed he had refused, but he was almost certainly eager for revenge on Darnley over his desertion of the Riccio conspirators. When Morton became Regent in 1572 he showed himself to be a crafty and unscrupulous ruler. His testimony must be regarded with great caution. It is nevertheless possible that he told the truth when he denied accepting Bothwell's invitation to join the conspirators. Another possibility could be that Morton refused Bothwell's proposal but agreed to assist Moray and Lethington in a plot against Darnley without informing Bothwell. According to Nau, Bothwell told Mary before leaving her at Carberry that Morton, Lethington, Balfour and some others were guilty of the death of Darnley.

It has perhaps been assumed too readily that the aim of the Craigmillar group was to kill Darnley, rather than warding him or arranging a divorce for Mary. Indeed, it would have been astonishing if those at Craigmillar had signed a Band specifically planning the murder of Darnley, as they had little trust in each other and the disclosure of such a document would have been highly embarrassing. It is also not certain that all of those who were at Craigmillar took concerted (or even any) action against Darnley at Kirk o'Field. It is perhaps unlikely that all of them continued as a group to plot against Darnley. They may, however, have acted as individuals or in smaller groups. What could have united them early in February 1567 was the apparent reconciliation of Mary and Darnley. All of them detested Darnley. The fear of a reconciliation may have accelerated their action against him and perhaps also the Queen. The timing may also have been influenced by their anxiety to ensure that Mary did not exercise the traditional right of Scottish monarchs to revoke grants of land awarded prior to their 25th birthday. Mary would be 25 in December 1567.

MORAY'S MOVEMENTS

Moray had much to lose from a reconciliation between Mary and Darnley and much to gain from the removal of Darnley. Contemporaries called Moray 'the good Regent', but this simply meant that he was godly or pious. He was certainly a staunch supporter of the Protestant religion, but nevertheless he was ambitious and avaricious, devious and deceitful. It is, however, most unlikely that he took an active part in the conspiracy. He had a reputation for 'looking through his fingers' and he would have carefully concealed his participation in a murder plot.

The departure of Moray from Edinburgh on the day before the murder has aroused speculation. According to Buchanan's *Indictment*, on the morning of Sunday 9 February he was told on his way to church that his wife had suffered a miscarriage and was in extreme peril of her life. He left Edinburgh immediately to visit her at St Andrews. (There is the interesting but perhaps fortuitous coincidence that Morton – according to his confession in 1581[31] – was at St Andrews visiting the Earl of Angus a little before the murder of Darnley.) On two other significant occasions it seems that Moray avoided being present when he did not wish to be seen as being involved. He returned from exile in England on the evening of 10 March just after the murder of Riccio. Early in April 1567 – shortly before the trial of Bothwell – he left Scotland for some weeks. These timings may have been by chance or otherwise.

Moray seems to have kept a low profile after the murder of Darnley. On 26 February Robert Melville wrote to Cecil informing him that the Queen had sent for Moray.[32] Then on 28 February Drury reported to Cecil that Moray had met Morton, Atholl and others at Dunkeld.[33] On 16 March the Papal Nuncio in Paris wrote to Rome stating he had learnt that Moray, Atholl and Morton were banded with Lennox under pretext of avenging Darnley's death and that Moray had been summoned by Mary but had refused to attend her.[34] It is not known precisely when Moray returned to Edinburgh, but on 11 March he attended the meeting of the Privy Council. On 13 March he wrote from Edinburgh to Cecil stating that he was 'touched himself' (ie he was suspected of involvement in the murder of Darnley) and requested a passport to be sent to him in haste.[35] According to the *Diurnal*, he left Edinburgh on 7 April, but the date in Moray's diary is 9 April.

There is the theory – set out emphatically in the Herries *History* – that Moray and Morton encouraged the idea that Mary should marry Bothwell in order to defame her through marriage to the reputed murderer of Darnley and at the same time to divert from themselves any allegation about their involvement in the murder. Bishop Leslie also pointed to Moray's guilt, alleging that he and his faction contrived the acquittal of Bothwell at his trial and also the marriage with Mary to achieve the utter undoing of both the Queen and Bothwell. There is no proof of such a plan and furthermore such an elaborate plot might easily have gone astray. Bothwell would not have been a stooge like Darnley might have been. It looks more like hindsight on the part of Leslie and the author of the Herries *History*. Yet suspicions of Moray's plans were current very quickly after the death of Darnley. On 16 March the Papal Nuncio in Paris wrote to the Grand Duke of Tuscany that Moray planned to kill Bothwell, make an attempt on the life of Mary and seize Prince James.[36] If there were any truth in these allegations, the plot turned out astonishingly well for Moray. It is more likely that Moray and his supporters planned one step at a time to gain power. In particular, Bothwell must have received help from another unscrupulous person in preparing the Band signed at the Aynesleyes Supper. When assessing the possible guilt of Moray it should be recollected that he had tried unsuccessfully in 1565 to overthrow Mary, and almost certainly he had expected to do so following the murder of Riccio. He and his associates could have used the cloak of the Craigmillar Band to plan a coup d'état against the Queen. Their fears that Mary would restore the Catholic Church and deprive them of their estates and political power were closely interwoven. It is very likely that the real target at Kirk o'Field was the Queen so that power would pass to Moray and his associates.

SIR JAMES BALFOUR

According to Nau, Balfour was one of the signatories of the Craigmillar Band. He had been one of the Protestant faction at the time of the siege of the Castle of St Andrews in 1547. After the capture of the Castle he was sent as a prisoner to France and rowed in the same galley as John Knox. He changed his religion after his release and supported the Catholic Regent, Mary of Guise. Balfour was steadily promoted in the judiciary following Mary's return to Scotland. It is difficult to know how Balfour was motivated: whether he aimed at the restoration of the Old Religion or acted just on the basis of self-interest.

In March 1580, Mary wrote to the Archbishop of Glasgow in Paris asking him to do what he could so that Balfour would write to her fully about the Band which he saw for the murder of the late King.[37] Although Balfour was probably not one of the main instigators of what happened at Kirk o'Field, he may have been the leading agent there for one or more of those present at Craigmillar. Balfour could have been involved in either a plot originated by Moray and other Protestant lords aiming at the death of Darnley (or both Mary and Darnley), or a plot organised by Bothwell against Darnley, or a Catholic plot devised by Darnley. There is a hint that Balfour had lost some favour at the Court in a letter to Cecil dated 24 June 1566 from Killigrew in Edinburgh.[38] He stated tersely: 'Balfour's credit decays'. Possibly Balfour began to look towards Darnley for further advancement of his own prospects. There is also the possibility that Balfour may have switched sides just before the night of the explosion and betrayed the arrangements to another party. That, however, is conjecture unsupported by any evidence except his tendency throughout his career to change sides. It is also difficult to explain why Balfour may have changed sides on the eve of the murder. Perhaps he had learnt that Darnley's plans had been leaked and that he himself would consequently be compromised.

If the gunpowder could have been brought into the Old Provost's Lodging only through an interconnecting passage from the vaults of the adjacent house, also owned by Robert Balfour, there would be strong circumstantial evidence against both of the Balfours. Irrespective of the placing of the gunpowder, those residing in the New Provost's Lodging would almost certainly have noticed or heard any unusual activities at the Old Provost's Lodging. Conspirators who intended to stage an elaborate murder plot at the Old Provost's Lodging must have looked to the Balfours for support or at least connivance. On 28 February 1567 Drury reported to Cecil that James Balfour had bought 60 Scots pounds worth of gunpowder from an Edinburgh man,[39] but Drury's information was often incorrect and may not prove James Balfour's involvement. Another query over Balfour's purchase of the gunpowder would be where he stored it without the secret being divulged or discovered.

Balfour, like Moray and Lethington, would have taken great care not to be openly incriminated over what happened at Kirk o'Field. His movements before and after the murders are not clear, but he was included in the placards as one of the murderers. Drury informed Cecil on 19 April 1567 that a servant of Balfour had been secretly killed and buried, apparently for uttering something which might lead to the whole discovery of Darnley's death.[40] He added that Balfour, due to some great fear, kept his house with great watch and ward. These allegations, of course, may have been mere gossip. There is no conclusive evidence against him. It is interesting that Melville in his *Memoirs* recollected that Balfour would not consent to be present nor take plain part with the murder of Darnley, but Melville quoted no source in support of his statement.

James Balfour's relationships with the other Scottish leaders at the time of the murder of Darnley and in subsequent months are far from clear. For some years he had not been aligned with the Protestant lords, and he seems to have been in some degree of danger from them at the time of the murder of Riccio. Yet possibly he was involved in their highly secret discussions at Craigmillar, and in June 1567 the rebel lords were willing to accept his help. His relationship with Bothwell was also mysterious. On 8 May 1567 Balfour was appointed Captain of Edinburgh Castle, and it is a reasonable assumption that Bothwell nominated him for such an important appointment. Perhaps Balfour had some incriminating information about Bothwell and blackmailed him to obtain the appointment. It is more likely that Bothwell still trusted him at that time, as, in early June, Bothwell entrusted the Casket to him. Balfour nevertheless switched his support away from Bothwell and Mary just before Carberry, and according to Nau he betrayed the Queen by giving her false assurances before she left Dunbar to proceed towards Edinburgh.

Balfour was devious. It is astonishing that Bothwell or anyone else trusted him. One person who would have been sufficiently foolish to trust him was Darnley. It was apparently at the sugggestion of Balfour that Darnley decided to reside at Kirk o'Field in a house belonging to Balfour's brother. This decision coupled with the near certainty that James Balfour was involved in the provision of the gunpowder suggests that Balfour was a participant in at least one plot.

THE HAMILTONS

In addition to those who were present at Craigmillar the Hamiltons had a motive for eliminating Darnley and also Mary, as they had a strong claim to the succession in Scotland following the deaths of Mary and her infant son. They would almost certainly have contested the succession of Darnley or Moray to the throne. They also had opportunities to plan the murder of Darnley in the house at Kirk o'Field as they owned a house nearby. If they took part in the murder, they could have escaped quickly to the Duke's house. It is not surprising that there were allegations of their involvement. Although the Duke himself was still in exile, his sons John and Claud were in Scotland. As early as 1 July 1567, Robert Melville reported to Cecil that the Hamiltons feared that Archbishop Hamilton, who was a half-brother of the Duke of Chatelherault, would be charged with Darnley's murder.[41] Then, in 1571, the Archbishop was arrested and executed for being party to the murders of Darnley and Moray. There is, however, no proper evidence to implicate any of the Hamiltons in the murder of Darnley.

A PARIS PLOT?

Mary's letter sent on 20 January 1567 to the Archbishop of Glasgow in Paris crossed with a letter from him written at Paris and dated 27 January.[42] Apparently she did not receive his letter (which was brought by an archer of the Royal Guard) until just after the murder of Darnley. The Archbishop informed Mary that the Spanish Ambassador had specifically required him to warn her to take heed to herself. The Archbishop had also heard some murmurings from others that some surprise was being trafficked against her. The Spanish Ambassador could not provide any details but he had been told to hasten to the Archbishop with the warning. The Archbishop had asked Catherine de Medici if she had received any information about a threat to Mary, but he had obtained nothing from her. The warning from the Spanish Ambassador could not have been related specifically to what happened at Kirk o'Field, as the move of Darnley to Kirk o'Field could not have been known in Paris as early as 27 January.

Several intriguing questions arise over this warning. It is not clear whether it related to Darnley's bid for Catholic backing against Mary or to a scheme devised by the Protestant lords. It is also not clear where and when the plot had been hatched and if it was receiving support from a foreign power. It is fairly clear that the Archbishop had expected Catherine to possess some further information but she had been either unable or unwilling to reveal anything. There is also mystery over why and whence and how the message was passed to the Spanish Ambassador. Why was the warning relayed with no details? Did the Ambassador obtain the news from a source in Paris or London or Madrid? His reticence suggests that revelation of the identity of at least one of the conspirators would have been embarrassing to Spain. Was the warning passed just to excuse Spain from any subsequent charge of complicity? Perhaps the originator of the warning was Mary's great friend during her years in France: Elisabeth de Valois, who had become the wife of Philip II, but she would have given Mary much more precise information. If it had been a hoax to incriminate another government or one of the factions in Scotland, it would have pointed more clearly in such a direction. The omission of any names meant that the warning was of little practical value to Mary.

Archbishop Beaton in his letter of 11 March 1567 to the Queen stated that the Spanish Ambassador had again passed to him a warning that he had been informed by the same means as before that Mary was to beware that there was some notable enterprise being planned against her.[43] The reiteration of the warning suggests that there was some substantial evidence to justify it, and also that the threat had not stemmed from Darnley as he was now dead.

If Mary genuinely believed that the explosion had been intended to kill her, the information from the Archbishop must have increased her anxiety over her own safety. According to her letter of 18 February 1567 to the Archbishop, she had also received a warning from the Spanish Ambassador in England, but she gave no details about when she received it or what was stated.[44] She repeated in her letter the belief that the events at Kirk o'Field 'may well appear to have been conspired against ourself'. It must again be stressed that the return of Morton and his ruffian henchmen such as Andrew Ker of Fawdonside had created danger for Mary as well as for Darnley.

In addition to the Archbishop's warnings there was a cryptic allusion to a plot originating in Paris in Cecil's letter of 21 March 1567 to Sir Henry Norris, the English Ambassador in Paris.[45] Cecil stated: 'we heard before your writing of the French attempt for the Prince'. The nature of this 'attempt' is not clear but the background may be the same as the statement in Norris' letter to Cecil dated 8 March 1567 that the King and the Queen Mother had 'caused an assembly of the nobility to consult for the getting of the Prince of Scotland into their regiment'.[46] Norris, in a letter of 5 April 1567 to Sir Nicholas Throckmorton in London, expressed the view that 'the origin of Darnley's murder came from hence, for besides their desire to have the Prince hither, those who were suspected were making this their chief refuge'.[47] He did not, however, give the names of these persons.

Spanish suspicions of French intentions at this time are shown in some other communications. On 16 December 1566, the Spanish Ambassador in London informed Philip II that it was quite clear the French would try to prevent a union of the two crowns in Britain.[48] After the murder of Darnley, the Ambassador wrote on 22 February to Philip, advising him that certain persons were not without suspicion that the whole affair might have been arranged by those who wished Mary to marry in France.[49] It is impossible to know whether these reports had any basis of substance.

Whatever may have been hatching in Paris, it is important to emphasise that there is no evidence that Darnley was plotting with the French. It should be noted that at the time of the Prince's baptism the French ambassador had refused to meet Darnley on the instructions of the French King.[50] Catherine de Medici, on hearing of Darnley's death, referred to him as 'that young madman'.[51] A French plot to place Darnley in power seems an unrealistic theory.

A more likely background for a plot concocted in Paris would have been a link between the French government and Moray aimed at avoiding the establishment of Spanish influence in Scotland. That might also explain the series of warnings from the Spanish Ambassadors and also the apparent indifference of Catherine de Medici when the Archbishop of Glasgow approached her. There is the curious interest of the French government during 1566 in trying to obtain the return of Morton and the other exiled Protestant lords who had become bitter enemies of Darnley and would give strong support to Moray. In August 1566, Bedford informed Cecil that Mauvissière had wrought very earnestly for the exiled lords.[52] (Michel de Castelnau, Sieur de la Mauvissière, was a French diplomat.) The pardon of Morton and his supporters (who were certainly not Mary's friends) was advocated by the French and English governments probably to weaken Mary's position and to strengthen opposition in Scotland to any pact with Spain. It should be added that their support for Morton would clash with any theory that these governments were backing a plot being put forward by Darnley.

Relationships between the French and English governments at this time had become less hostile due to mutual fear of Spain and the possibility of a Spanish invasion of England with backing from Mary.[53] In early 1567, the French and English governments and the Scottish Protestant lords all shared the same fear of a Catholic Britain ruled over by Mary and allied to Spain. The hostile attitude of Catherine de Medici to Mary should also be kept in mind. As Sir Henry Norris stated on 23 July 1567 in a despatch to Queen Elizabeth, 'the Queen-Mother loves not the Queen of Scots'.[54] Moray undoubtedly had good friends in Paris and London. When he was out of Scotland in 1567 neither the French nor the English governments took the opportunity to detain him as a hostage to secure the release of Mary from Lochleven Castle or at least to safeguard her life.

AN ENGLISH PLOT?

English backing for a plot instigated by Moray and the Scottish Protestant lords is a distinct possibility which cannot be discounted. The English government was frequently trying to interfere in Scottish affairs and had a track-record of helping Mary's opponents either overtly or secretly. Elizabeth and Cecil had attempted to topple Mary through Moray's rebellion in 1565, and they had foreknowledge of the plot against Riccio and even a threat to Mary's own person.[55] Yet no attempt was made to alert Mary. Then, on 30 December 1566, Bedford wrote to Cecil about Mary's agreement to the return of Morton and other exiles and referred to his own pleading for them 'by your advice'.[56] The influence of the English government was confirmed in the letter from Queen Elizabeth to Throckmorton dated 27 July 1567 stating that Morton 'was restored to his pardon for gratifying us, upon instance made by our order at the Earl of Bedford's being with the Queen'.[57] When considering Mary's motives for allowing Morton to return, the extent of English pressure should be noted, especially at a time when Elizabeth was raising Mary's hopes of being recognised as her successor.

The English Protestant leaders would have had strong motives for getting rid of both Mary and Darnley. Their elimination would have been a major setback for those who wished to restore the Catholic religion in England. They were aware of Darnley's schemes to facilitate a Spanish invasion by seizing the Scilly Isles and Scarborough. The deaths of Mary and Darnley would have removed the possibility of a Catholic succession in England after the death of Queen Elizabeth, as Prince James would have been brought up as a Protestant. Elizabeth's rude and unpleasant letter of 24 February 1567 to Mary[58] shows that she was very content to stir up trouble by casting slurs on Mary over the death of Darnley. There is, however, no proof of English involvement at Kirk o'Field.

THE IMPORTANCE OF PRINCE JAMES

The birth of Prince James had almost certainly increased the insecurity of Mary's position. If the Queen were killed, there would no longer be the risk of a dispute between rival claimants to the succession. Mary's own life had hitherto stood as a barrier to civil war in Scotland between rival factions. Henceforth she was in even greater jeopardy.

The historian RH Mahon suggested in 1923 that the true explanation of the tragedy of Mary will probably be found in the plots around the possession of Prince James. Whatever party controlled his upbringing would have been able to ensure that he would adhere to their religion. There was the additional factor of great consequence for western Europe that James was in direct line for the succession to the English Throne. Both the English and the French were interested in the possibility of James being brought up in their own country to promote their future influence in Scotland, and there was widespread speculation in western Europe about their intentions. The elimination of Mary or of both Mary and Darnley would have created a new situation with an infant monarch on the throne. The background to the events at Kirk o'Field was undoubtedly very complex. There may have been several undercurrents to what happened at Kirk o'Field, and either the English or the French government or both may have been involved.

The plot against Mary mentioned by the Spanish Ambassadors may never have existed or it may have been linked to Darnley's plans about the time of the Prince's baptism or it may have been due to take place at a later date than 10 February 1567. Any ruler in those turbulent times was perpetually liable to be the sudden victim of a plot, and it was also difficult to check the substance of any rumour of a plot. It is, however, clear that Archbishop Beaton had no doubt about the gravity of the warnings from the Spanish Ambassador in Paris. These warnings certainly add another dimension to the mystery of what happened at Kirk o'Field. It is remarkable that many distinguished historians have either ignored the Archbishop's letters or failed to consider their implications.

The issues at stake in this crisis were of great significance. It is therefore not surprising that Mary's opponents subsequently used every means available to them to justify their own actions and ensure that guilt was pinned on Mary and Bothwell.

Part 2
The Casket Letters

5. THE DISCOVERY AND DISCLOSURE OF THE CASKET LETTERS

THE DISCOVERY OF THE CASKET

ACCORDING TO THE DECLARATION which Morton made at Westminster on 9 December 1568, he arranged for the arrest of George Dalgleish, a servant of Bothwell, on 19 June 1567 in Edinburgh. This followed a tip-off from Sir James Balfour, Captain of Edinburgh Castle.[1] Apparently Bothwell had asked Dalgleish to collect from the Castle a Casket which he had left there. Morton asserted that on 20 June Dalgleish agreed to give evidence before there was any rigorous demeaning (torture) of his person. In the early evening he was taken to a house where he produced a silver Casket. It therefore seems probable that Dalgleish was subjected for the greater part of a day to interrogation and at least the threat of torture. Morton kept the Casket overnight and broke it open next morning in the presence of several nobles and also Lethington and Archibald Douglas. Morton's delay in opening the Casket seems a little contrived, and it suggests that he may have obtained prior knowledge of the contents, perhaps from James Balfour. The Letters in the Casket were examined and then returned to Morton for safekeeping, but there is no record that a list of the contents was taken. At Westminster in December 1568 Lethington was the only other person who had also been present at the opening of the Casket. It is most unlikely that Lethington in December 1568 would have repudiated Morton's account of the discovery of the Casket Letters. As Morton's Declaration did not become public knowledge at the time, it could not be challenged by other contemporaries. It was not published until 1889.[2] There is no certainty that the contents were not initially manipulated in various ways between 15 June (Mary's surrender at Carberry) and 20 June.

There are several points in the story of the discovery of the Casket which must be queried. There is no information about the dates on which Bothwell entrusted the Casket to Balfour, asked Dalgleish to collect the Casket, and realised that Balfour had deserted to the rebel lords. Morton's account of Dalgleish's role has several significant omissions, such as how Dalgleish was permitted to enter the Castle and take away the Casket. It is strange that Balfour himself took no direct action to apprehend Dalgleish. It is almost inconceivable that the astute Balfour allowed a Casket belonging to Bothwell to slip out of his grasp. It is curious that it was Dalgleish, just a chamber-servant to Bothwell, who took the Casket rather than Mr Thomas Hepburn, the parson of Oldhamstocks, or John Cockburn, brother to the laird of Skirling, who had, according to Morton, gone to the Castle with Dalgleish. It is also surprising and suspicious that the deposition of Dalgleish taken on 26 June (concerning his role in helping Bothwell at Kirk o'Field) contained no reference to his visit to the Castle and his removal of the Casket. As Dalgleish was executed in January 1568, he could not be subjected to cross-examination in the conferences at York and Westminster. The story of Dalgleish and the Casket may be partially or even totally fabricated. If so, the true story of the discovery of the Casket Letters must be sought elsewhere.

THE DISCLOSURE OF THE LETTERS

There was no immediate and sensational publication of the Letters. Neither Robert Birrel nor the author of the *Diurnal* ever mentioned the Casket Letters. No rumour reached Drury at Berwick. Lethington on 21 June sent Robert Melville to London with a letter to Cecil asking for Queen Elizabeth's support in doing justice on the murderers of Darnley,[3] but there is no reference to the Casket Letters. Yet the Casket had been opened that morning in the presence of Lethington according to Morton. Within a few weeks, however, the news began to circulate, at least in official circles, that some Letters incriminating Mary had been found.

On 12 July, Guzman de Silva, the Spanish Ambassador in London, wrote to Philip II informing him that he had learnt from M de la Forrest (the French Ambassador in London) who had met M du Croc (the French Ambassador in Scotland) on his way back from Scotland to France, that Mary's adversaries asserted positively that they knew she had been concerned in the murder of Darnley from Letters under her own hand.[4] Copies of these were 'in his possession', but whose possession is not clear from the despatch.

Possibly the passage was deciphered incorrectly.[5] It is not known if M du Croc had been given copies of all the Letters eventually produced at Westminster in December 1568; whether they were copies in the Original French or translations into Scots; what happened to these copies; and if they were identical to the final versions. It is surprising that de Silva did not see the copies or at least obtain more details of what were, if authentic, very important documents. It is also surprising that the Scottish lords at this time apparently did not send copies to the

English and Spanish governments. Furthermore, the release of copies to M du Croc is curiously at variance with the subsequent reluctance, for over a year, of the Scottish lords to display the Letters. The evidence is tantalising and inconclusive.

On 21 July de Silva wrote again to Philip II.[6] He had mentioned to Queen Elizabeth that the Scottish lords held certain Letters which incriminated Mary. The Queen replied that it was not true, although Lethington had acted badly in the matter and that when she saw him she would say some words to him which would not give him much pleasure. The meaning of Elizabeth's reply is not clear, and she did not disclose the source of her information. Perhaps she obtained it through John a Forret, who carried a letter from Robert Melville in Fife to Cecil dated 8 July 1567 stating that the bearer knew all occurrents.[7] Then on 25 July Throckmorton sent a despatch from Scotland to Queen Elizabeth informing her that the Protestant lords intended to charge Mary with the murder of Darnley, asserting they had proof by the testimony of her own handwriting.[8] On 2 August, de Silva reported to Philip a conversation in which Moray had told him about a Letter from Mary to Bothwell proving she had been cognisant of the murder.[9] Apparently Moray did not mention any of the other Casket Letters. It is surprising he did not refer to them if he knew that they existed. It is important to realise that French and Spanish sources at that time did not immediately reject the claims made by the Scottish lords that Letters had been found incriminating Mary. Her standing in Catholic countries had fallen due to her failure to restore the Catholic religion. Her reputation had fallen further by her hasty marriage to the reputed murderer of Darnley. Assertions about the incriminating contents of the Casket Letters therefore had a receptive audience in some quarters abroad.

There seems to have been a lull in the disclosure of the Casket Letters until December 1567 when Moray and his Council presented to the Scottish Parliament an Act which referred to the Queen's 'Privy Letters wholly written with her own hand'.[10] The Letters were not described as being signed by her although in the record of the Secret Council held earlier in the month it was stated that she had subscribed them.[11] This omission in the Act may or may not be important. It is not clear what were Moray's motives in drawing attention to the Letters at this stage, but probably he wanted to justify the continuing imprisonment of Mary. It is also not clear how far the Letters were circulated to those present, nor which Letters were produced, nor to what extent they were examined. It seems that there was no specific mention of the Sonnets and the Marriage Contracts until the conference at York in October 1568 when the Casket Letters were shown privately to the English Commissioners. It must also be pointed out that, apparently until December 1568, the precise number of the Letters was not revealed. This gave Mary's enemies ample time to make adjustments to the list.

The reason why Moray and his associates did not release the Casket Letters officially until the conference at Westminster in December 1568 is not known, but there are at least four possible explanations. One is that they may not have been sure of Elizabeth's reactions to their publication; another is that Moray and his associates did not wish to sour too far their relationships with Mary in case she returned to power; they may have held them back as some form of pressure on Mary; or that time was needed to edit and forge the final versions of the Letters in similar handwriting.

THE SUPPRESSED LETTER

An indication that the final version of the most important of the Casket Letters – the long Glasgow Letter – had not yet been decided in the summer of 1567 is given in the despatch dated 2 August 1567 from de Silva to Philip II.[12] He related the details of a letter which Moray had described to him. This letter was written in Mary's own hand and signed by her. It said that Bothwell was not to delay putting into execution what he had arranged. She herself would go and fetch Darnley and would stop at a house on the road, where she would try to give him a draught, but if this could not be done she would put him in the house where the explosion was arranged for the night upon which one of her servants was to be married. In the meanwhile Bothwell must contrive to get rid of his wife either by a divorce or by giving her some drink to cause her death. Moray had told de Silva that he had heard about the letter from a man who had read it, and the rest was notorious.

There were important differences between this alleged letter and the long Glasgow Letter produced in 1568 to the English Commissioners. The 'suppressed' version could not have been written in Glasgow as Mary was volunteering to go and fetch Darnley (who was in Glasgow). Unlike the 1568 version this letter was signed by Mary. There were also other differences. The 1568 version contained no indication that an attempt might be made to poison Darnley on the way to Edinburgh, nor about the intended explosion at Kirk o'Field, nor about Bothwell getting rid of Lady Bothwell by a divorce or by murder. These are not minor, petty differences which could easily have arisen through Moray receiving a description of the letter from another person and then relaying it to de Silva. They are points of major substance. It should also be noted that virtually everything which the Ambassador recorded about the letter is different from the final version of the long Glasgow Letter. De Silva's despatch is certainly not conclusive evidence of the existence of a 'suppressed' letter, but his account cannot be ignored. Moray should have been fully briefed about the contents of any Letters allegedly found in the Casket on 21 June, and the major discrepancies cannot be dismissed.

There is further evidence, though also not conclusive, for the existence of an early suppressed version of the long Glasgow Letter. In the *First Narrative* prepared by Lennox, probably late in May 1568, there is a description of the contents of a letter sent to Bothwell by Mary from Glasgow. This version (like de Silva's) stated that Mary proposed the night of Bastian's marriage for the murder, and also that Bothwell should not fail in the meantime to despatch his wife and to give her the drink as they had devised before.

Both Lennox's version and Moray's assert that Mary had proposed the night of Bastian's marriage for the murder, and that she had done so before her return from Glasgow. This, however, clashes with the alleged deposition of John Hay. He is supposed to have stated that the deed would have been executed on the night of Saturday 8 February but was delayed because all things were not ready. The choice of the wedding night would have given Mary an excuse for leaving Darnley on that night, but she did not stay every night at Kirk o'Field and did not really need an excuse to leave him. Mary's proposal, if inserted at a later date into a forged letter, would of course have fitted neatly into what actually took place. The choice of such a date so far in advance seems very improbable. Mary could not have been certain before leaving Edinburgh that Darnley would still be convalescing on the night of 9/10 February and would be in the house at Kirk o'Field. The discrepancy with Hay's account may point to a lack of collusion in preparing the version subsequently suppressed. The reliability of Hay's deposition, however, is questionable.

The Lennox version and the version quoted by Moray have much in common and almost certainly came from the same source.[13] It should also be noted that there was about a year's gap between Moray's remark and Lennox's statement. The suppressed version was therefore under consideration for quite a long time. It is very difficult to accept that the suppressed version was a genuine letter written by Mary. The contents of such a murderous letter would have been far too incriminating not to have been produced as evidence against her. It must be emphasised that nothing similar to the suppressed letter was mentioned in either the *Detection* or the *Indictment* or the *Hopetoun Manuscript*. At some time in the summer of 1568 it was presumably rejected and put aside. The rejection of this version implies that the final form of the long Glasgow Letter had not been produced by June 1568.

MORAY'S DESPATCH OF COPIES TO ENGLAND

Mary's escape into England in May 1568 forced Moray and his associates to produce evidence which would convince Queen Elizabeth that their deposition of Mary from the throne had been justified and also provide her with an excuse to keep Mary under surveillance in England. Their approach, however, was remarkably cautious. They did not immediately send Elizabeth copies of the Casket Letters in the Original French. On 22 June Moray informed Mr Henry Middlemore, an emissary from Queen Elizabeth, that he had sent to Mr John Wood, Moray's envoy in London, a set of the Letters translated into Scots to be considered by the English judges who would have examination and commission of the matter. Moray hoped that the judges would resolve that, provided the originals agreed with the copies, he had proved the case against Mary.[14] It is not known which Letters were sent. It is also not known which persons in England, apart from Cecil, saw the copies nor what happened subsequently to these copies. Apparently there was no written reply from the English Queen to this astonishing and revealing enquiry.

The approach raises doubts about Moray's confidence in both the acceptability of the Casket Letters and the consistency of Queen Elizabeth's support for him. It is also remarkable that the copies were sent not in the Original French but in a Scots translation. If Moray had sent copies in the Original French, it could reasonably be argued that he was merely being wary of Queen Elizabeth's overall reaction to the Letters. The despatch of translations – not even in English but in Scots – raises question-marks against his integrity. Moray may have reckoned that if the contents were deemed inadequate to prove Mary's guilt, suitable adjustments could still be made to the originals and the differences attributed to errors in copying or translating. The significant divergences between the Scots and English translations of the Casket Letters reveal the standard of accuracy of translators at that time. It would therefore have been easy to claim that the translation of Letters sent in June 1568 had been faulty. Furthermore, if the Letters shown to the English had been deemed inadequate to prove Mary's guilt, it would not have been difficult for Lethington or someone else to produce more 'Casket Letters'. Moray could have expected some collusion from Elizabeth and Cecil. It should be appreciated that relations between Elizabeth and Moray were very cordial at this time. On 13 July, Moray wrote to her stating that John Wood had conveyed her gracious inclination, upright dealing and just zeal, and Moray had resolved to prosecute the cause so far as Queen Elizabeth should think expedient.[15]

THE PROBLEMS FACING THE COMMISSIONERS

All the participants in the conferences at York and Westminster were facing possible pitfalls. The English Commissioners had to be cautious in their statements in case they offended Elizabeth (who was reluctant to condemn another monarch) or Secretary Cecil (who was anxious over the potential threat to Protestant England from Mary). Another unpredictable pitfall was that their Queen was prone to change her attitude.

Moray and his associates also had their problems. They were hesitant about pushing their accusations against Mary and producing the Casket Letters either from lack of confidence in their case or from uncertainty over Elizabeth's long-term support from them. At York no formal declaration was made by Moray accusing Mary of complicity in the murder of Darnley. Moray concentrated on justifying the action of the Confederate lords in rebelling against her on the grounds of a shameful marriage with Bothwell.

Mary's Commissioners were hampered by having to negotiate at some distance from where Mary was being kept in confinement. This problem was aggravated when the proceedings were transferred to Westminster in midwinter. They also faced the disadvantage that there was a measure of understanding and underhand dealing between the English Commissioners and Moray and his associates.

All the Scots had a further problem. The proceedings held in England with the semblance of a trial encouraged the English to revive their old claim of suzerainty over Scotland. Mary consistently maintained her rights as an independent sovereign. In the Instructions to her Commissioners at York she stated that she was willing to use Queen Elizabeth's counsel towards her subjects without prejudice to her honour, estate, crown, authority and title, and that she was a free Princess acknowledging no other superior.[16] Lethington also stoutly refuted the ill-founded English pretensions.[17]

THE PROCEEDINGS AT YORK

In September 1568, Moray received from Morton a silver Casket containing the Letters to take to England.[18] The precise number of the documents was not recorded. There is also no record of any copies having been taken and retained in Scotland at this time. On 11 October the English commissioners at York wrote to Queen Elizabeth stating that they had been secretly shown (without Mary's Commissioners being informed) certain Letters. They specifically referred to the two Glasgow Letters, Letter IV, two of the Stirling Letters, the two Marriage

Contracts, the Sonnets, the Band allegedly signed at Aynesleyes's Tavern, the Queen's prior warrant for the signing of that Band, and a letter arranging a duel between Darnley and Mary's half-brother Lord Robert.[19] It was not disclosed which of the Stirling Letters were shown.

It is not known if Letters III and V and the other Stirling Letter were divulged at this time. If those three Letters were not shown at York, there is no record of any surprise being displayed by the English when they were produced at Westminster. Possibly they were not ready in October 1568. Although Letters III and V contain very little of significance and might not have attracted much attention at York, it is very odd that the English Commissioners at York referred specifically to only two 'Stirling' Letters being shown to them at that time.

The English Commissioners enclosed extracts of the most incriminating passages with their letter.[20] They stated:

> they showed unto us one horrible and long letter of her own hand, as they say, containing foul matter, and abominable to be either thought of or to be written by a prince, with divers fond ballads of her own hand; which letters, ballads, and other writings before specified, were closed in a little coffer of silver, and gilt, heretofore given by her to Bothwell. The said ballads and letters do discover such inordinate and filthy love between her and Bothwell, her loathsomeness and abhorring of her husband that was murdered, in such sort as every good and godly man cannot but detest and abhor the same. And these men here do constantly affirm the said letters and other writings which they produce of her own hand, to be of her own hand indeed, and do offer to swear and take their oaths thereupon, the matter contained in them being such as could hardly be invented or devised by any other than by herself; for that they discourse of some things which were unknown to any other than to herself and Bothwell. And as it is hard to counterfeit so many, so the matter of them, and the manner how these men came by them, is such, as it seemeth that God (in whose sight murder and bloodshed of the innocent is abominable) would not permit the same to be hid or concealed.[21]

It would seem that the Letters were presented as having been written in Mary's own hand. Yet the extracts sent to London were in Scots. Possibly the wording of the letter to London is misleading. Either the English Commissioners did not understand what the Scots had said to them or Moray and his associates misled them for some purpose. The English Commissioners must have known that Mary would have written any private letters in French. It is again highly suspicious that the original Letters in French were still not produced.

Despite the shocked tone of the letter to Elizabeth it is not certain what were the private reactions of the English Commissioners. Some passages in their letter to Elizabeth were very carefully erased or disguised, though not rendered completely illegible.[22] It seems that the Commissioners had originally believed that the Letters were genuine, but before despatching their report they decided to be much more guarded on their authenticity. Furthermore, the Duke of Norfolk within a few days of seeing the Letters was becoming interested in the possibility of a marriage with Mary, although the Letters portrayed her as having planned the murder of her previous husband. Another English Commissioner, the Earl of Sussex, had doubts about the likely outcome of the conference. On 22 October he wrote to Cecil pointing out:

> if her adverse party accuse her of the murder by producing of
> her letters, she will deny them, and accuse the most of them of
> manifest consent to the murder, hardly to be denied; so as,
> upon the trial on both sides, her proofs will judicially fall best
> out, as it is thought.[23]

It should be noted that the English Commissioners at York gave no indication that they were already aware of the existence of the Casket Letters. Yet in June 1568 Moray had sent copies to Cecil. It is strange that apparently Cecil had not revealed the existence of these copies to the English Commissioners, but this may be typical of his cautious approach. It is, however, much more surprising that Moray and his associates did not point out in October that the English government had already received copies. Possibly this indicates that some modifications to the Casket Letters had been made since June.

THE PROCEEDINGS AT WESTMINSTER

The three English Commissioners were joined at Westminster by a further ten English Commissioners, including Sir William Cecil. On 6 December, Moray read the Book of Articles to the English Commissioners. This was a list of accusations against Mary. Moray and his associates must have been fully aware that much of the material was false, and the English Commissioners should have spotted at least some of the lies and misrepresentations.[24] After 6 December, Mary's Commissioners took no further part in the proceedings in protest against Elizabeth's refusal to allow Mary to be present. Then, on 7 December, Moray and his associates produced:

> a small gilded coffer of not fully one foot long, being garnished
> in many places with the Roman letter F set under a Royal
> Crown wherein were certain letters and writings.[25]

The Letters were the originals in French of those numbered I to VIII
in this book and were the final versions of the Casket Letters. They
comprised five of the Letters shown informally at York and three others.
On 7 December, the English were shown the two Glasgow Letters and
the two Marriage Contracts. On the next day the other six Letters and
the Sonnets were produced and were avowed to have been written by
Mary.[26] These

> seven writings, being copied, were read in French, and a due
> collation made thereof as near as could be by reading and
> inspection, and made to accord with the originals, which the
> said Earl of Murray required to be redelivered.

The depositions from Bothwell's followers were also shown to the
English Commissioners. On 9 December, the conference heard state-
ments written by Thomas Nelson (Darnley's servant) and Thomas
Crawford (one of Lennox's followers).[27]

Moray and his associates did not produce two of the documents they
had shown to the English at York. The originals and any copies of these
two documents have disappeared, and their precise contents are not
known. One was the warrant, allegedly signed by Mary and specifically
dated 19 April, authorising the nobles to sign the Band which approved
the proposed marriage with Bothwell.[28] At York it had been alleged that
none of the nobles at the supper, apart from Huntly, would sign the
Band before they had the Queen's warrant to do so. Yet, according to
Buchanan's *History*, the warrant was signed retrospectively. As Herries
and Boyd had signed the Band and were there at Westminster, they
would have been able to confirm or dispute the authenticity of such a
warrant. The English Commissioners who were present at both York
and Westminster must have been aware that such an important document
was being withheld. Their integrity must be questioned. Buchanan, who
was present at York, must have been another party to this act of deceit.

The other missing document was a letter alleged to contain a reference
to a quarrel at Kirk o'Field, provoked by Mary, between Darnley and
Lord Robert Stewart. This was intended to lead to Darnley's death in a
duel, but Mary had intervened by summoning Moray. Buchanan in his
History asserted that Lord Robert informed Darnley at Kirk o'Field
that he was in danger. Darnley repeated this to Mary. Then Lord Robert
denied that he had said so. The story is also mentioned briefly in the

Detection, the *Indictment*, the *Hopetoun Manuscript* and Melville's *Memoirs*. Lord Robert had been one of Darnley's cronies after he arrived in Scotland in 1565, though the extent of their friendship in early 1567 is not clear.[29] Possibly there was a quarrel between Lord Robert and Darnley, and the story may have some basis. Details may have been added to incriminate Mary. Probably the missing letter is Letter IV which was shown at York and has a very obscure sentence just conceivably relating to the quarrel. It was certainly an ingenious interpretation of the sentence to link it to the alleged quarrel. If the story was true it is astonishing that Darnley did not take adequate precautions for his own safety during the rest of his stay at Kirk o'Field.

It is curious that Moray and his associates did not show the English Commissioners a letter which Melville mentioned in his *Memoirs*. He related that on the night of Mary's surrender at Carberry she wrote a letter to Bothwell. According to Melville, she called Bothwell her dear heart whom she would never forget nor abandon. She promised a reward to one of her keepers to see it safely conveyed to Bothwell at Dunbar, but he delivered it to the rebel lords, who used it to justify sending her to imprisonment at Lochleven. Melville asserted that the letter had subsequently been shown to Kirkcaldy of Grange, who had been angry over the rebel lords' breach of the promises he had given to the Queen at Carberry, but the letter 'had stopped his mouth'. The whole story, however, depends on the reliability of Melville's account, and there must be considerable doubt over the existence and authenticity of such a letter.

It is far from clear how carefully the English Commissioners studied the Casket Letters when they were produced at Westminster. The Casket Letters were not released until after Mary's Commissioners had withdrawn. So there was no one present to challenge their authenticity. The English Commissioners should have been able to understand them in French, but English translations were also available at least by 9 December.[30]

THE PROCEEDINGS AT HAMPTON COURT

After an interval in the proceedings, a meeting of the English Privy Council was held at Hampton Court, where the English Commissioners were joined by six more earls. On 14 December

> there were produced sundry letters written in French supposed to be written by the Queen of Scots' own hand, to the Earl of Bothwell — of which letters the originals were then also

> presently produced and perused; and being read, were duly
> conferred and compared, for the manner of writing and fashion
> of orthography, with sundry other letters long since heretofore
> written, and sent by the said Queen of Scots to the Queen's
> Majesty, — In collation whereof no difference was found —
> And forasmuch as the night approached, it was thought good to
> defer the further declaration of the rest until the next day
> following.[31]

It may be inferred from the comparison with other letters written by
Mary that the Casket Letters were either genuine or carefully written
forgeries. The English Commissioners, however, did not have the skill
of modern handwriting experts, and their opinions are not conclusive
proof on this point.

Cecil described what happened on the following day when further
documents (including the Book of Articles and the Contract dated 5
April) were produced:

> it is to be noted, that at the time of the producing, showing and
> reading of all these foresaid writings, there was no special
> choice nor regard had to the order of the producing thereof, but
> the whole writings lying all together upon the Council table, the
> same were one after another showed rather by hap, as the same
> did lie upon the table, than with any choice made, as by the
> natures thereof, if time had so served, might have been.[32]

Cecil's record is remarkably candid. The scene presented by him is
that on a day in midwinter (long before the provision of electric lights)
there were 19 English Commissioners around the Council table
examining the papers of great importance lying scattered on it. Presumably Moray and his associates were also present as they would not
have parted with the originals. There seems to have been a 'guillotine'
on the time allowed for perusal of the Letters, judging from Cecil's
comment 'if time had so served'. It is astonishing that Cecil recorded
such an admission, unless he had some special reason for doing so. It
should also be noted that in none of the records of the proceedings in
England is there any indication of questions being asked about the
contents of the various documents. The extent of the examination of
the Letters cannot stand comparison with the minute scrutiny given by
many historians in subsequent centuries. Furthermore, at Westminster
and Hampton Court the Letters were not scrutinised by impartial judges.
The English Commissioners knew that their findings would have to be
acceptable to their Queen. It was basically a political, not a judicial
process.

The English earls wrote to Elizabeth stating:

> they had seen such foul matters as they thought truly in their consciences that Her Majesty's had just cause herein given to make the said Commissioners such an answer [her refusal to meet Mary] being as reasonable as the case might bear; and the rather [sic] for that they could not allow it as meet for Her Majesty's honour to admit the said Queen to Her Majesty's presence as the case now did stand'.[33]

MARY'S DEFENCE

The statements made by Mary and her Commissioners have been carefully scrutinised by historians to see if any admissions were made about the genuineness of the Casket Letters and also how far her own Commissioners were convinced of her innocence. Her leading Commissioners were Herries and Bishop Leslie. Some have assumed that when Herries asked Queen Elizabeth in June 1568 what would happen to Mary if it appeared she was guilty, he was admitting his own doubts. Such an assumption seems unwarranted. In the first place he reported the conversation to Mary[34] and it is unlikely that he would have revealed to her any lack of conviction in her innocence. Secondly, he added 'que Dieu ne veuille' (equivalent to 'God forbid') to his question to Elizabeth about the possibility of Mary being deemed guilty. Thirdly, in May he had tried to dissuade Mary from crossing the Solway as he feared what might happen to her in England. Clearly he was not convinced that Mary would get a fair hearing. It is also relevant to add that he had just risked his life at the Battle of Langside fighting for Mary. At York he made the enigmatic statement that he would say nothing but what was just and true but would in no ways say all in this matter that he knew to be true.[35] It is not known what he was refusing to divulge. It might be surmised that he was intending to shield Mary from some unhelpful testimony such as what he may have heard about the Craigmillar discussions. When Bishop Leslie was examined in London in November 1571, he stated that in September 1568 he had feared that Moray and his associates would utter all that they could for their own defences even though it were to the Queen's dishonour.[36] He said he had therefore told Mary he wished that the whole matter should first be treated by way of agreement before any accusations were uttered. The Queen had replied that there was no such danger in the matter for she trusted that Leslie would find the judges favourable, especially the Duke of Norfolk. It should, however, be appreciated that in November 1571 Leslie was being questioned by the English government which was gathering evidence to make a case against Norfolk for treason.

At Westminster on 4 December, Mary's Commissioners, acting on their own initiative and without consulting her, suggested to Elizabeth that there should be some arrangement to settle the dispute,[37] but Elizabeth insisted that Mary's honour was at stake in view of the charge of murder and that Moray must proceed to produce his proofs. The compromise proposed by Leslie and Herries has usually been interpreted as indicating their acceptance of the authenticity of the Casket Letters. It is equally possible that they realised that the publication of the Letters (whether authentic or forged) was bound to besmirch Mary across Europe. It should be noted that they stated clearly that their proposals did not come from Mary, and there is no sound evidence that they believed their Queen was guilty of complicity in Darnley's murder. It is also very relevant that apparently Herries was willing to fight a duel on 23 December 1568 against those in Moray's party whom he considered guilty of the murder of Darnley, but his cartel was not accepted.[38]

Mary's own statements were firm and specific. The instructions she gave to her Commissioners at York included:

> in case they allege they have any writings of mine, which may infer presumptions against me in that cause, you shall desire the principals to be produced, and that I myself may have inspection thereof, and make answer thereto. For you shall affirm, in my name, I never wrote anything concerning that matter to any creature. And if there are any such writings, they are false and feigned, forged and invented by themselves only to my dishonour and slander; and there are several in Scotland, both men and women, that can counterfeit my handwriting, and write the same manner of writing which I use as well as myself, and principally such as are in company with themselves [this may be a reference to Lethington]. And I doubt not, if I had remained in my own realm, that I would have got knowledge of the inventors and writers of such writings.[39]

Mary's answer, dated 19 December, to the Eik presented by Moray was also a firm rebuttal:

> in all times, when the Earl of Moray and his accomplices have said, spoken, or written, that we knew, concealed, devised, persuaded, or commanded the said murder, they have falsely, traitorously, and wickedly lied, imputing unto us maliciously the crime whereof they themselves are authors, inventors, doers, and some of them proper executors.[40]

She instructed her Commissioners to ask for the inspection and doubles of all that they had produced against her, and also to ask that she should see the originals of the alleged writings in order to make her answer to them so far that her innocence would be known to Elizabeth and all other Princes. It is difficult to perceive how Mary could have been more positive in repudiating the Casket Letters, especially when she was not allowed to see them. Yet some historians have had such a strong in-built presumption of Mary's guilt that they have rejected her denials as insufficiently positive.

THE CONCLUSION OF THE CONFERENCE

At the end of the conference in January 1569, Queen Elizabeth secured exactly what she had almost certainly wanted from the start of the proceedings. There would be a friendly regime under Moray's control in Scotland, posing no threat to Protestant England. Mary would remain in England as a virtual prisoner with the question of her innocence left unresolved. That stain on her character would act as a deterrent to some of her potential supporters in both kingdoms and on the continent. Moray also obtained a reasonably satisfactory outcome from the conference, as he remained in power in Scotland. The conference was a disaster for Mary, as she regained neither her reputation nor her liberty nor her throne. She was nevertheless fortunate that the proceedings did not take place a few years later after the Massacre of St Bartholomew in France in August 1572, when fears and passions ran high in England against Catholics.

It is difficult to be certain what were the reactions of all the English Commissioners to the evidence presented to them by Moray and his associates. They were under strong pressure from Cecil, who wished to ruin Mary, but there seems to have been some reluctance to proceed too far against Mary.[41] Although the English Commissioners denounced Mary, they refrained from recommending her execution.

The procedural wrangling between Elizabeth and Mary, which resulted in Mary not being allowed to appear herself to challenge her accusers, can be held to point to Mary's innocence or guilt. Plausible cases can be made in either direction. It is, however, obvious that Mary and her Commissioners were not given full opportunities to clear the charges against her. Elizabeth was not impartial and was adept at deceiving Mary over her real intentions. In order to retain her Scottish rival in custody, she was reluctant to allow Mary the opportunity to prove her innocence. It is, however, far from certain that Mary could have proved her innocence. In her counter-charges against Moray,

Morton and Lethington, the Queen never produced any supporting evidence. On the other hand, apart from the highly questionable Casket Letters, only circumstantial evidence was produced against Mary. It is very doubtful whether either of the parties could have produced conclusive evidence. It must, however, be stressed again that the conferences at York and Westminster were basically not judicial proceedings. The issues at stake were essentially political. In addition to the conferences there was considerable discussion and correspondence between the parties about a settlement. In the background there was also the constant threat to Elizabeth's own security from the existence of Mary. A further complication was that by January 1569 relations between England and Spain had become very tense following the English retention in December 1568 of a treasure-fleet carrying money for Spanish troops in the Netherlands. Elizabeth could not risk setting Mary free.

THE DISAPPEARANCE OF THE CASKET LETTERS

At the end of the Westminster conference, Moray took the originals of the Casket Letters back to Scotland. After Moray's death in January 1570, the next Regent, the Earl of Lennox (Darnley's father), recovered them from Moray's servants. Then, in February 1571, Morton was entrusted with the Casket and Letters on a mission to London to oppose a settlement which would have been advantageous to Mary. Before his departure, the Casket Letters were copied and subscribed by Lennox and the Lords of the Council. These copies were to remain with Lennox, but there is no record of what happened to them.[42] By that time, one of the original documents may have disappeared, as Morton was given only 21 instead of 22 (counting eight Letters, two Marriage Contracts and 12 Sonnets as 22). It is not known which was missing nor when and how it was lost. The missing document was not one of the two Marriage Contracts, as the record of the Privy Council referred to marriage contracts as well as missive letters, sonnets and other letters to the number of 21. Possibly the discrepancy was just an error. Perhaps some historians have been at fault in counting each Sonnet to reach a neat total of 22. In 1571 the documents may have been counted in a very different way. Unfortunately the wording of the Council's record is not sufficiently precise to settle this point. The apparent discrepancy may or may not be significant. If the missive letters were the eight Casket Letters, there is the interesting question of what were 'the other letters'? Another intriguing possibility is that one document may have been surreptitiously removed when 'the whole writings' were lying haphazardly on the table at Hampton Court on 15 December – that might account for Cecil's remarkable description of the scene. It has been assumed that Morton brought the Casket and the Letters back to Scotland a few weeks later and retained custody of them after he became Regent in October 1572.

It is not known why Morton took the Casket Letters to England early in 1571, nor whether this was initially at the request of the Scottish or the English government. It is also not known if the Letters were shown to anyone during Morton's visit. It is astonishing that Morton took the Letters with him. Travelling was difficult and dangerous in those times, and he risked being waylaid and losing the Casket. He must have had strong reasons for taking the Letters. Probably Morton took them to reinforce his arguments against a settlement with Mary. This would mean that there had not been outright rejection nor much criticism of the Letters at Westminster in 1568. Yet it is puzzling that Morton considered that something could be gained from producing them again unless the plan was to barter them for some advantage in the negotiations.

After Morton's death in 1581, it seems that the Letters passed into the control of the Earl of Gowrie. He was the son of the Lord Ruthven who had led the murderers of Riccio. He himself had bullied Mary into abdicating in July 1567. In November 1582 Sir Robert Bowes, Queen Elizabeth's envoy, tried to obtain the Letters for Elizabeth from Gowrie.[43] Their location had been unknown until Bowes ascertained from the Prior of Pluscarden, an illegitimate son of Morton,[44] that Gowrie held the Casket and the Letters. At first Gowrie was loath to admit that they were in his possession, but Bowes convinced Gowrie that he knew he had them. Gowrie said he could not deliver them to anyone without the permission of the King and also the noblemen who had taken action against Mary. Bowes tried to persuade Gowrie to hand them over to him, but Gowrie reiterated that he could not do so and asserted that the King knew where they were. Bowes never saw the Letters and there can be no certainty that Gowrie did hold them. It can only be conjectured why Elizabeth wished to obtain the Letters, why Gowrie tried to deny possessing them, and why he refused to part with them.

There is no record of what happened to the Casket Letters after Gowrie was executed in 1584 (for his part in conspiracies to gain control of the government). There has been speculation that the Letters were destroyed, because they were authentic or forged. Possibly James VI obtained them, but his motives in getting rid of them can be only a matter of surmise. The last occasion when it is certain that they existed was Morton's embassy to England in 1571. It is, however, unlikely that Morton would have destroyed them while the possibility of Mary being restored still existed, as he would have again produced them as evidence against her.

THE DISAPPEARANCE OF THE CASKET

There is also uncertainty over what happened to the Casket. It may be a mistake to assume too readily that the Letters were kept in the original Casket after Moray's return from England in 1569. That Casket had been forced open in June 1567 and unless it had been repaired it would not have been secure. On the other hand, it seems that a degree of mystique was attached to the original Casket as it was taken to England in 1568 by Moray and again in 1571 by Morton as part of the evidence. So it may have been preserved. There is also no conclusive proof that the Casket now at Lennoxlove in East Lothian is the Casket which contained the Casket Letters. There is a long gap in its pedigree and there are some differences in appearance. It is, however, very similar.[45]

THE PUBLICATION OF THE LETTERS

The Letters were published late in 1571 and probably in London. In retrospect, the delay is surprising. The reason can only be surmised. Both the Scottish and the English governments could have published them earlier, but for a time there must have been some collusion between them not to do so. Perhaps there was a lack of confidence in exposing them to widespread scrutiny; or their publication might have offended foreign governments; or the Letters may have been withheld as a form of pressure on Mary. The decision of the English government to proceed with their publication was probably part of the process of building a case against the Duke of Norfolk, who had been arrested on 7 September 1571 for treason. The English government believed that Mary was involved in Norfolk's plotting, and it was therefore opportune to besmirch her reputation through the publication of George Buchanan's *Detection*[46] and the Casket Letters.

The earliest surviving edition of the *Detection* gives no indication of the place of printing or the date or the printer. Presumably this was to shield the English government from any resulting opprobrium, as such a book could not have been openly published at that time without official approval. The *Detection* was printed in Latin in this edition. The volume also contained the *Actio*[47] and Letters I, II and IV, all in Latin. It did not include the Sonnets. Those three Letters were the only Letters translated into Latin. The Latin translations seem to be based on the Scots versions of the Letters. It is not known why only three of the Casket Letters were included, though it might be surmised that they were deemed to be the most incriminating. This edition may have been printed about October 1571, as Cecil (now Lord Burghley) sent a copy of it to Walsingham, the English Ambassador in Paris, with his letter of 1 November 1571.[48]

Several more editions of the *Detection* were published in the ensuing months. The next contained the *Detection*, the *Actio* and all the Casket Letters in Anglicised Scots, the Sonnets in both French and Anglicised Scots and the 5 April 1567 Marriage Contract. There were two editions of this version, and they can be identified by some variations on the title pages.[49] These two editions also show neither place of printing nor the printer's name nor the year of publication. Copies of the Latin edition and the two subsequent editions are available in several major libraries.

Early in 1572 an edition in correct Scots was printed by Lekprevik at St Andrews. It is included in James Anderson's *Collections relating to the History of Mary, Queen of Scotland* (1727). It also contains all the Casket Letters, the *Actio*, the Sonnets and the 5 April Marriage Contract. There has tended to be an assumption that the published Scots translations were precise copies of the original 1568 Scots translations. This assumption is probably correct as the English translator in 1568 clearly had access to the Scots translation, judging from a comparison of the two translations. It cannot, however, be proved that the published Scots version was completely identical to the Scots translation made in 1568.

Apart from the opening lines of each Casket Letter, these early editions did not include the Original French versions of the eight Letters. The version of the Casket Letters known as the 'Published French' was published in France in 1572. It is ascribed to a Huguenot lawyer of La Rochelle called Camuz, and it is often referred to as the Rochelle version.[50]

It is not known how or in what form the printers of the early editions of the *Detection* in London and St Andrews obtained the copies of the Casket Letters. There are several other points which are uncertain. The authorship of the *Actio* (which is very polemical in style) is disputed. Possibly the author was George Buchanan or Dr Thomas Wilson, an Englishman who in 1577 became a Secretary of State. There is also the question of who translated the *Detection* and the *Actio* into Anglicised Scots or what has been called 'sham Scots'. Again, the translator may have been Dr Wilson or even Buchanan himself.[51] Another question which lacks a definite answer is why the *Detection* and the *Actio* were produced in sham Scots instead of English or genuine Scots. Possibly the English government wished to pretend that the books had been produced in Scotland to avoid any opprobrium being ascribed to England. The whole matter is not edifying.

In retrospect it is surprising that contemporaries did not become involved in a closer scrutiny of the authenticity of the Casket Letters.

There was no attempt by Mary's supporters to disprove them by a detailed analysis. This might indicate acceptance of their authenticity or fear of reprisals from Morton and Cecil or unwillingness to embarrass Mary in some way or just lack of interest in their continuing relevance. Perhaps the question of their authenticity did not seem so crucial to contemporaries as to later generations. By the time King James was old enough to rule Scotland there was the additional hazard that he might not have welcomed any proof of their authenticity or manipulation.

6. A STUDY OF THE CASKET LETTERS

> The Letters have never been examined with so
> much strictness, before. A regular survey of
> them was much needed. Great mistakes had
> been made, concerning their meaning and their
> language.
>
> John Whitaker (1787)[1]

THE SURVIVING COPIES

AS THE ORIGINALS OF the Casket Letters disappeared over 400 years ago,
it is therefore necessary to rely on the surviving contemporary copies
of the Original French version and the translations into Scots and
English. Further complications are that there are no copies of the
Original French for Letters I, II, VII or VIII; no copies of the 1568
English translations of Letters III, VII or VIII; and none of any of the
1568 Scots translations, apart from a few sentences relayed from York
to London. Scots translations were published in 1572.

In the Public Record Office in London there are copies of Letters III
and V in the Original French and also the 1568 translations in English
of Letters I, II and V.[2] At Hatfield House in Hertfordshire there are
copies in the Original French of Letters IV and VI and also the 1568
English translations of those Letters. The earliest versions of Letters
VII and VIII and the Sonnets are those in some of the editions of George
Buchanan's *Detection* published in 1571–72. A contemporary copy of
the Marriage Contract, written in French, is in the Cottonian collection
in the British Library, but the Marriage Contract written in Scots is
available only in the published form. Scots translations of all of the
eight Letters and the Sonnets were published by Lekprevik at St
Andrews in his 1572 edition of the *Detection*.[3]

The importance of Lekprevik's publication must be stressed. It
provided the earliest versions of the eight Letters in correct Scots. In
addition, its versions of Letters VII and VIII are especially valuable as
no 1568 versions of those Letters in the Original French or as English
translations have survived.

107

It is unfortunate that the texts of the Original French versions are not available for four very important Letters. It is puzzling that the publishers of the early editions of the *Detection* did not print the eight Letters in the Original French, especially as the Sonnets were printed in French. It is also curious that in the early editions of Buchanan's *Detection*, the initial three or four lines of each Casket Letter in what is presumably the Original French were shown before each Letter. It is not clear why they were included.[4] What is called the Published French or Rochelle version of the Letters was translated not from the Original French but from the Latin and Scots translations. There is, however, no Published French version of Letter III. The reason for this omission is a matter of conjecture. Perhaps the content was too obviously improbable.

The authors of the books written on the Casket Letters in the eighteenth century and the first seven decades of the nineteenth century were not aware of the Original French copies in the PRO and at Hatfield. Some of their theories and arguments relating to the Published French translations subsequently became obsolete.

The fact that no copies of the Original French version and the 1568 English translations of certain Letters have survived does not prove that such copies were never made. It would be almost incredible if Cecil had overlooked obtaining those copies or if he did not have sufficient clerks available. The surviving copies, moreover, seem to be a slightly haphazard collection. There must be a presumption that somehow the other copies were subsequently lost or destroyed, but in contrast to the disappearance of the original Casket Letters there may be nothing sinister about their loss. It is interesting that Cecil kept copies of at least some of the Letters in his own papers.

THE FORM OF THE LETTERS

It was claimed by Moray and his associates that, apart from the Contract allegedly written by Huntly at Seton on 5 April 1567, all the documents were in Mary's handwriting. As the originals can no longer be examined, it is impossible for modern handwriting experts to give their opinions. Mary's handwriting, however, would have been quite easy to imitate as it was in the italic (not the intricate gothic) style, and at that time there were skilled forgers whose work would have deceived most people. There was a clear refutation of the allegation that the Letters were in Mary's handwriting in the Instructions to her Commissioners issued from her Scottish supporters in September 1568:

And if it be alleged that Her Majesty's writing produced in

108

> Parliament, should prove Her Grace culpable, it may be
> answered, That there is no place mention made in it by the
> which she may be convict, albeit it were her own handwriting,
> as it is not. And also the same is devised by themselves in some
> principal and substantial clauses.[5]

The texts of the Letters are curiously devoid of the usual preambles and appendages. In 1569, Bishop Leslie pointed out:

> there is neither subscription of the writer, nor subscription
> unto whom they were directed, they are neither sealed nor
> signed; there appears neither date wherein they were dated,
> neither day nor month.[6]

The only exception to the absence of dating is Letter I, in which the last sentence purports to show that it was sent from Glasgow on a Saturday morning. The opening sentence of Letter V refers to the addressee as 'my heart' and those of Letters III, VI and VIII as 'my lord', but these phrases do not reveal identities. It is very intriguing that none of the eight Letters was addressed and signed and that only one had any form of dating. Perhaps Mary wished to conceal her authorship in case they fell into the wrong hands, but the contents of at least the two Glasgow Letters would have clearly pointed to her as the author. If she did omit to address, date and sign all eight Letters, it is surprising that her opponents did not remedy her omissions. Possibly the copyists were afraid to forge the Queen's signature in case she returned to power and they were tried for forgery.[7] While it is just possible that the Queen did not address and sign certain Letters to Bothwell for reasons of security, it is very unlikely that the French lady would have omitted to do so.

One possible explanation for omitting the signatures would be that if, by chance, the French lady's name was also Marie she wrote her name with a capital M whereas in the Queen's signature the M was the same size as the other letters in Marie. It is, however, much more probable that the French lady had a different name and therefore her signature had to be removed. That still leaves the question of whether Mary signed any of the Casket Letters which she actually wrote.

In Letters I and II, the Queen would have addressed Bothwell in a different style from the way in which the French lady would have addressed him in some of the other Letters. It therefore seems highly likely that at least the opening and closing passages of the Letters were rewritten to obscure such glaring differences. The absence of signatures etc nevertheless remains a mystery.

The original appearance of each of the Casket Letters was not recorded. It is not known what sizes of paper were used, nor where there may have been blank spaces available for inserting incriminating passages. The English translation of Letter II in the PRO covers seven sides of quarto paper, but allowances must be made for differences in spacing and size of writing between that and the Original French version.

The contemporary copies of the Letters, like other correspondence at that time, were not divided into paragraphs. The modern reader, however, is accustomed to reading documents which are divided into paragraphs, and such divisions greatly facilitate understanding of the Letters. Some of the Letters which have been printed in Appendix 1 are therefore shown for convenience in numbered paragraphs. It should be noted that the numbering of the paragraphs and the punctuation used may not always be the same as those shown in other editions of the Casket Letters. There are, however, pitfalls when introducing paragraphs and trying to clarify punctuation. Such emendations are not infallible and may distort the original meaning or flow of thought.

THE TRANSLATIONS

The translations into Scots and English can be criticised for many omissions and misrenderings (especially in Letter II). Even in the copies of the Original French versions, the sense of some passages is hard to understand due mainly to careless copying. Some editors have suggested alternative words or spelling or even rearrangements in the sequence of the content to clarify the meaning. The copies and translations (including omissions, mistranslations, errors and manipulated material) have nevertheless become historical documents in their own right, as for centuries the issue of Mary's involvement has been judged on their basis. It is therefore essential to study what is shown in the versions copied in 1568 or published in the next few years.

It is not known precisely when nor by whom the final versions of the Scots and English translations were made. Moray sent Scots translations of some, though perhaps not all, of the final set of the Casket Letters to London in June 1568. There is no certainty that these translations were identical to those produced later at York and Westminster. It is, however, likely that the Scots translations in their final form preceded the English translations. The latter were available at least by 9 December 1568, according to Cecil's record of the conference at Westminster.[8] Presumably the French copies were taken and the English translations made on 7 and 8 December by some of Cecil's clerks.

Cecil used several clerks to do this work. The handwriting in the French copies in the PRO is different to that in the English copies held there. At Hatfield the French copy of Letter IV is in the same handwriting as the French copies in the PRO, but the French copy of Letter VI is in the entirely different italic style.

There are a few indications that the English translators referred to the Scots translations and consequently made errors.[9] At times, however, the English translations are more accurate.[10] It is interesting that the two translations of Letters V and VI are much closer together than those of Letters I, II and IV, but this may just have been fortuitous. A full examination and comparison of the translations is rendered impossible by the absence of the Original French versions of Letters I, II, VII and VIII, and unfortunately these include some of the most important of the Casket Letters.

WAYS OF EXAMINING THE CASKET LETTERS

For centuries there has been a curious assumption – stemming from Buchanan's legacy – that the Casket Letters are genuine unless it can be proved otherwise. The onus of the proof has lain on those who have questioned their authenticity. It is, however, equally valid – perhaps even more so in the absence of the originals – to insist that the burden of proof should rest on those who assert they were genuine.

Consideration must be given to how far proof of the authenticity or otherwise of one Letter can be extended to apply to the other Letters. It is usually held by historians that if just Letter II – the long Glasgow Letter – is authentic, the Queen was clearly incriminated in the murder plot against Darnley and was also passionately in love with Bothwell. There is, however, another aspect to be considered. If it can be proved that even one of the eight Letters was manipulated in a fraudulent way, that must cast grave doubts on the other Letters being entirely genuine. It would also lead to major queries against the diligence of the English Commissioners who examined the Letters.

One of the basic tests is to consider the overall style and contents of the Letters. It is necessary to examine how far these show that the contents are in or out of line with Mary's style, personality and regal position. Unfortunately one important test of authenticity of the Casket Letters is not available. No other correspondence between the Queen and Bothwell which is undoubtedly genuine has survived. It is therefore not possible to compare the Casket Letters with such letters. This is disappointing as so many other letters written by Mary have survived, but there may never have been any other letters between them. At least her authentic letters to other persons can be studied to obtain some appreciation of her style. It should, however, be kept in mind that some of her letters were drafted for her by officials such as Lethington, and that letters written after she became captive reflect the very changed circumstances of her life. Her usual style between 1561 and 1567 seems to have been refined in tone and clear in expression and certainly not coarse or turgid.

The style of the Sonnets must also be considered. Pierre Brantôme (c1540–1614), the French soldier and biographer, who was in the party accompanying Mary on her return to Scotland in 1561, commented in his *Recueil des Dames* that the Sonnets were too coarse and badly polished to have come from her, and that they did not resemble her own verses which he had seen. Brantôme said he had discussed them with Ronsard, the French poet, who was strongly of the same opinion. Possibly they were prejudiced in Mary's favour, but their views should at least be noted.[11]

The Letters should be scrutinised to see if they could have been written on the dates asserted by Mary's opponents. There are three distinct groups. The first two Letters are said to have been written by Mary while she was in Glasgow visiting Darnley. The precise dating of the next three Letters is obscure. Moray and his associates made no attempt to date Letter III; asserted that Letter IV was related to an alleged quarrel at Kirk o'Field on 8 February; and implied that Letter V was written on an unspecified date prior to the wedding of the Queen's servant, Margaret Carwod, on 11 February 1567. These three Letters contain nothing which can be clearly seen as incriminating Mary. It is most unlikely that anyone would have deliberately concocted the entire contents of those three Letters, but possibly a few additions were made to the original versions. The last three Letters (which can be called the Stirling Letters) are said to have shown that Mary was aware of Bothwell's intention to waylay her when returning from Stirling to Edinburgh. There could not have been an earlier and abortive abduction, as there was no other occasion between the murder of Darnley and the actual abduction when the Queen resided elsewhere than at Edinburgh or nearby at Seton. The Stirling Letters must therefore be scrutinised at least initially in relation to the circumstances of 21–24 April.

The Casket Letters are very complicated documents and require very careful analysis. It is impossible to accept that they were either entirely genuine or entirely forged. It is necessary to dissect what may have been genuine material written by Mary from what was inserted or altered. Another major point to consider is that the original settings of the Letters may be very different from those alleged by Moray and his adherents. It must therefore be investigated whether the original background to all the Letters could have been those claimed by Mary's foes.

LETTER I

This relatively brief Letter is usually referred to as 'the short Glasgow Letter'. At the end it is marked 'From Glasgow this Saturday in the morning'. When considering any dates for this Letter, it should be kept in mind that the reference to a Saturday morning in Glasgow was at the very end of the Letter and could easily have been added by a forger.

The insinuation was that Mary wrote this Letter to Bothwell on Saturday 25 January 1567 about the plans for Darnley's convalescence. The content of the first paragraph shows that such a date was impossible. Mary stated in the Letter that yesterday (the 24th) she was looking for news from Bothwell and she chided him for being forgetful, not writing to her as he had promised, and delaying his return longer than promised. Yet according to Moray's *Diary*, the Queen had arrived with Huntly and Bothwell at Callendar House on the 21st and had remained there till the 23rd, when Mary proceeded to Glasgow while Huntly and Bothwell returned that same night to Edinburgh. Then, on the night of the 24th, Bothwell 'took journey towards Liddesdale'. It is unlikely that Mary was looking for a letter as early as the 24th, and inconceivable that she could allege he was prolonging his absence.

There is the possibility that Mary left Edinburgh on the 20th (as stated in the *Diurnal* and Birrel's *Diary*) and arrived in Glasgow on the 21st or 22nd. The real flaw in trying to make dates fit the content of the Letter is the allusion to Bothwell prolonging his return. That simply does not fit into the period of 22–25 January 1567. It would also be wrong to assume too readily that Moray's *Diary* was produced carelessly and without some attempt at verification. The content of Letter I cannot be that of a Letter written on the 25th, and that date was the only Saturday in January 1567 when Mary was in Glasgow.

The second paragraph reiterated that Mary had received no further news from Bothwell 'according to my commission'. That meant according to her royal instructions to him. She then stated she would bring 'l'homme' (the man) to Craigmillar on Monday where he would be all Wednesday (or on Wednesday, depending on the translation). The significance of the emphasis on Wednesday is not clear. The reference to Craigmillar, however, clearly conflicts with the alleged plot to murder Darnley at Kirk o'Field. It is astonishing that in Letter II yet another reference to Craigmillar was in one of the incriminating passages sent to Queen Elizabeth by her Commissioners in York.

If 'the man' was Darnley, this implies that the decision to lodge him at Kirk o'Field had not yet been taken by the time Mary and Bothwell parted at Callendar House, and also that on the 25th Mary was still un-aware of the change from Craigmillar to Kirk o'Field. It is therefore surprising that on the 24th Bothwell (according to Moray's *Diary*) was examining the lodging (presumably at Kirk o'Field) being prepared for Darnley. Mary's opponents were inept in concocting the details of an incriminating case against her.

There are also difficulties over the anticipated date of arrival at Craigmillar. Both the Scots and English translations could give the impression that Mary and 'the man' would arrive at Craigmillar on Monday. Possibly the correct translation was that they would set out on the Monday (presumably 27 January) and arrive early on Wednesday 29 January. It would have been difficult to keep to such a timetable when conveying an invalid on a horse-litter in midwinter. According to Moray's *Diary* and Lennox's letter in June 1568, the Queen spent three nights on the way from Glasgow to Edinburgh.[1] There is also no certainty that they did leave Glasgow on the 27th, though in Moray's *Diary* that is shown as the date of their departure. There is further uncertainty over when they arrived in Edinburgh. The earliest of three contemporary dates for their arrival in Edinburgh was Thursday 30 January. It could, of course, be asserted that when Mary wrote the Letter on the 25th she had been intending to reach Craigmillar early on Wednesday 29th.

The transition from the second to the third paragraph seems abrupt. Possibly there was another sentence at the start of the third paragraph and this was excised so that the content could be interpreted as relating to Darnley. If the third paragraph referred to Darnley, the description of him as being merry would certainly conflict with his mood in the weeks prior to Mary's visit to Glasgow and during the early days of Mary's stay in Glasgow. Possibly, however, his attitude had changed by 25 January. It is nevertheless curious that Mary should have referred to Darnley as 'the man'. In paragraph 5 of Letter II she referred to him as 'the King', and in official, authentic correspondence that was also the term she used. On the other hand, 'the man' might have been a familiar term for the infant Prince James.[2] Mary stated that 'the man' was the merriest you ever saw him and seemed to be making love to her. This may have been a doting mother's view of her baby son, but such an interpretation can only be conjecture. The wording, moreover, suggests the description of an adult rather than a baby. Unfortunately the Original French is not available, and the translations cannot be checked. It is therefore unwise to be dogmatic about any interpretation of the third paragraph including what caused Mary's pain in her side to recur.

In the fourth paragraph, Mary again asked for news and enquired what she should do in case Bothwell had not returned by the time she arrived (presumably at Holyrood or Craigmillar). She envisaged that the whole burden would fall on her shoulders, but it is not indicated what arrangements she was discussing.

In the fifth paragraph – according to the Scots translation – it is stated that the Letter was to be taken by Beaton, whereas in the English translation it is stated that she was sending the Letter to Lethington to be delivered to the recipient (Bothwell) by Beaton. This is a most curious discrepancy. Why was the reference to such an important person in Scotland as Lethington omitted in the Scots version? The omission of his name could have been just an oversight by an English translator (who might not have known Lethington), but such a mistake by a Scottish translator would have been unlikely. Unless it was just a mistake, it may have been an attempt to conceal an embarrassing reference to Lethington in what was being portrayed as an incriminating Letter. There is also the possibility that Mary was simply sending the Letter to her secretary's castle at Lethington near Haddington in East Lothian to be collected by Beaton.

There are two possible settings for this Letter. The earlier is that Mary wrote it on a date between 20 November and 7 December 1566 while she was at Craigmillar.[3] The background would refer to the arrangements for the baptism of the Prince to be held on 17 December. Bothwell had been put in charge of these important arrangements,[4] presumably because Mary considered him reliable, whereas the father – Darnley – was neither competent nor trustworthy. It is possible that Bothwell may have gone to Stirling to make arrangements for the baptism for some days while the Queen was residing at Craigmillar, though there is no record that he did so. The content of the Letter would indicate that Bothwell was being dilatory in making arrangements for the baptism and giving her extra burdens. In such a setting 'the man' would be Darnley, who was at Craigmillar for about a week in late November and early December.[5] Buchanan, in his *Detection*, stated that the King had returned from Stirling to Craigmillar, but found that the Queen's anger had not mollified. It is, however, very difficult to imagine Darnley at that time in a merry mood.

The other (and more likely) date could have been Saturday 11 January 1567 when the Queen was in Stirling and apparently Bothwell was arranging to contact Morton on his return from exile in England.[6] Mary would have been anxious to receive news of this meeting. She may have wished to ensure that Morton would stay away from Darnley and herself or to obtain Morton's support for warding Darnley, or his assistance if Darnley started a rebellion. The reference to bringing 'the man' to Craigmillar could relate to Mary's journey with James from Stirling to

Edinburgh. The *Diurnal* stated that 'upon the fourtene day of Januar ... our soverane ladie come with James prince of Scotland towart Edinburgh'. Birrel, however, stated that it was on the 13th that the Queen and the Prince came to Edinburgh. As 13 January was a Monday, that date may fit the Letter. It is at least clear that the Letter was written while Mary was away from Edinburgh, as she envisaged the possibility that Bothwell would not have returned when 'I am come there'.

The Letter was certainly written at a time when both Mary and Bothwell were away from Edinburgh. That may point to either a date in late November when Mary was at Craigmillar and Bothwell may have been in Stirling or a date in January when Mary was in Stirling and Bothwell was meeting Morton at Whittingehame. There must be strong support for these alternative dates from the reference to Beaton delivering the Letter to Bothwell. It is much more likely that Beaton could have been expected to contact Bothwell in East Lothian or Stirling than in remote Liddesdale. It should be added that there is no indication in the Letter where Beaton was to deliver it to Bothwell. The reference in paragraph 4 to 'the whole burden' might mean either the arrangements for the baptism or safeguards against further trouble from Morton. Both of these dates provide more likely settings for the Letter than the Queen's visit to Glasgow, but a definite date cannot be given unless the identity of 'the man' can be established. It is perhaps more probable that Bothwell would have retained a letter concerning his negotiations with Morton than one relating to the baptism. It is, however, impossible that this Letter was written from Glasgow on Saturday 25 January owing to the inclusion of the comment that Bothwell was prolonging his return from Liddesdale. Probably the forger added the date and the place without realising the embarrassing implications of such an addition.

The original text of this Letter is not available, and the translations of certain passages may be poor or even deliberately corrupted. The text is so confused that it is impossible to state definitely what was the context of the Letter. It does not, however, contain evidence of Mary's complicity in a murder-plot. Indeed the reference to Craigmillar could be held to show her innocence of a plan to dispose of Darnley at Kirk o'Field. Furthermore, the inbuilt flaws must cast strong doubts on the integrity and intelligence of her accusers.

LETTER II

This Letter is aptly called 'the long Glasgow Letter' as it is exceedingly long. Its length and complexity suggest that it is either genuine or an amalgamation of forged and genuine material. It is most unlikely that anyone would have deliberately forged the whole of such a long, rambling and disjointed Letter. On the other hand, if there was manipulation of the various Casket Letters, the meandering content of Letter II and some inconsistencies may have been the result of inept work by a forger.

THE DATE OF THE LETTER

It is clear that Mary wrote the Letter on two successive evenings from the content of paragraphs 15 and 28. What is not entirely clear is which date she regarded as the first day. In paragraph 5 she wrote that Darnley had asked Joachim the previous night why she was not staying in the same house as himself. This would imply that she started the Letter on the day after her arrival unless Joachim had been sent in advance of the Queen to prepare her accommodation.[1] In paragraph 6 she indicated that she had started her conversations with Darnley on the day of her arrival and had broken off to have supper. In paragraph 7 (according to the Scots version) she wrote: 'as to the rest of Willie Hiegait's, he confessed it, but it was the morn after my coming or he did it.' (Unfortunately the English translation of that passage is meaningless, and possibly the Scots translation is also faulty.) At the start of paragraph 13 she wrote: 'This is my first day's work, I will end to-morrow.' Provided the Scots translation of paragraph 7 is correct and both paragraphs 7 and 13 are in their proper positions in the Letter, her first day's work was the day after her arrival. If she arrived at Glasgow on Thursday 23 January, it therefore seems that she did not complete the Letter until the evening of Saturday 25 January.

Further evidence (though of very dubious reliability) on the dating of Letter II is contained in the deposition of French Paris. He stated that Mary gave him a letter to take to Bothwell in Edinburgh. That letter was presumably not Letter I, as Beaton was to be the bearer of that Letter. It was either Letter II or a letter which has not survived in any form. If Mary finished Letter II on the evening of the 25th, Paris could not have arrived with it in Edinburgh until the afternoon of the 26th. Meanwhile, according to Moray's *Diary*, Bothwell had left Edinburgh for Liddesdale on the 24th. Yet Paris stated that he himself delivered the letter to Bothwell. Either Moray's *Diary* or Paris' confession or the content of Letter II is incorrect, unless there was yet another letter and that seems unlikely in the time-span. It would also be very odd that Mary had not known Bothwell's intended movements, as he had escorted her to Callendar House on her way to Glasgow.

If Mary did not complete Letter II until the evening of 25 January, that would cast doubt on the dating of Letter I which was alleged to

117

have been sent from Glasgow on the morning of 25 January. It would mean that she despatched Letter I before completing Letter II, which had been started on the previous evening. Although that might be explained in some ingenious way, a convincing explanation seems improbable.

As with Letter I there is the possibility that the whole timetable is earlier than shown in Moray's *Diary* (which asserted that the Queen left Edinburgh on 21 January and arrived in Glasgow on 23 January) and instead that she arrived in Glasgow on the 21st or 22nd. Letter II, however, relates an after-supper conversation at Callendar House, and the content (if genuine) suggests that Mary stayed two nights there. It is indicated that Bothwell had left earlier in the day. It is unlikely that he would have escorted the Queen to Callendar House and travelled about 25 miles back to Edinburgh on the same day at that time of the year. It seems a reasonable assumption that Bothwell stayed at Callendar House for at least one night. Even if Mary had left Edinburgh on the 20th (as shown in the *Diurnal* and Birrel's *Diary*) she would therefore have arrived in Glasgow on Wednesday 22nd. She would have started Letter II on the 23rd and completed it on the evening of Friday 24th, but Paris would still have missed finding Bothwell in Edinburgh as he could not have arrived there until the 25th.

All these snags over dates could, of course, be airily dismissed as explicable in some way, but these dates are nevertheless part of the case presented against the Queen. Although it may have been difficult late in 1568 to ascertain precise dates in January 1567, Mary's opponents and Elizabeth's Commissioners failed to perceive the inbuilt inconsistencies and the consequent implications for the validity of the case against Mary.

AN OUTLINE OF THE LETTER

The opening paragraphs of the Letter cover Mary's journey from Callendar House to Glasgow and relate how she was met by a supporter of the Earl of Lennox (who was Thomas Crawford according to his deposition) and then by Sir James Hamilton and others. There is a long and detailed account of her conversations in Glasgow with Darnley and the points of contention between them. Halfway through the Letter there is a list of topics already mentioned in the Letter. This seems curiously out of place. It is probable that Mary jotted down these headings before starting the Letter and subsequently used the sheet on which she had written them on the reverse side.[2] Apparently she was short of paper as at the end of the Letter she wrote: 'Excuse that thing

1. The Morton Portrait of
Mary Queen of Scots.
Artist unknown.
Glasgow Museums.

2. The Palace of Holyrood
House, by courtesy of
Mr John F. Walker.

3. Craigmillar Castle.
© Crown Copyright. Reproduced courtesy of Historic Scotland.

4. View of Bishop Cameron's Tower, Glasgow, by courtesy of the
Mitchell Library, Glasgow City Libraries and Archives.

5. Exterior of Provand's Lordship, Glasgow.
Glasgow Museums.

6. A room in Provand's Lordship, Glasgow.
Glasgow Museums.

7. James Hepburn, 4th Earl of Bothwell, by Unknown Artist. Scottish National Portrait Gallery.

8. William Maitland of Lethington, by the 11th Earl of Buchan after Unknown Artist. Scottish National Portrait Gallery.

9. James Stewart, Earl of Moray, by Hugh Monro after Unknown Artist. Scottish National Portrait Gallery.

10. James Douglas, 4th Earl of Morton, by Unknown Artist. Scottish National Portrait Gallery.

11 & 12. Models of Kirk o'Field before and after the explosion.
Illustrations 11, 12 and 13 are copied from R. H. Mahon, The Tragedy
of Kirk o' Field (1930) published by the Cambridge University Press.

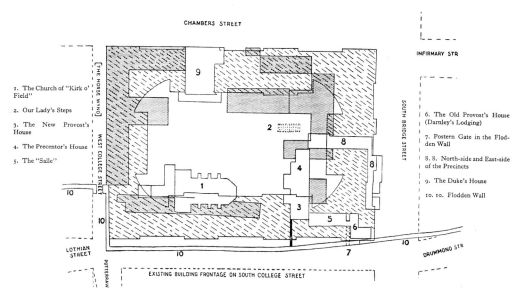

13. Plan of Kirk o'Field, superimposed on the present Old Quadrangle (hatched) and earlier buildings (dotted) of Edinburgh University.

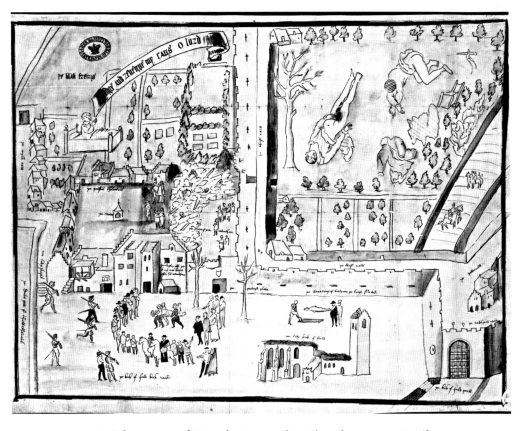

14. The scene of Darnley's murder. Sketch sent to Cecil.
Public Record Office

15. Sir William Cecil,
1st Baron Burghley.
Painting by Brounckhorst,
courtesy of the
National Portrait Gallery,
London

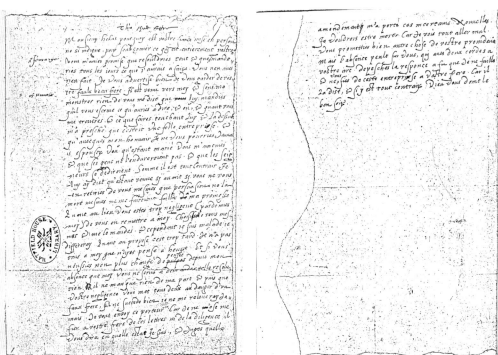

16. Casket Letter VI in French. By courtesy of the Marquess of Salisbury

that is scriblit, for I had no paper yesterday when I wrote that of the memorial.'

On the assumption that the Letter was written on two successive nights the second half may begin at paragraph 18 or 19 or 20. The precise break is not clear. It may be significant that in the English translation held in the PRO, there is a gap equivalent to three lines after the words at the end of paragraph 17. That is the only gap in the English translation. In the second half there is a certain amount of repetition of her conversations with Darnley. At the end of the Letter there are several very passionate sentences in which the writer expresses her love for the recipient. These sentences are similar in tone to the Letters which can be associated with the French lady kept in seclusion by Bothwell. In the Scots version the Letter concludes with what seems to be a list of additional points to be mentioned by the bearer.

COMMENTS ON SPECIFIC PASSAGES

There are several passages which require detailed comment or elucidation.

According to the first paragraph the Queen had been in a bad mood after departing from the place (which is not specified) where she had left her heart. This may refer to being away from Bothwell and was probably intended to do so. Yet is seems that he left Callendar House on the previous day. Perhaps the correct meaning is that she was on a dangerous mission and had left behind her courage. In the sixteenth century the meanings of 'coeur' included courage.

There are references in paragraph 3 and in the list at paragraph 16 to Sir James Hamilton. The identity of Sir James is not known. Perhaps he was Sir James Hamilton of Crawfordjohn who had supported Mary during the Chaseabout Raid in the autumn of 1565.[3] The comment from Sir James Hamilton in paragraph 3 that on the other time, when Lennox heard that Mary was coming, he had avoided a meeting, is too vague to identify the date of such a visit or proposed visit, but it may relate to Mary's growing concern about the Lennox faction. In the list at paragraph 16 there are variations between the Scots and English versions as the latter refers to 'the talk of Sir James of the ambassador' and the Scots to 'the purpose of Sir James Hamilton'. The word 'purpois' in Scots, however, can mean matter or subject or talk. Mary did not specify which ambassador, but he may have been an emissary attending the baptism of the Prince. It is curious that in Mary's account of the conversations with Sir James in paragraph 3 she did not mention any ambassador.

In paragraph 5 Mary wrote that Darnley had enquired if she had made her 'state'. (This is omitted in the English version perhaps because the translator did not understand the meaning.) The reference is to Mary's list of salaries and pensions paid from her own very substantial income from France as Queen-Dowager.[4] This source of income was of very considerable significance to the royal finances.

In the same paragraph Mary mentioned that Darnley said she would send Joseph away or send Joseph (depending on the translation). This almost certainly referred to Joseph Lutini (a member of the Queen's household) or Joseph Riccio (the younger brother of the murdered David Riccio). On 6 January 1567 Lutini had been given a passport to go to France on the Queen's business (which was not specified). Lutini became ill on the way and stopped at Berwick. Mary requested his detention at Berwick, as she suspected he had stolen some of her bracelets, though she simply alleged to Drury that Lutini was indebted to some poor merchants and others. Drury thought that Mary had really wanted Lutini back in Scotland in case he should offer his services to the English government and then disclose something to her detriment. Meanwhile it was discovered that the real culprit was Joseph Riccio who had put the blame for the theft of the bracelets on Lutini. After a delay Lutini was allowed to return to Edinburgh during February, escorted by one of Drury's officers. It seems that Lutini settled his alleged debts, refused an offer by Bothwell to tarry, and departed for England again. It is not clear what happened subsequently to Riccio and Lutini.[5]

The whole affair of the two Josephs is obscure and mysterious, but possibly some historians have erred in inferring too much from it. There is no evidence that it was connected with any plot being engineered by or against Darnley. It should, however, be noted that there is an interesting allusion to the departure of Joseph in Paris' Second Deposition. In an improbable story he alleged that the Queen conspired with him to make Joseph flee. This may point to an attempt by Mary's enemies to turn the episode into something sinister and incriminating.

There are several paragraphs relating the conversations between Mary and Darnley. He asked that his faults might be forgiven on account of his youth. Mary then questioned him about the English ship lying in the Clyde and the statements made by Hiegate and Walker. She wrote that she had drawn information out of Darnley about a bishop and the Earl of Sutherland. The Letter does not reveal what information Mary obtained from Darnley, but the passage probably related to Mary's fears that Darnley was plotting to overthrow her with Catholic help from abroad. The bishop may have been William Chisholm, Bishop of Dunblane. According to the *Diurnal*, Chisholm had assisted at the baptism of Prince James. Sutherland's religious stance in early 1567 is not clear, but his deceased second wife was the sister of Lennox. This link might explain why Sutherland had been approached to take part in a plot being hatched by Lennox and Darnley. As Sutherland died in July 1567, he would not see before his death the references to him in this Letter and also Letter VIII when they were published in 1571–72.

In paragraph 6 there is the first of three specific allusions to Darnley's alleged insistence that he and Mary must be 'at bed and board together'. The other two are in paragraphs 19 and 20. The close proximity of these two allusions should be noted. The repetition may indicate that they were written at different times. If so, they would mark the break between the two halves of the Letter. Darnley's demand is also implied at the end of paragraph 8. It is interesting that Mary did not reveal in the Letter her own private feelings over Darnley's demand. If she and Bothwell had been secret lovers or partners in a plot to get rid of Darnley, it might be expected that she would at least have hinted that Darnley would not be readmitted.

In paragraph 11 the writer warns Bothwell in case his heart is won by 'that false race', presumably a reference to Lady Jane Gordon. Yet Mary probably knew that Bothwell was showing no infatuation for his new wife. There is a similar passage in paragraph 14, in which the writer stated 'we are tied by two false races'. It can be assumed that this was intended to refer to the Lennox and Gordon families. By January 1567 Mary had strong reasons to distrust the Lennox family, but it is not clear why she would have described Bothwell's in-laws as false. Some years had passed since the rebellion of the previous Earl of Huntly in 1562. During 1566 the Queen had been on friendly terms with the new Earl of Huntly and his sister. Yet near the end of the Letter, in paragraph 27, there is a reference to Bothwell's false brother-in-law (the Earl of Huntly). There is a similar reference in Letter VI, and it is highly probable that the same person wrote or forged all these passages. It is also curious that in paragraph 25 of Letter II the writer referred to 'your brother' in a passage which is not damaging to Mary. (Bothwell did not have a brother and the reference is clearly to Huntly). Possibly these two descriptions of Huntly within the same Letter came from two different writers. There are no reasons to doubt Huntly's loyalty to the Queen, though it is possible that by late May 1567 he was becoming apprehensive about continuing to support Mary and Bothwell. On 31 May, Drury reported to Cecil that 'Huntly of late renewed his suit to repair into his country, which is not well taken.'[6] That, however, was long after January 1567.

There is a rather isolated remark in paragraph 12 that Darnley and someone else had been at school (école) together. This must have been an error in translating the French idiom 'faire éclore un projet' (to hatch a plot). It is curious that the mistake was not detected at York or West-minster. The other person in the plot was presumably Lennox. Perhaps the phrase was deliberately mistranslated to avoid any embarrassment to Lennox. This paragraph has a curious inconsistency with paragraph 9 as it states that Darnley was saluting every man, whereas in the earlier paragraph he desired to see nobody.

There are references to Lady Reres in paragraphs 17 and 23 and (in the Scots version) the list at the end of 28. She was the aunt of Mary Beaton, one of the four Scottish girls with Mary in France. George Buchanan alleged that she was a go-between in arranging the illicit meetings of Mary and Bothwell. In paragraph 23 the writer recorded Darnley's hope that Lady Reres would serve Mary to her honour. This may have been an allusion to the allegation or a sarcasm to arouse Mary's doubts over the loyalty of Lady Reres. There may subsequently have been a rift between the Queen and Lady Reres. On 20 May 1567, Drury reported to Cecil that Lady Reres was railing marvellously in both writing and speech at the Queen and Bothwell.[7]

At the end of the list in paragraph 16 is a reference to Lord Livingstone. It might have been possible to add his name and also the ensuing paragraph, which relates to him, in a blank space below the list of headings, but this is conjecture. If paragraph 17 is an addition to the original text, it would throw in doubt whether Mary stayed at Callendar House for two nights or just one night.

It is related in paragraph 17, apparently as an after-thought, how Lord Livingstone was over-familiar with the Queen after supper in Callendar House, nudging her while he insinuated that she was missing the pre-sence of Bothwell, who had left earlier that day. This is a rather odd story to be related by the Queen herself, who did not have a reputation for being vulgar. Another doubt about this story is that it clashes with Moray's *Diary*, which stated that Bothwell and Huntly returned to Edinburgh on the 23rd, the same day as Mary left Callendar House. Either the story in the Letter or the information in the *Diary* is inaccurate. If the *Diary* is faulty, it follows that Bothwell and Huntly set out (in line with the story) to return to Edinburgh on the 22nd instead of the 23rd. There is yet another apparent flaw in this paragraph as it insinuates that Mary's affair with Bothwell was well known, whereas in the next paragraph her gift of a bracelet to him was not to be revealed.

Letter II is such a complicated document that almost every phrase warrants scrutiny. In paragraph 18 it is difficult to understand the background to the writer's warning to Bothwell not to let any of those who were in her presence while she was making the bracelet see him wearing it. If the Queen wrote this passage in Glasgow, presumably only a few of her own servants would have been present and they must have known about any illicit relationship with Bothwell. Yet if the French lady wrote such a passage, those in her presence must also have known about her connection with Bothwell. Another difficulty is why the bracelet was made 'in haste'. These points would probably be clarified if the original setting for paragraph 18 were known.

It is not clear what kind of bracelet was being made. The Queen would not have had the technical skill to make a gold or silver bracelet, and presumably the French lady also lacked such expertise. It has, however, been suggested that the writer was making a bracelet of woven hair as a love-token.[8] It is worth adding that in the second deposition of French Paris it is asserted that he took bracelets from the Queen in Glasgow to hand to Bothwell in Edinburgh. Yet all the references in both translations of Letter II are just to one bracelet. In paragraph 18, however, the writer says she will make 'a fairer'. Perhaps she did so, and gave both to Paris to take to Bothwell. Such a conjecture would clash with her haste in making the first bracelet and also with her enquiry if Bothwell would accept the first bracelet.

Paragraph 18 is almost certainly an addition to the original text. The insertion was made clumsily as it has no connection with either the preceding or the following paragraph. Furthermore, it may have been transposed with paragraph 24. The writer states that this day she had been working till 2 o'clock (presumably in the afternoon) fitting the key and lock on a bracelet for the recipient of the Letter. Yet in paragraph 24 she states that she can find no locks for it. It should be noted that the English translation refers to clasps instead of locks, and that both locks and clasps are in the plural. Unfortunately the correct translation cannot be established as the Original French version has not survived. On balance, the wording of paragraph 18 gives the impression that the bracelet was finished, whereas the writer admits in paragraph 24 that it was not yet ready. The two references to the bracelet may have been reversed in sequence through careless manipulation.

Another query is why the writer could not find any locks or clasps for the bracelet. If the Queen wrote this passage, it implies that she could not obtain them in Glasgow. It is not known where the French lady resided, but Bothwell would have kept her in a secluded place away from shops.

In paragraph 19 the writer revealed that she would rather be dead if it were not that she was obeying the recipient. Possibly the iron-willed Bothwell was pushing the over-trusting Mary into taking strong measures against Darnley, such as warding him or arraigning him for high treason. The Letter continues with an account of conversations with Darnley and relates how Mary tried to lull his suspicions and persuade him to trust her.

In paragraph 22 Mary claimed that she could draw some information (which is not stated) out of Darnley if she disclosed everything to him. This enigmatic sentence may conflict with the penultimate sentence in the Scots translation of paragraph 13 that she had drawn it all out of him. It is not clear what Mary might have disclosed, but possibly Bothwell – as indicated in paragraph 13 – had discovered something about the bishop and Sutherland in relation to Darnley's schemes.

In paragraph 24 there is a reference to money, in which the two translations seem to conflict. In the Scots translation, the writer asks if Bothwell will have more silver; in the English version, it could mean that Bothwell was to send her more money. As there is no copy of the Original French for Letter II, the translations cannot be checked. Obviously the Queen would not expect Bothwell to send money to her. If she knew that Bothwell was heading towards Liddesdale, it is perhaps unlikely that she would have enquired if he needed more money for a journey which would take him to the vicinity of Hermitage Castle as he was the Keeper of the Castle. The secluded French lady, however, may have needed money from him.

In the same paragraph the writer asks Bothwell when she should return and how far she may speak. If the Queen wrote this passage, it is not clear why Bothwell was to decide the date of her return or what she was to discuss with Darnley. It is most unlikely that Mary received a reply to these questions before leaving Glasgow probably on 27 January. It is also curious that Mary asked such questions if she knew that Bothwell had proceeded to Liddesdale. Again it is much more probable that the French lady put these questions to Bothwell.

At the end of paragraph 24 there is another discrepancy between the two translations, as the next sentence in the English version is not shown in the Scots: 'Now as far as I perceive, I may do much with you; guess you whether I shall not be suspected.' The translation of 'I may do much with you' should strictly be 'I am very popular with you', as Cecil wrote in the margin 'j'ay bien la vogue avec vous'. The meaning of this sentence, however, is far from clear. Probably it is intended to hint again at the alleged illicit relationship between Mary and Bothwell. It seems very likely that this sentence and the preceding sentences in this paragraph about a bracelet and 'more money' and when to return were inserted in the original text of Letter II. They were probably taken from a letter written by the French lady.

At the end of the Letter the writer describes herself as Bothwell's humble and faithful lover and advises him not to see the other woman (who was presumably Lady Bothwell) nor to regard her feigned tears. She prays that Bothwell will write often to her. Paragraphs 27 and 28 are similar in tone to the Letters which can be associated with the French lady kept in seclusion by Bothwell.

At the end of paragraph 28 there is another very conspicuous difference between the two translations. The Scots version has a list of what seem to be directions for the bearer. The list is curious and no obvious thread runs through it. It is certainly not a list of headings for points to be mentioned in the Letter like the list in paragraph 16. The omission of the list from the English version may have been an oversight as the translator had already reached the end of a sheet, or he may have written the list on an eighth sheet which has disappeared.

The list commences with 'the purpois of the Lady Reres'. According to paragraph 17, she accompanied the Queen at least as far as Callendar House, and possibly she also went to Glasgow. The word 'purpois' in Scots probably means here talk or conversation. The list then refers to 'the Englishmen'. These might be some of Darnley's English companions or a reference to the English ship in the Clyde mentioned in paragraph 7 of this Letter. Another enigmatic reference is to 'his mother'. She may have been Bothwell's mother or Lady Lennox (Darnley's mother) or someone else. It is also difficult to suggest why the Earl of Argyll is on the list. He was hostile to Darnley but sided with Moray rather than with Bothwell. The list concludes with references to Bothwell and 'the lodging in Edinburgh'. There is the obvious question of why Mary in a Letter to Bothwell should have added his name, but there might have been some special message to be conveyed to him. If, however, the rest of the Letter is genuine, there seems to have been no need to withhold from it any more incriminating messages. The reference to the lodging is clearly intended to be an incriminating allusion to the house at Kirk o'Field. That, however, would conflict with the statement in Letter I that Mary would bring Darnley to Craigmillar and also with the statement in paragraph 21 of this Letter that Darnley would take medicine and the bath (marking the end of his convalescence) at Craigmillar. The reference to the lodging in Edinburgh is the only conceivable allusion to the house at Kirk o'Field in Letters I and II. It is relevant to comment that the references to Bothwell and the lodging in Edinburgh are not merely at the end of the list but also at the end of the Letter. These references (and indeed the entire list) could easily have been added by a forger, and that is almost certainly what happened. The authenticity of the list must be rated as highly dubious. The forger may have obtained the idea from the list towards the end of the first half.

It seems unlikely that two rather obscure passages were the work of a forger. One is the enigmatic allusion in paragraph 13 to a bishop and the Earl of Sutherland (which has already been discussed); the other is in paragraph 20 and refers to Darnley knowing about something (which is not specified) said by one of Mary's half-brothers to her at Stirling.

These passages, however, do not appear to implicate Mary in a plot against Darnley.

PASSAGES ALLEGEDLY INCRIMINATING MARY

Scattered in the Letter are a few passages, which, if genuine, were alleged to incriminate Mary in the murder of her husband. There are also expressions of the writer's alleged strong passion for Bothwell. These passages were relayed in October 1568 from York to Queen Elizabeth.[9]

The most dramatic (though also enigmatic) sentences are those in paragraph 21:

> Think also if you will not find some more secret invention than
> by medicine; for he should take medicine and the bath at
> Craigmillar. He may not come out of the house for a long time.

The first sentence, however, might simply be a suggestion for the use of a quicker 'magical' cure. This was not the age of modern medicine! It should also be noted that in paragraph 8 of this Letter, Mary had already referred to a mediciner and herself helping him at Craigmillar. The second sentence might just imply that Darnley would not be sufficiently fit to leave Craigmillar for some weeks. It is unfortunate that a copy of the Original French has not survived, as the translations of this passage are not very clear. What is abundantly clear is that at the time the Letter was written it was assumed that Darnley would go to Craigmillar and not to Kirk o'Field or some other lodging in Edinburgh.

Another dramatic sentence is in paragraph 26 which may have been the original end of the Letter: 'Burn this Letter for it is too dangerous.' Such a sentence is perhaps too melodramatic to be authentic. On the other hand, Letter II, even if it was not written in the setting of a plot to murder Darnley, was still a dangerous document as it clearly indicated the Queen's intention to keep Darnley under her surveillance. The interpretation of such passages can be significantly influenced by prior suggestions that they show Mary's guilt. It is therefore difficult to study them impartially and free from such a predisposition.

CRAWFORD'S DEPOSITION

The section of the Letter from paragraph 6 to paragraph 9 is remarkably similar to the deposition of Thomas Crawford, an adherent of the Lennox family, which was presented at Westminster in December 1568 as part of the case against Mary.[10] The similarities have provoked heated arguments between historians over their significance for the integrity of Letter II.

Crawford claimed that he made a record of the conversations between Mary and Darnley in Glasgow from what Darnley told him immediately afterwards. The purpose was to relay the details to Darnley's father. No reasons were given for making such a record when Lennox was in Glasgow at the time (and presumably living in the same house as Darnley as indicated in paragraph 12) and for keeping the record after Lennox had been informed. It is also suspicious that in June 1568 Lennox wrote from England to Thomas Crawford asking for details of Mary's visit to Glasgow and journey back to Edinburgh.[11] His letter was probably written after consultation with John Wood, Moray's emissary in England. Lennox should already have known what happened in Glasgow.

Sentence after sentence in Crawford's long deposition and Letter II are in the same sequence and contain many identical or very similar words and phrases. It should also be noted that the account of Crawford's conversation with the Queen on her way to Glasgow has some words identical to those in paragraph 2 of the Letter. In particular, there is one almost inexplicable coincidence. Crawford stated: 'my opinion was that she took him away more like a prisoner than her husband'. Mary allegedly wrote in the Letter: 'I trow [think] he believed that I would have sent him away as a prisoner.' It is highly improbable that Mary and Crawford would not only have had identical thoughts on this point but also have recorded them.[12] Furthermore, there is the remarkable fact that this sentence appears just in the Scots translation and not in the English translation of the Letter. It was either omitted for some reason from the English version or deliberately added to the Scots version.

Unless Darnley dictated the deposition to Crawford, there is the extraordinary chain of coincidences that what Crawford recollected and recorded in Scots (and then Anglicised in 1568) from Darnley's recall and translation of his conversations with Mary (which were probably conducted in French or perhaps in Scots) was almost identical to Mary's recall and record of it in French, which was translated into Scots and English.[13]

The extent of the similarities between Crawford's deposition and the Letter is too great to be accepted even as a random coincidence. Either part of Letter II was copied from Crawford's deposition or his deposition was copied from Letter II. The entire story that Crawford recorded and retained an independent but virtually identical account of lengthy conversations is implausible. It seems highly probable that the deposition was concocted or manipulated to help to prove the authenticity of Letter

II. There can be little doubt that Mary's opponents did not realise the complications and pitfalls they were creating for themselves in their zeal to prove her guilt. The rejection of Crawford's deposition as corroborative evidence also points to Mary's opponents not having confidence in the acceptability of those parts of Letter II which are not covered by the deposition.

Andrew Lang, after a long controversy with TF Henderson early in the twentieth century, conceded that Mary wrote the whole of Letter II and that none of it was forged.[14] The vital point providing positive proof for him was that Crawford repeated Darnley's self-defence over the possibility of leaving on the English ship:

> He answered that he had spoken with the Englishman, but not of mind to go away with him. And, if he had, it had not been without cause, considering how he was used. For he had neither [means] to sustain himself nor his servants, and need not make further rehearsal thereof, seeing she knew it as well as he.

As this passage is not repeated in Letter II, Lang considered it proved that Crawford reported Darnley's actual words in his deposition. Andrew Lang on reflection might have considered how such a difference between the contents of the Letter and the deposition rendered valid everything else in the Letter, including all the other content which was not even mentioned in the deposition. Furthermore, any information in Crawford's statement which was not included in Letter II does not account for the very positive correlation between certain passages in the two documents. The inclusion of the additional passage does not prove anything of substance.

Hitherto the crucial question in Letter II for many historians has been whether Crawford's deposition confirms the authenticity of Letter II. This has been a highly controversial issue, but its significance has been considerably overemphasised. The authenticity or otherwise of the deposition neither proves nor disproves the authenticity of the whole of Letter II. That is the vital point overlooked in the long, bitter, and largely unnecessary, controversy between TF Henderson and Andrew Lang. If the deposition was genuine, it could be regarded as corroboration of the corresponding part of Letter II, but it still does not prove that the rest of Letter II was genuine. If the deposition was not genuine, the possibilities still remain that Letter II was either genuine or manipulated.

The controversy over the relation between Letter II and Crawford's deposition has tended to obscure the very important points that the equivalent part of Letter II was almost certainly genuine and that it confirms Mary's deep concern over Darnley's behaviour and plotting. That was the real background to the original form of Letter II before it was manipulated to incriminate Mary. It must also be emphasised that the passages which are common to both the deposition and Letter II do not include anything which obviously incriminates Mary. It is interesting that this was one part of the Letter which appears to be authentic and yet contains nothing incriminatory. Any compromising passages follow further on in the Letter.

THE BEARER OF THE LETTER

It is not known who was entrusted by Mary with taking the Letter to Bothwell. There are references to the bearer in paragraphs 5, 6, 20, 21 and 26. Apparently Mary accepted Bothwell's word that he was reliable. Possibly he was French Paris. The references to the bearer in the Letter state that he was to relay more on her arrival and on the matter of the Englishmen; to mention 'many small things'; to tell the rest of her news; and to explain the reason why she was continuing to stay in Glasgow. These points should be compared and contrasted with the apparent list of instructions to the bearer shown only in the Scots version at the end of the Letter. That list looks more and more like an addition to the original Letter. The points which the bearer was entrusted to mention are vague but nevertheless intriguing such as the reason for prolonging her stay in Glasgow. It is not known how long she had originally intended to be in Glasgow, nor how far the length of her stay was related to a decision to take Darnley to Edinburgh.

CONCLUSIONS

It is probable that Mary wrote much of this Letter, but improbable that the background is that of a murder plot against Darnley. A very substantial part of the Letter is related to Mary's unravelling of Darnley's activities. Mary's prime concern at Glasgow was to ascertain from Darnley precisely what he had been planning. Hence her questions to him about the English ship, the statements of Walker and Hiegait, and the bishop and Sutherland. The Letter is essentially in line with that interpretation as far as the statement 'You have heard the rest' at the end of paragraph 13. Increasingly from that point the forger added material of an incriminating nature, partly taken from correspondence to Bothwell from another woman. The tone also becomes more emotional and less impersonal.

When assessing the authenticity and significance of the passages in which Mary recorded her conversations with Darnley, it should be appreciated that the Letter is very one-sided. Darnley's excuses and denials and explanations are given, but the Letter does not contain much of the case against him. This may or may not indicate some manipulation. Perhaps Mary knew that the recipient was well aware of Darnley's record. The extent of the sincerity of Darnley's avowed repentance should also be closely scrutinised. Although Darnley confessed in paragraph 6 that he had done wrong, it is not clear which fault or faults he was admitting. Furthermore, in the same paragraph he continued to deny some un-specified accusation which he claimed he had always disavowed. Possibly he was referring to an aspect of the conspiracy against Riccio.

There have been a few attempts to reconstruct Letter II in a more meaningful way, but any reconstructions have been based on a con-siderable degree of conjecture. If the sequence of the paragraphs as shown in the Scots and English translations is incorrect, both the trans-lators were at fault. It would also mean that neither Moray and his asso-ciates nor the English Commissioners noticed their errors. That, however, is quite possible! Another explanation of the curious sequence of the content is that the forgers carried out their work clumsily and without considering the overall implications. There is also the theory that Letter II was put together from two letters: the first part addressed to Lethington or Moray, and the second part from about paragraph 19 to Bothwell.[15] This might explain some repetition in the second part and the more informal style as Mary at that time still trusted Bothwell. If part of Letter II had originally been a letter from Mary to Lethington, that might explain Queen Elizabeth's remark in July 1567 on Lethington's bad behaviour. It is, however, much more probable that the core of Letter II was addressed to Bothwell as Mary must have had doubts about the loyalty and discretion of Moray and Lethington over such confidential matters. Yet another possibility is that an additional letter from the French lady or unused material from one of the shorter Casket Letters, such as V, was inserted to add material to Letter II. The presence of such material may exist in the whole or parts of paragraphs 14, 18, 24, 27 and 28. The sequence would not invariably be in that order; for example, paragraphs 18 and 24 about the bracelet were possibly reversed due to clumsy manipulation. Those two paragraphs and paragraph 14 are also abrupt intrusions into the flow of the Letter. Paragraphs 27 and 28 look as if they have been tagged onto the original ending of the Letter in paragraph 26. It should also be noted that the contents of some of these passages are particularly incriminating though they do not include all the incriminating material in this Letter. Other insertions to the original Letter would include the last sentence in paragraph 11, the reference to Livingstone, at the end of paragraph 16, and paragraph 17. These theories on the construction of this Letter cannot be proved, and all of them must be viewed with caution.

Letter II remains an astonishing, long, rambling, disjointed document containing several obscure allusions. It is probable that the Letter consists mainly of authentic material mingled, at times clumsily, with additions from other sources, and with no perception of the consequences for the validity of the case being concocted against the Queen.

Interest in Letter II has focused in the past primarily on passages which appear to reveal Mary's guilt in the murder plot and her passion for Bothwell. A much fuller and deeper understanding of Letter II can be grasped if it is considered as basically an account of how Mary unravelled information from Darnley about his plotting against her and how she succeeded in bringing him again under her control.

LETTER III

This Letter is much shorter than Letter II. The tone is mournful, submissive and unhappy. The writer reproaches Bothwell for his absence, forgetfulness, broken promises and the coldness of his writing. She also laments her own cruel lot and continual misfortune. It is not possible to pinpoint any time when Mary could have written such a Letter to Bothwell. Although the reproachful tone of the Letter, if written by the Queen, might reflect her attitude to Bothwell in the short period between their marriage and departure from Edinburgh in the following month, Bothwell was not away from Mary during that time. As regards the submissive passages, Mary's letters to the Duke of Norfolk in 1569–70 (when she anticipated being married to him) also contained such passages. The entire tone of those letters, however, is completely different from this doleful Letter which is so full of reproaches.

In this Letter there is no indication of the writer's jealousy of Lady Jane Gordon in contrast to Letter IV and the Sonnets which strongly reflect that hostility. This suggests that Letter III was written prior to Bothwell's marriage to Lady Jane in February 1566. The possibility that the Queen wrote such a Letter to Bothwell would therefore become even more remote, as there was no allegation of such an early romance between them.[1]

There is nothing in this Letter which might indicate that the writer could be Mary apart from the inclusion of a brief mention of French Paris as the bearer of a lock of hair, but he could also have conveyed letters between Bothwell and the French lady. The reference to Paris, moreover, could easily have been an addition to the original text. The writer also sent a black enamelled ring or more probably a locket (apparently containing the lock of hair) to Bothwell, referring to it as her only wealth. It is, however, incredible that the Queen would have referred to that jewel as her only treasure.

The Letter can only be understood if it is assumed that the writer was not Mary but the mysterious French lady, who believed that she was privately married to Bothwell and possessed some form of marriage document from him as indicated near the end of the Letter. The Queen would not have obtained such a document while she was married to Darnley.

It is astonishing that anyone has believed that Mary wrote this Letter. The contents, however, reveal much about Bothwell's iniquity towards another woman.

LETTER IV

In this Letter there are some of the most baffling passages in the Casket Letters. At least there are clear reasons for rejecting the claim that Mary wrote it. On the assumption that it was addressed to Bothwell, the author states that Bothwell had commanded her not to write to him. That would have been a most unlikely order to have given to the Queen, but much more credible if given to another woman, especially a foreigner kept in a degree of seclusion. If Bothwell did not wish the Queen to send him letters (which might incriminate him in the murder of Darnley) it is difficult to understand why he kept this Letter and others which appear to be much more prejudicial to him. It is also very difficult to accept that the reference to all the evils that Bothwell had caused the writer could conceivably apply to the relationships between Mary and Bothwell in early February 1567. Furthermore, the tone of the Letter is similar to Letter III and suggests another Letter from the French lady.

There is also a problem over why and when the Letter was sent to Bothwell. It was implied by Mary's accusers that she wrote the Letter from Kirk o'Field on the evening of Friday 7 February (the second of the two nights she slept there). Bothwell was staying at this time in the Palace. Mary could have spoken to Bothwell earlier in the day or on the following morning. There seems to have been little need to send a letter to Bothwell that evening.

The Letter begins with the author stating that she had watched later up there than she would have done if it had not been to prepare what the bearer was to tell Bothwell. The setting could have been the Queen's chamber at Kirk o'Field below Darnley's room. It could not have been written at Glasgow in the previous month, as in paragraph 3 the writer stated that she expected to see Bothwell the next day. There are no indications who was the bearer and what was the information to be taken to Bothwell. The entire meaning of this sentence is far from clear. It is followed by another cryptic sentence which has attracted much interest: 'I have promised him to bring him to-morrow.' It must have been suggested by Moray and his associates in London that this referred to the alleged quarrel between Lord Robert Stewart (Mary's half-brother and Commendator of the Abbey of Holyrood) and Darnley on 8 February.[1] Cecil's copy of the Letter was endorsed that it concerned Holyrood House, which presumably was a reference to Lord Robert. There are also alternative and more accurate translations of this sentence: 'I have promised him [the bearer] to bring it [what she had prepared] to him [the bearer] to-morrow'; or even 'I have promised her to bring him to her tomorrow'. These opening sentences seem to relate to different circumstances to those in the rest of the Letter, and it is possible that they were added to the original text. Perhaps Letter IV is a modified version of the Letter shown secretly at York concerning the alleged quarrel. That Letter may have been subsequently withdrawn as too absurd to be credible.

Another cryptic passage refers to some other woman as the second lover of Jason (in Greek mythology). If this Letter was written a few days before the murder of Darnley, it is most unlikely that Mary was thinking of herself as Medea, the deserted first wife of Jason, in her relationship with Bothwell. On the other hand, Bothwell's wife or the French woman might have written such a passage. It is, however, unlikely that Lady Jane would have written in French.

The English Commissioners at York drew the attention of Queen Elizabeth to yet another cryptic passage.[2] This was to keep good watch in case the bird left its cage without its mate, like the turtle-dove it will stay alone to lament the absence howsoever short it may be. The whole passage is obscure, and perhaps the Original French was copied incorrectly. The Scots translation shows two distinct sentences and seems to make more sense than either the French or the English versions. Another possibility is that, as the passage was intended to be particularly incriminating, it may have been manipulated slightly without appreciating the impact on the rest of the meaning.

It is curious that in a poem 'Gif Languor makis Men licht' attributed to Darnley there are the lines:

> The turtour [turtle-dove] for hir maik [mate],
> Mair dule [sorrow] may noch indure.
> Nor I do for hir saik.

There is, however, nothing in this very mournful poem which links it specifically to anyone.[3]

The English translation refers to 'his cage' and this may have been deliberately misleading, so that the passage could be read to imply that Darnley was 'the bird'. It is more probable that the allusion was to the female writing the Letter. This might indicate that the writer was in a degree of seclusion or confinement. Such a condition is impossible to relate to the Queen early in 1567, but it could have referred very appropriately to the French lady who might have been threatening to leave.

Another point of uncertainty is the translation of 'per'. Originally it was shown as 'père' and as 'father', but altered or more probably corrected to 'per' and 'mate'. Presumably 'per' would be the French word 'pair', meaning in this passage the mate of a bird. If the meaning is 'mate' and Darnley is 'the bird', the insinuation would have been that he could escape from the control of his wife if Bothwell did not take care.

The second half of the passage, which is the second sentence in the Scots version, might again point to the author being the French lady. She might have lamented Bothwell's absence even for a short time, whereas it is very difficult to believe that Mary would have grieved for Darnley early in February 1567.[4] Any link between the two halves of the passage is nevertheless obscure and uncertain. The whole passage is not clear, and its meaning remains a matter for conjecture.

It is curious that one of the nicknames given to Lethington was 'The Bird in the Cage'.[5] It is, however, not easy to interpret the passage as an allusion to him. It might nevertheless have been an ingenious insertion by Lethington himself.

There is nothing in this Letter which identifies Mary with it apart from mentioning some of her servants in the last sentence, but that would have been a curious sentence for a Queen to write. It is also surprising that the Queen had to hide a letter to Bothwell from the prying eyes of Joseph and Bastian, who were subsequently on Lennox's list of persons whom he greatly suspected.[6] The concluding sentence and also the opening sentences could possibly have been added quite easily. It is significant that the last lines in Letters I and II are also prejudicial to Mary. A further possibility is that the original version of this Letter terminated at the end of paragraph 3 with the writer bidding good night to Bothwell and asking him to contact her in the morning. This would mean that the sentence referring to the bird in the cage was also added to the original Letter. The mental ingenuity required in realising that the original version of this Letter could be manipulated and interpreted to fit the circumstances of Mary's stay at Kirk o'Field may point to a person with the abilities of Lethington.

LETTER V

This is a relatively short Letter. Again it does not seem to contain any incriminating evidence against Mary and there is nothing in the Letter which shows that she was its author.

The Letter appears to deal with the problem of a servant who had been ungrateful to the author and had also done something foolish which had displeased Bothwell. The precise cause of his annoyance is not clear. When it was produced in England in 1568 it was said to be concerning the departure of Margaret Carwod. She was Mary's favourite servant and must have known most of the details of her personal life. According to the Letter, the servant was about to be married. On 11 February 1567, Margaret Carwod was married to John Stewart of Tullypowreis. Yet Mary regarded Margaret Carwod highly and paid for her wedding dress. There is no evidence that Mary was dissatisfied with her or that Margaret Carwod was ungrateful or disloyal to the Queen.[1] The allusion to Margaret Carwod was simply a way of trying to link the Letter with the Queen. There was devilish ingenuity in doing so.

The tone of the Letter does not give the impression that the Queen was the author. It is most unlikely that Mary would have asked Bothwell to find another servant for her. It seems much more probable that the author was the French lady who was being kept in seclusion and could have had difficulty in obtaining another servant.

Another aspect of the Letter which raises doubts about the Queen's authorship is that the writer is concerned that Bothwell will be swayed by another person's opinion of her and that he will doubt her constancy. If Mary was infatuated with Bothwell in 1566–67, it is improbable that she gave him cause to doubt her loyalty to him. Furthermore, anyone who carried some tale about her to Bothwell at that time would have incurred the Queen's wrath. The passage does not fit the alleged relationship between them.

There is one passage in the Letter which is particularly obscure:

> if you do not send me word this night what you want me to do,
> I will rid myself of it and risk causing to be enterprised and
> taken in hand what might be hurtful to what we both aim at.

Possibly this passage provides the key to why Bothwell retained the Letter. It can be surmised that the servant held some information which would be prejudicial to the author and Bothwell, but it is impossible to decide what this information was. Perhaps the intended meaning was that the writer would get rid of the servant who might then expose some secret.[2]

There is no indication in the Letter about when and where it was written. If the Queen did write this Letter to Bothwell, that would raise questions over when the problem stated in it could have arisen during 1566–67 and why she needed to write to him on this matter instead of discussing it with him.

It is astonishing that any reputable historian could have accepted this as an authentic letter from the Queen.

LETTER VI

This has been assumed to be the first of three relatively short Letters which Mary's accusers claimed she had written during her visit to Stirling in April 1567. They asserted that these Letters proved she knew in advance about Bothwell's intention to abduct her.

The chronological sequence of the three Stirling Letters is not entirely clear from their contents. Letter VIII is (judging from its agitated tone) intended to be the last, but the sequence of Letters VI and VII requires consideration. Possibly they should be reversed. It should also be re-collected that for some undisclosed reason only two of the Stirling Letters were shown to the English Commissioners at York.

A major objection to accepting this group of Letters as genuine is simply why so many Letters were written in such a short time. Mary had seen Bothwell on 20 April at Seton. On the 21st she travelled to Stirling and arrived there either on the 21st or on the 22nd. She may have left on the 23rd, stopping for the night on the way back to Edinburgh. It is surprising that they did not make the arrangements for the abduction while they were at Seton, and that Mary had to send Bothwell a series of Letters. According to this Letter and Letter VII, she was expecting Bothwell to inform her when and where he would meet her. The entire background of the Letters, however, is thrown in doubt by Buchanan's statement in his *History* that before she left Edinburgh she arranged with Bothwell that on her return journey he would seize her at the Bridge of Almond.

The authenticity of the Letters and the claim that Huntly knew before the 24th about the proposed abduction are also thrown in doubt by Drury's despatch to Cecil on 30 April, stating that Bothwell was secretly at Linlithgow the night before the abduction, and on the following morning had told Huntly what he intended to do.[1] This could mean that Huntly did not know about the abduction until the morning of the 24th and that the references to him in the three Stirling Letters as a participant in the plan were false. It would also mean that Mary wrote Letter VIII fairly early on the 23rd and that compresses even further the

136

tight time-scale for the three Letters to about 24 hours (from the morning of the 22nd to the early afternoon of the 23rd). If Drury's information was incorrect, that at least shows the extent of the rumours circulating over the details of the abduction.

A superficial perusal of this Letter could give the impression that it had been written by Mary, but a detailed study reveals various flaws. Mary warned Bothwell to take heed of his false brother-in-law, who had told her it was a foolish enterprise. In Letter II there is also a reference to a false brother-in-law. Presumably this was Huntly who was in attendance on Mary at Stirling. Yet all the evidence points to willing collusion between Huntly and Bothwell in arranging the divorce of Huntly's sister from Bothwell. According to Nau, at that time the Earl of Huntly was a warm partisan of Bothwell; there is no indication in Nau's account that Mary regarded Huntly as having been false. It is improbable that Mary would have involved someone she distrusted in making secret and highly compromising arrangements. If the references to Huntly as false in Letters II and VI represent Mary's genuine opinion of him, it means that she distrusted him between at least January and April 1567. Yet there is no corroborating evidence to support this. In contrast, it is very probable that the French lady who was so jealous of Lady Jane would have viewed Huntly with great suspicion. If the Letter was forged, part of the purpose may have been to offend Huntly by such an aspersion and so deprive Mary of any further support from him.

One particular passage in the translated versions needs careful study.[2] The translation of 'amenies' as 'carry away' is incorrect as the verb 'amener' means 'to bring'. The passage therefore relates not to an abduction but to the recipient of the Letter having brought the writer. This could point to the author being the mysterious French lady and the Letter being written after Bothwell's marriage to Lady Jane, possibly in the context of bringing the French lady under the same roof as Lady Jane. Such an arrangement would certainly have aroused concern among the supporters of Bothwell and Huntly.

There are further queries against accepting this as a genuine letter written by Mary. Bothwell had asked Huntly to write to tell him what were Mary's proposals for the enterprise. Such a procedure seems unlikely in making arrangements involving the Queen and most unlikely if in fact there was a romantic relationship between Mary and Bothwell. It would have been much more probable if the enterprise had involved the French lady.

Another query arises over the author's assertion that Bothwell had changed his mind during her absence more than she had. Yet in none of the three Stirling Letters is there any clear indication of messages or letters having been received from Bothwell. The absence of such a letter seems to be confirmed at the start of Letter VI with the reproach that he had promised to send word every day and had done nothing. The complaint about Bothwell changing his mind, moreover, is difficult to fit into the tight time-scale of the brief visit to Stirling. It is also not disclosed about what he had changed his mind.

It should be noted that the English translation of this Letter at Hatfield is virtually identical to the Scots translation, apart from the process of turning it into English.[3] It is, however, clear from the copy of the English translation of Letter IV, also at Hatfield, that the same translator did not follow so closely the Scots translation of Letter IV. Perhaps he was under greater pressure to finish Letter VI.

It is difficult to comprehend the details of the content of this Letter if it is read on the assumption that Mary wrote it from Stirling. The Letter is more meaningful if it is assumed that the secluded French lady wrote it. The querulous and mournful tone of this Letter, moreover, is similar to that in Letters III, IV and V and suggests strongly that the basis of Letter VI was also a Letter from the French lady. Two reservations to such an explanation are that it is difficult to conceive what arrangements Bothwell was making for her and why he was involving Huntly.

Letter VII

The tone of this Letter is very different from both Letter VI and Letter VIII. It is far more confident and authoritative than the plaintive and reproachful tone of those Letters. It is difficult to imagine this Letter being written within about 24 hours of the other two. Another fundamental difference between Letter VI and Letter VII is that in the former the writer repeats the reasons given by the brother-in-law why she could not expect to marry Bothwell, whereas in Letter VII the writer is addressing a loyal servant who might aspire one day to marry her. The stances are very far apart. It must also be stated that this Letter could not have been written by the French lady. The style is very different from Letters III, IV and V, and the content could not possibly be related to her circumstances.

If this was a Letter from Mary to Bothwell, she stated that his brother (presumably Huntly, his brother-in-law) was finding many difficulties, but Mary would follow him and not fail in her part of the plan. Mary's willingness to entrust herself to Huntly is a sudden and significant transformation from her attitude to Huntly in Letter VI. In that Letter she stated that she dared not trust Huntly with her letters and claimed that Bothwell's negligence put both of them in danger from Huntly. Yet no reason is given for the change. It is again difficult to accept that the same person wrote these two Letters.

In this Letter, Mary referred to Bothwell's services and the goodwill in which he was held by the other lords. He should make himself sure of the lords and free to marry. He was also to say many fair words to Lethington. Mary was clearly not expecting an early marriage as she mentioned Bothwell's hope that one day his service would make that possible. This is a very significant point as perhaps the only rational explanation of Mary's complicity in her abduction would have been the knowledge that she was already pregnant and required an excuse for a hastily arranged marriage to obscure her predicament.

Mary's references to Bothwell's services and aspirations are reminiscent of some of her comments about him in the Instructions for the French Court given to the Bishop of Dunblane after her marriage to Bothwell. Several key words are identical: 'dewtie', 'persuasiounis' and 'importune'.[1] The same person almost certainly drafted Letter VII and the Instructions, and this points to Lethington who would have been responsible for drafting the Instructions. It should be recollected that for comparative purposes there are no surviving copies of the Original French (apart from the opening lines) of this Letter, nor of the 1568 English translation. This Letter may have been originally drafted in Scots. The 'Original French' of Letter VII could have been a translation from the Scots draft. That would account for the similarities between the Scots 'translation' of Letter VII and the Instructions for the French Court (which were recorded in Scots in the Register of the Privy Council).

The deliberate reference to Lethington in Letter VII could indicate that he was the author of the forgery. The remark is curious as it is not clear exactly when Mary expected Bothwell to speak to Lethington, who was with her at Stirling. The insertion of Lethington's name might have been intended to show that he was not involved in the plans for the abduction. Perhaps Lethington tried to be too clever and consequently revealed his own participation in forging Letter VII.

An alternative explanation for this Letter which has been suggested is that it was written by Mary during her captivity in Lochleven Castle and was addressed to George Douglas after he had been banished from the Castle in March 1568 for trying to help her to escape.[2] He was the younger brother of Sir William Douglas, Mary's jailer, and he should not be confused with George Douglas the Postulate,[3] who was one of the ringleaders in the murder of Riccio. It seems that George was captivated by Mary's charm and tried to arrange her escape. During Mary's captivity there were rumours of a romance between Mary and George. On 28 October 1567, in a letter to Cecil, Drury reported suspicions of the over-great familiarity between them, and in April 1568 he reported talk of a possible marriage.[4] There is, however, no sound evidence on the extent of Mary's interest in him.

It is not inconceivable that Sir William connived at Mary's escape. That could explain the opening sentences of the Letter. Nau related that young Willie Douglas (an orphan member of the family who had also become devoted to the Queen) secretly removed the keys of the Castle as he was handing Sir William his drink, but their loss from the table should have been quickly detected. Perhaps Sir William may have been content to avoid noticing their removal and so allow the Queen to escape. His motive may have been a fear that he would be pressurised into killing her and would subsequently be punished for her murder. According to Melville, the mother of Sir William was also staying in the Castle and was thought to have been in the plot. After Mary's escape her baggage was promptly sent to her from Lochleven.[5] This also suggests that her captors wished to keep on good terms with her.[6]

Any letter written by Mary at Lochleven could not have been in the Casket when it was opened in June 1567. Such a letter must have been intercepted while the Queen was at Lochleven. Someone must then have realised that it could be related to the planning of the abduction instead of an escape from captivity. This is a possible explanation of Letter VII, but the use of such a letter would have been highly embarrassing to Sir William and also to the Earl of Moray. Sir William's mother was also Moray's mother as she had been the mistress of James V. Perhaps the opportunity to use the letter against Mary overcame Moray's objections. It is, however, impossible to prove or disprove that this was a letter from Mary to George Douglas. Although the possibility should not be dismissed, it is much more probable that Lethington drafted Letter VII some time after the abduction.

Letter VIII

The intended interpretation of this Letter was to show Mary's concern that there might be resistance to the proposed abduction. She pointed out that there were many persons present, including the Earl of Sutherland, who would not allow her to be carried away. She was anxious about Huntly's attitude as he was worried in case he would be charged with treason. Mary nevertheless thought he would play the part of an honest man – a marked contrast to her description of him in Letter VI as a false brother-in-law. She exhorted Bothwell to bring plenty of followers and have more power than her own escort. At first glance it seems very convincing as a genuine letter written by Mary before she left Stirling on 23 April or at Linlithgow on the evening of that day. The content, moreover, cannot be related to the situation of the French lady. There are, however, several doubts over its authenticity.

The Letter begins by mentioning a previous letter (to Bothwell), but it is not clear whether this was Letter VI or Letter VII or even another letter. Then there is a reference to 'your brother-in-law that was'. At the time of the abduction Huntly was still Bothwell's brother-in-law, although it should be noted that on 20 March 1567 Lady Jane Gordon had appointed procurators for her intended divorce and any actions to be pursued against her.[1] Either this description of Huntly was a slip on the part of the forger or Mary was anticipating the result of the divorce proceedings or the Letter was written at a later date. It is not an error in translation. Although no complete copy of Letter VIII in the Original French has survived, the Scots translation of the Letters published in 1572 included the first sentence from the Original French of each Letter. This showed 'vostre beau frere qui fust.' It is also surprising that Mary did not refer to Huntly as Bothwell's brother-in-law as in Letter VI or as his brother as in Letters VI and VII. Within two days she referred to Huntly in three different styles.

Another query is the reference to the presence of Sutherland and Livingstone. It is not known why they were at Stirling (or Linlithgow), and it is not recorded that they were conducting the Queen when she was abducted. It might, of course, be suggested that she had ordered them not to accompany her. It may or may not be significant that Sutherland and Livingstone were also mentioned in Letter II. Although it was indicated in Letter VIII that they would oppose the abduction, both attended the royal wedding in May 1567 according to the *Diurnal*. That would have been a mark against them in the minds of Mary's opponents. The specific reference to Sutherland implying his special loyalty to the Queen (or his dislike of Bothwell) seems to clash with the hint in Letter II that he was involved in a plot against her. This may point to inept editing of the Letters.

There is a discrepancy between this Letter which stated that Huntly and Livingstone had assembled (presumably at Stirling) more than 300 of their followers and the actual number in the Queen's escort on the return journey. A body of 300 horsemen was quite a large force. It is not clear what happened to them. The Letter refers to their presence 'yesterday' – probably the 22nd. Yet on the 24th the actual escort was 'ane few number' according to the *Diurnal*, and Robert Melville wrote in May 1567 to Throckmorton that it was 'but 30 horse'.[2] It should also be noted that there is no breakdown of the 300 between Huntly's men and those of Livingstone. Presumably Huntly could have ordered most of his own followers to stay at Stirling, but it might have been difficult for the Queen to avoid accepting the offer of an escort from Livingstone. Perhaps the large escort accompanied the Queen only as far as Linlithgow on the 23rd. If Mary deliberately shunned the protection of a large escort on the 24th, it is very surprising that none of her detractors, such as Buchanan, emphasised the point and connected their absence with the reference to them in this Letter.

It has been suggested that an alternative date for this Letter was 8 June 1567, when an attack on Borthwick Castle by the rebel lords was anticipated.[3] Mary might have written it at Borthwick and sent it to Bothwell, who was away in the Borders trying to recruit forces. Such a date would explain the reference to Huntly as a former brother-in-law, and it would also match the one occasion when Bothwell was away from Mary after their marriage. There are, however, several major difficulties in accepting such a date. Most of the content seems very clearly related to the abduction in April. There is no evidence to suggest that Huntly, Sutherland and Livingstone were at or even near Borthwick. Huntly could not have feared being charged with treason for rescuing the Queen from Borthwick Castle. Furthermore, the exhortation to Bothwell to bring more power than the 300 horsemen of Huntly and Livingstone would have been completely meaningless in June, as those two nobles would have supported the Queen against the rebel lords. There is also the question of how such a Letter could have been found in the Casket as it could not have been placed in it by Bothwell before leaving Edinburgh. Possibly the rebels captured the messenger taking the Letter to Bothwell. It is, however, highly improbable that a letter resembling Letter VIII was written at Borthwick. Either Mary wrote Letter VIII at Stirling or Linlithgow or someone forged it.

If the three Stirling Letters were written by Mary, they give the impression that she was not reluctant to take part in the proposed abduction and that she was willing to go ahead with it despite the forebodings of Huntly and other difficulties. In contrast, the Letters portray Bothwell as indecisive, dilatory, negligent and ill-organised. This is a curious portrayal of Bothwell who had a reputation for being bold, resolute and impetuous. These impressions provoke the question of whether Bothwell or Mary suggested that abduction. The Letters could be interpreted as indicating that Mary proposed her own abduction.

None of the three Stirling Letters gives any indication why this almost incredible abduction was being planned. Likewise, these Letters do not provide an overall view of the plan nor explain what would be the next steps to be taken by Mary and Bothwell. It should also be appreciated that if Mary did not write any of these Letters this radically weakens the assumption held by many contemporaries and historians that she had prior knowledge of Bothwell's intention to abduct her.

An examination of the three Stirling Letters does not reveal why Moray and his associates produced only two of those Letters at York, nor can it prove which was the Letter added at Westminster. There can have been little confidence in the impact of the first two Letters for some reason which has not been recorded. It must also be emphasised that the English Commissioners did not send Queen Elizabeth any extracts from the two Stirling Letters shown to them at York. It is curious that they found nothing worth extracting from them. It is difficult even to guess which was the additional Letter produced in December 1568. Possibly Letter VI was shown at York, as that Letter is so similar in style and tone to the other Letters written by the French lady and therefore should have been available. Either Letter VII or Letter VIII may have been added after York to strengthen the evidence showing Mary's collusion in her abduction.

Mary's foes did not have the aptitude to be consistent in their fabrications. Possibly this was because they took $1^1/_2$ years to produce the final version of the Casket Letters and too many persons were involved in the process. It seems, moreover, that they took a long time before deciding to assert that the Queen connived at her abduction. Despite the alleged discovery of the Letters on 21 June 1567, they stated in their summons against Bothwell on 30 June 1567 that he had taken the Queen by force to Dunbar, detained her and made her promise to marry him through fear of her life.[4] Then, on 20 July 1567, they wrote to Sir Nicholas Throckmorton stating

> how shamefully the Queen our Sovereign was led captive; and
> by fear, force, and, as by many conjectures may be well
> suspected, other extraordinary and more unlawful means,
> compelled to become bedfellow to another wife's husband.[5]

They did not mention any of the three Stirling Letters. Their assertions that the Queen had not been a willing accomplice in her abduction cannot be reconciled with the contents of the Stirling Letters. It is also remarkable that neither the Act of Secret Council nor the Act of Parliament in December 1567 made any allusion to the Queen's alleged connivance in her abduction. These omissions throw considerable doubt on the genuineness of all of the three Stirling Letters.

THE MARRIAGE CONTRACTS

Two Marriage Contracts between Mary and Bothwell were said to have been found in the Casket.

143

One of the Contracts was written in French. It was undated but shown as having been signed just by Mary. The copy of this Contract in the Cottonian Collection was written by one of Cecil's clerks, who also transcribed most of the surviving Original French versions of the Letters.[1] It is interesting that, in contrast to the Letters, he showed the Queen's signature on the Contract. In this Contract, she promised to take Bothwell as her husband and alluded to her freedom to do so since the death of Darnley. The document referred to Mary's late husband as 'Henry Stuart, called Darnley'. That was a style which she did not use when referring to him, but perhaps she had no control over the drafting of the Contract.[2] There are some other peculiar points in the drafting. The Contract starts with the royal 'Nous' but subsequently reverts to 'Je'. The references to relatives and friends, moreover, do not have a regal tone. In this Contract there was no specific reference to Bothwell's divorce, but Mary's promise would be operative when Bothwell had the same liberty.

A key to the date of the French Contract is that Mary made her promise to marry Bothwell 'without constraint'. This suggests that it was drafted during or after her abduction. Prior to that event the inclusion of such a phrase would have been unnecessary. The presence of this phrase is a very significant pointer to the pressure on Mary at Dunbar.

Although the content clearly indicated that the document had been written after Darnley's death, this did not deter Moray and his associates from stating on 7 December 1568 to the English Commissioners their assumption that it had been written by Mary before the death of Darnley.[3] Presumably their insinuation was that the Queen had signed this Contract as a pledge to Bothwell to secure his help in murdering Darnley. It seems that Moray and his colleagues did not produce any evidence to support their insinuation, and it is much more likely that Mary was forced to sign this Contract at Dunbar.

The other Contract, which was written in Scots, was published in the early editions of the *Detection*. It was shown as having been signed by both Mary and Bothwell at Seton on 5 April 1567. This was before the abduction later in the month. It referred to the intended process of divorce between Bothwell and Lady Jane. Bothwell promised to prosecute and set forward in all diligence the process of divorce already begun. It has been suggested that Bothwell tried to persuade Mary to sign it on 5 April but she did not do so until after her abduction.[4] If Mary did sign such a contract on 5 April, it is surprising that Bothwell needed to abduct her later in the month to force her into marrying him. The dating of this Contract must therefore be queried.

The Scots Contract is much longer than the French Contract, and is significantly different in two ways: it includes a justification of the marriage and it binds Bothwell as well as Mary to the proposed marriage.

If the Contracts are authentic it is difficult to perceive why both were required. Perhaps the shorter French Contract is an indication of Bothwell's pressure on Mary during the early days of her abduction at Dunbar. Possibly Bothwell had doubts about the legality of that document, or one of the Contracts may have remained as an unsigned draft.

It is difficult to see any advantage to Mary's enemies in forging two Contracts or adding a forged Contract to go with a genuine Contract. There is little reason to suppose that the actual texts were forged at a later date by Mary's opponents. The key questions (which unfortunately cannot be answered) are whether Mary signed these Contracts and, if so, when and in what circumstances.

It is unlikely that Bothwell personally drafted these two documents, especially the long 5 April Contract. He probably received help from someone more skilled in this type of work, such as Lethington or James Balfour. One passage in the 5 April Contract has similarities to the Aynesleyes Band and to the Instructions which the Queen sent to the Bishop of Dunblane in Paris after her marriage to Bothwell. All three documents indicated the Queen's inclination to marry again, dismissed marriage with a foreign prince and referred to Bothwell's good qualities. As there are also similarities between Letter VII and the Instructions sent to the Bishop (as already shown), it is very possible that the same person drafted all four documents. Lethington, as the Secretary, would have been responsible for drafting the Instructions. It is therefore a possibility that he drafted the 5 April Contract, but this cannot be proved.

It was avowed by Moray and his colleagues at Westminster on 7 December 1568 that the Scots Contract was wholly written by the Earl of Huntly.[5] It is not possible to verify this assertion, and it is surprising that such an important person should have performed the task of writing such a lengthy and very formal document, especially when the Parson of Oldhamstocks was present and presumably could have done so. Furthermore, it is not certain that Huntly had the skill to draft such a document. If he himself did not prepare the Contract, it is curious that he subsequently copied it. Bothwell himself could have copied it.

The reasons for claiming that Huntly wrote the Contract can only be a subject for conjecture. It is nevertheless clear that emphasis was placed on Huntly's involvement, as the same point had been impressed on the English Commissioners at York.[6] Possibly Moray wished to enhance the authenticity of the Contract by claiming it was in Huntly's handwriting. Perhaps Moray, who was certainly not Huntly's friend, sought to blacken his name by emphasising his involvement in the arrangements between

Bothwell and the Queen. Yet the assertion that Huntly wrote the Contract clashes with his alleged reluctance to become involved in the abduction as shown in the Stirling Letters.

The English Commissioners seem to have accepted with little, if any, questioning the assertions that the French Contract was signed before Darnley's death, and that Huntly wrote the Scots Contract. Clearly they were receptive to any allegations which helped to incriminate Mary and were not anxious to ask awkward questions. As, by 7 December, Mary's Commissioners were no longer present to challenge the statements of her opponents, Moray and his colleagues were able to assert their interpretation of the Contracts without contradiction.

Whatever may be the degree of authenticity in these two Contracts, they reflect the great pressure which Bothwell put on the Queen to marry him and his anxiety to ensure she did not subsequently revoke her consent.

THE SONNETS

Moray and his associates claimed that the Casket contained 12 love Sonnets written by Mary to Bothwell. There is no record of any statement about when she was supposed to have composed them. It is highly improbable that anyone deliberately forged all of these Sonnets to incriminate Mary, but there may have been a little manipulation. When considering the Sonnets it should be kept in mind that the only available versions are those published in the years after the conferences in 1568–69. The meaning of some lines is not entirely clear and, of course, any possible alterations to the original Sonnets cannot be confirmed, as the original versions disappeared.

The unhappy and jealous tone of the Sonnets suggests that the person who wrote Letters III, IV, V and VI also composed the Sonnets. The recurring theme is jealousy of Lady Bothwell.

There are several passages which prove that the author was not the Queen. In the Third Sonnet the author wrote:

> she makes use of constancy just for her advantage,
> for it is no small honour to be mistress of your possessions.

Despite Bothwell's strong position in the Borders there is no indication that he was a very wealthy nobleman. It is most unlikely that Mary would have regarded Bothwell's wealth as significant, but the mysterious French lady kept in seclusion by Bothwell could have envied Lady Bothwell's position as mistress of Bothwell's possessions.

In the Fourth Sonnet the following lines (referring to Lady Jane) could not have been addressed to Bothwell by the Queen:

> By you, my dear, and by your marriage
> she has restored her family to honour.

Mary herself had restored Huntly to his father's title in 1565, months before his sister's marriage to Bothwell, but the French lady may not have known the full story of the fortunes of the Gordon family. Likewise the next two lines:

> She has enjoyed through you the grandeur
> of which her own relations had no assurance

surely do not reflect Mary's knowledge of the House of Huntly.

In the Ninth Sonnet, the author wrote that for him she had left all her kin and friends. Both of Mary's parents had died long before 1567. She had left her French relatives in France in 1561. There was also no question of Mary losing all her friends on account of her reliance on Bothwell up to the time of their marriage. On the other hand, the French lady would have left all her family and friends in France.

There are, however, a few lines which could be held to incriminate Mary provided they were authentic. These are in the Second Sonnet:

> In his hands and his full power
> I place my son, my honour, and my life,
> my country, my subjects, my soul,
> subjected all to him.

The French version of the third and fourth lines quoted above is shown in the early editions of the *Detection* as follows:

> mon pais, mes subjectz, mon ame
> assubiectie est tout à luy.

If the Queen composed this Sonnet, it is surprising that she referred to 'mon pais' rather than 'mon royaume'.[1] Possibly the words 'mes subjectz' could have been inserted or substituted for another phrase. A further query against an interpretation of these lines which would incriminate Mary is that she did not place Prince James in the care of Bothwell. The reference to a son, moreover, does not necessarily mean Prince James. Although Bothwell had no legitimate children, he had an illegitimate son called William.[2] It is not known who was William's mother, nor when and where he was born. It might be a reasonable

147

conjecture that he was entrusted to Bothwell's mother when his own mother returned to her own country. When considering these lines in the Second Sonnet it should also be noted that, unless a measure of poetic licence has been used, there is a grammatical fault with the singular verb 'est' in the fourth line of the Second Sonnet. This may point to some corruption in the text of the third line. The persons who tampered with the Casket Letters did not always realise the complications they created.

It has been pointed out that Sonnets 1, 2, 8 and 9 refer to 'him', whereas the others refer to 'you'.[3] Those four Sonnets relate to the feelings of the author for Bothwell; Sonnets 3, 4, 5 and 6 to the jealousy of the author for Lady Jane Gordon; and the remainder again to the author's feelings for Bothwell. It is a curious structure, which may point to some manipulation or just to the emotional state of the author. It is difficult to be convinced that the first group was forged and added to the others. Sonnets 1, 2, 8 and 9 do not contain material which is sufficiently damaging to the Queen to have justified forging them. What may be more likely is that the sequence of the Sonnets was altered, or that Sonnets 1, 2, 8 and 9 were composed at a different time from the others.

The Sonnets do not contain anything which shows the Queen's involvement in the murder of Darnley, but in the opinion of Fénélon, the French Ambassador in London, the Sonnets were worse than all the other contents in the *Detection*.[4] That edition of the *Detection* presumably included at least the important Letters I, II and IV. Fénélon's opinion should certainly be kept in mind when the impact of the Sonnets on the reputation of Mary is being considered.

The overwhelming impression after reading the Sonnets is that it is easy to follow their content by assuming they were written by the unhappy French lady, but very difficult to accept that the Queen could even possibly have written them.

7. AN ASSESSMENT OF THE CASKET LETTERS

IT IS VERY DIFFICULT to consider the Casket Letters free from an inbuilt conditioning that their contents revealed or were supposed to reveal an illicit romance between Mary and Bothwell, a plot to murder Darnley and Mary's connivance with her abduction. It is very easy to accept that passages in the Letters showed Mary's passionate and jealous love for Bothwell, her complicity in the murder of Darnley and her almost frantic anxiety over the arrangements of her own abduction. Contradictions and discrepancies can be dismissed by asserting that such details could stem from faulty translations or could have explanations which escape modern readers. Another argument in support of the authenticity of the Casket Letters is simply that it would have been difficult to compose and forge so many Letters and Sonnets. Perhaps the strongest argument for their authenticity is that Mary and her defenders never produced a detailed rebuttal of them, but that would not have been easy to organise during her captivity.

A closer and more critical study does not support the view that the Letters were what Mary's enemies claimed. There are too many points of detail which cast doubt on their authenticity. The overall content of the Letters also raises very strong doubts. It must be asked whether the portraits of Mary and Bothwell which emerge from the Casket Letters resemble what is otherwise known of their personalities and behaviour.

It is not too difficult to disentangle the authentic material from the fabrications. Some innocent passages in genuine Letters from Mary could simply have been given an incriminating interpretation by a few alterations such as substituting 'l'homme' for 'le Prince' in Letter I. The more emotional passages allegedly showing her passion for Bothwell and her intense jealousy of Lady Jane were extracted from letters to him from the secluded French lady. It is probable that Mary wrote Letter I, but it is impossible that its content referred to plans to murder Darnley. Much of Letter II, especially in the first half, was almost certainly written by Mary but in the setting of ascertaining information about plots against her and the infant Prince. It is highly likely that Letters III, V and VI, the Sonnets, most of IV, and parts of II were written to Bothwell by the French lady. The tone of Letter VII suggests that the Queen could have written it, but the patronising attitude towards the recipient clashes with the alleged setting of an immediate abduction and early marriage. It was probably a forgery by Lethington, who was familiar with the Queen's style of writing. Letter VIII has several significant queries against its authenticity. An overall study of the three Stirling Letters raises further doubts. Likewise, consideration of the two Marriage Contracts raises queries over whether Mary signed them and, if so, whether voluntarily and without any constraint. It is too simplistic to hold that the Casket Letters were either completely authentic or entirely forged. There is, however, sufficient evidence to endorse the view that there was extensive manipulation and forgery.

One strong impression is that here and there the manipulators went too far and introduced contradictions and inconsistencies. These may have arisen because after the alleged discovery of the Letters in June 1567 there was a long time-lag before the final set of documents was displayed. Moray and his supporters were desperate to ensure the survival of the Protestant Revolution for various reasons. That required the removal from Mary of the control of Scotland. They also had to justify their deposition of a monarch by providing damning evidence of her guilt. They had plenty of time to concoct a set of incriminating Letters, and there are very strong indications that they did so. There was, however, no eagerness to expose them to scrutiny by others. For a long time, Moray and his associates seem to have lacked confidence in displaying the Letters. They tried to obtain advance assurances that the Letters would be accepted in England as sufficient proof of Mary's guilt. Neither the originals nor even copies were allowed to be subjected at York and Westminster and Hampton Court to critical analysis by supporters of Mary. There is also no evidence that the English Commissioners scrutinised them inquisitively. The discovery of flaws was avoided.

Arguments have raged for centuries over the authenticity or otherwise of the Casket Letters and the innocence or guilt of Mary. The Casket Letters can no longer be considered as sound evidence against her. In future there should be greater interest in considering two other aspects of the Casket Letters: first of all, what did Letter II and perhaps also Letter I reveal about Mary's concern over Darnley's plotting against her; and secondly, what were Bothwell's motives in retaining a selection of Letters and Sonnets and entrusting them to the very dubious safe-keeping of James Balfour.

MARY AND THE CASKET LETTERS

The portrayal of Mary as shown in some of the Casket Letters is that of a woman who is infatuated with her lover and deeply jealous of his wife.

She looks for a letter from him after he has been away for only a day or two. Yet the relationship between them is far from happy. She reproaches him for his coldness and forgetfulness, his suspicions and broken promises. She upbraids him for his lack of resolution. She refers to the evils he has caused her and laments her cruel lot and continual misfortune. If these Casket Letters are genuine, they present a remarkable picture of the Queen in a state of frenzied love, while Bothwell remains almost coldly indifferent to her approaches. The Queen is running after him with no display of demure or regal decorum.

It is remarkable that contemporaries gave no hint of Mary showing such passionate feelings for Bothwell in the weeks immediately before and after the murder of Darnley. It is highly unlikely that such an emotional relationship could have been kept secret. Mary had too many enemies who would immediately have relayed such gossip across Scotland and the rest of western Europe. Although Mary was certainly relying more and more on Bothwell, there is no reputable evidence which indicates any infatuation with him. The unrealistic portrayal of the Queen in some of the Casket Letters shows that one of the other women in Bothwell's life wrote those Letters and all the Sonnets.

The real portrait of Mary which emerges from the authentic passages in Letter II is that of a Queen determined to ensure that her scheming husband would not usurp her throne. She went to Glasgow not as party to a murder plot but as a deeply-perturbed monarch anxious to bring Darnley under control without creating a scandal which would wreck her claim to the English throne. The visit to a Lennox stronghold needed a considerable measure of courage. It also required a degree of deception which she did not relish, and she may have undertaken this only at the insistence of Bothwell.

BOTHWELL AND THE CASKET LETTERS

The portrait of Bothwell which emerges from the Casket Letters is just as unbelievable as that of Mary. Four of the Letters – III, IV, V and VI – reveal him as cold, forgetful, distrustful and ungrateful towards the devoted writer. It is inconceivable that Bothwell would have treated the Queen in such a way until she was securely married to him. Bothwell's ill behaviour to Mary immediately after their marriage shows how he must have behaved to the secluded French lady who was the real author of these reproachful passages.

The most intriguing point about the Casket Letters is why Bothwell had been keeping those which were genuine. Yet little consideration has hitherto been given to his motives for retaining them. If some Letters to him from another woman had been stolen from him after his marriage to the Queen, they could have been used to blackmail him. If others were Letters from Mary incriminating herself, they also involved him. Bothwell must have had strong reasons for retaining such potentially damaging papers. Although Bothwell may have had sentimental reasons for keeping Letters from another woman, this seems unlikely from what is known of his personality and behaviour to women and especially as the comments were not flattering to him! He probably had other reasons for retaining them, though these are difficult to perceive. It is also most unlikely that he kept any Letters from Mary for purely sentimental reasons. His interest in Mary lay in the goal of the crown matrimonial. There is no evidence indicating any passion or even strong affection on his part for Mary.

Bothwell may have had one very potent reason for retaining certain Letters from Mary. That would have been his involvement in what happened at Kirk o'Field. Possibly his intention was to keep the Letters as a safeguard in case Mary repudiated him or allowed fresh proceedings to be taken against him for the murder of Darnley. Buchanan stated in his *History* that Bothwell kept the Letters because he had seen in the past few years many examples of the Queen's capriciousness. That, however, may just be another of Buchanan's slurs on Mary, who erred on the side of being too loyal to some of her entourage. Furthermore, Buchanan's statement can only have been surmise, as he was not in Bothwell's confidence. Bothwell should have considered himself secure after his acquittal at his trial and then his marriage to the Queen. The retention of the Letters indicates his continuing insecurity and a guilty conscience. It suggests that he had little reason to assume that Mary would trust and support him, and also implies that Mary was far from being passionately in love with him. Reports (if true) that he was very suspicious of Mary's conversations with anyone else after their marriage would be in line with this interpretation of his attitude.[1]

There is the possibility of other serious charges against Bothwell. It must be asked why he placed Letters from the Queen and the French lady in the same Casket. He should have realised that if these Letters were discovered together they would cause even greater embarrassment to the Queen. Their presence in the Casket may also have given Morton and his accomplices the idea of combining them into a set of Letters to incriminate Mary. It must also be asked what Bothwell was planning to do with the various letters, and why he entrusted the Casket to Balfour. His decision to leave it in Edinburgh Castle suggests that he was very anxious to avoid the Queen discovering the contents of the Casket. Unless the Casket contained only his title-deeds, Bothwell's conduct must be regarded with deep suspicion.

It must again be emphasised that the whole story of the Casket being left in the Castle may have been fabricated, and also that the Casket may have contained none or only some of the Letters when Morton opened it. First of all, it is very probable that the Casket did not contain all of the eight Letters eventually shown at Westminster. Some may have been subsequently forged; others may have been found elsewhere. An additional letter from the unknown lady may also have been available. Such a letter could have been used to insert material into some of the Casket Letters such as the second half of Letter II. There is also the possibility that the Casket did not contain any of the eight Letters. Bothwell may have left other important papers in the Casket.

According to Morton's *Declaration*, various title deeds belonging to Bothwell were found in Dalgleish's possession when he was apprehended. Perhaps these had been in the Casket. Other documents which may have been in the Casket included Bothwell's copy of the Band allegedly signed at Craigmillar. The Herries *History* stated that, according to the Queen's party, the Casket contained that Band, and the Letters were counterfeit. It is not known what happened to the original of the Band signed at the supper-party on 19 April, and it is conceivable that it was also in the Casket. The Casket, however, was not very large, and that raises the question of how many papers it could have contained. The contents of the Casket remain uncertain.

As a final assessment, those who concocted the Casket Letters were very successful – despite the obvious inbuilt flaws and errors – in besmirching Mary's reputation for the rest of her life and in hoodwinking many historians up to present times. The Letters provided plausible justification for keeping her as a prisoner, and also ensured that the Protestant lords remained in power in Scotland. This in turn safeguarded England from facing a hostile government in Scotland backed by France or Spain. Another important aspect of the Letters is that their correct interpretation is an essential step towards understanding the reasons for Mary's policy and actions from December 1566 until the death of Darnley.

In retrospect the conduct of Mary's opponents over the Letters leaves an ugly stain on their own characters. Their obvious lack of integrity should give Mary the benefit of the doubt in the interpretation of any ambiguous or obscure passages in the Casket Letters. Her own account of the crisis must also be given much fuller consideration.

8. Mary's Own Version

It is important to appreciate that Mary's enemies held power from June 1567 onwards in both Scotland and England, and that it was difficult and dangerous for most of her supporters to give testimony in her favour.[1] Furthermore, the opportunities for making public denials were far fewer than in more modern times. Most of the surviving evidence therefore comes from her opponents. Many historians have consequently neglected considering the events from Mary's standpoint. This has perpetuated a slanted view of what happened.

The four main pillars of the case produced against Mary by her opponents must be judged as flawed and unsound: the circumstantial evidence, the depositions, the writings of George Buchanan and, especially, the Casket Letters. The traditional version should no longer form the basis for any sound historical account. An alternative approach, which provides a more reliable starting-point for a revised interpretation of the events, is based on an examination of Mary's own statements. These are contained primarily in her correspondence, the Instructions to her Ambassadors after her marriage and to her Commissioners at York and Westminster and the conversations with Nau.

After Darnley's participation in the murder of Riccio, Mary had very good cause to take seriously any rumours of further plots being hatched by him. By the autumn of 1566, she was very concerned about the intentions of Darnley and the possibility that he might go abroad or attempt a coup against her and Prince James. It would be a foolish error to minimise or ignore her concern over the threat from Darnley in late 1566 and early 1567. It must again be stressed that the consequences of their marital rift stretched far further than the breakdown of their own personal relationship. The conflict endangered the government of her realm. Her deep dismay is revealed by Buchanan in his *Detection*. He stated that about 5 November 1566 a man came to Kelso with letters from Darnley which the Queen read in the presence of Moray, Huntly and Lethington. Then she cast a piteous look and miserably tormented herself. She protested that unless she might by some means or other be despatched of the King, she should never have another good day; and if by no other way she could attain it, rather than abide to live in such sorrow she would slay herself. (It is not known what Darnley said in those letters.) Buchanan's account was almost certainly intended to be detrimental to Mary, but if it was broadly true, his statement reveals the depth of her misery. At Craigmillar the Queen was fully justified in consulting her principal councillors about the political threat from Darnley.

Mary's anxiety over Darnley led to her confrontation with him in the presence of her nobles on 30 September 1566, the discussions at Craigmillar in early December, her measures in late December to strengthen her position, the removal of the Prince to Edinburgh, and then her journey to Glasgow. For many weeks it was the key to her activities. In her letter of 20 January 1567 to the Archbishop of Glasgow in Paris, she stated her concern about Darnley's plans:

> Always we perceive him occupied and busy enough to have inquisition of our doings, which, God willing, shall aye be such as none shall have occasion to be offended with them, or to report of us any way but honourably; howsoever he, his father, and their fautors [supporters] speak, which we know want no good will to make us have ado, if their power were equivalent to their minds.[2]

From the accounts of Bishop Leslie and Nau it seems that Mary claimed there had been a perfect reconciliation between Darnley and herself following their conversations in Glasgow and Kirk o'Field. There may indeed have been a reconciliation but that does not necessarily mean much more than the repair of a breach. It is very unlikely that Mary recovered any trust in Darnley, and it is highly probable that she was still deeply suspicious of him.

In January 1567, the Queen was facing not only the hostility of Darnley and the Lennox faction but also the perpetual potential threat from Moray, Morton and their Protestant supporters, backed by England and even France. Mary's security was being sandwiched. By this time she must have been very aware of the danger of plots against her own life. Since her return in 1561 she had overcome three rebellions. In 1565 there may also have been an attempt to kidnap her. At Kirk o'Field, according to Nau, Darnley told her that certain persons had advised him to make an attempt upon her life. Although this statement by Nau should be treated with caution, it is nevertheless not surprising that her reaction to the murder of Darnley – as shown in her letter of 10 or 11 February to the Archbishop of Glasgow – was that the explosion was intended to kill her as well as Darnley. She had been there until midnight, and she claimed it was by very chance she had not tarried there all night. Mary's opinion that the plot was also aimed at herself should be given greater consideration and not be dismissed.

It is not known whom Mary regarded as the likely murderers of Darnley immediately after the deed. At first she does not seem to have suspected Lethington, and she protected him against the enmity of Huntly and Bothwell until early June 1567 when he fled from the court, but according to Nau the Queen told Lethington just after Carberry that Morton, Balfour, Lethington himself and others of the Council had been the actual murderers. A year later, on 14 June 1568, Middlemore reported to Cecil that Mary had told him she wished to confront Lethington and Moray in the presence of Queen Elizabeth and that 'Lethington would be very loath of that commission'.[3] Mary's accusation against Morton and others after Carberry was probably derived from information not available in the immediate aftermath of the murder. Her list may have been accurate at least as regards the planning of the deed. It is unlikely that Argyll, Bothwell and Huntly (none of whom she specifically mentioned) would have visited that evening a house already mined or being mined with gunpowder. In contrast, it seems that those named by her stayed away from Kirk o'Field on the night of the murder. It is, however, impossible to know how far her opinions, as recorded by Nau, were just hindsight on her part.

Nau recorded Mary's belief that the plan of her opponents was to persuade her to marry Bothwell so that they might charge her with conspiring against Darnley and consenting to his death. Bishop Leslie, in 1569, had already made the same accusation against Mary's opponents. It is, however, not clear if Mary had realised before her abduction the trap which it was alleged that her enemies had laid for her.

Mary's justification of her marriage to Bothwell – as set out in her Instructions for the Bishop of Dunblane to present at the French court[4] – has the tone of being apologetic and defensive. That is not surprising. It is nevertheless a long and detailed statement in which Mary claimed she had assumed that Bothwell's ready willingness to fulfil all her commands came from his duty to her as her subject; she had rebuffed his advances to her after he had obtained the support of the nobles for a marriage with her; she had reproached him and remonstrated with him for his abduction of her; and at Dunbar she had been left alone as it were a prey to him. She emphasised that the Band, which was signed at the Aynesleys Supper by many of the leading nobles, exhorted her to marry Bothwell and that there was no attempt to rescue her at Dunbar.

What is most surprising and also very significant in the Instructions is that they included several uncomplimentary remarks about Bothwell such as this passage:

> While of late, since the decease of the King our husband, that,
> as his pretensions began to be higher so we found his
> proceedings somewhat strange; although now since we are so far
> proceeded with him, we must interpret all things to the best.
> Yet we have been highly offended first with his presumption
> that thought we could not sufficiently reward him, unless we
> should give ourself to him for the recompense of his service,
> next for his practices and secret means, and at length the plain
> attempting of force to have us in his power, for fear to be
> disappointed of his purpose.

That was not written in the submissive style of the author of several of the Casket Letters. Her Instructions merit further study free from inbuilt assumptions of her guilt.

In March 1571 Mary sent a message to the Pope supplicating to be relieved of the indignity of her marriage to Bothwell.[5] She stated that he carried her as a prisoner to Dunbar Castle and then Edinburgh Castle. She had been kept against her will in the Earl's control until he had procured a pretended divorce from his wife. She was also constrained to give her consent, although against her will, to marrying Bothwell. It is difficult to disprove her version of these events. A substantial measure of confirmation is provided through the accounts of her abject misery immediately after the marriage.

It should be noted that Mary did not plead her own ill-health to account for her failure to discover and arrest the murderers of Darnley. In her Instructions to the Bishop of Dunblane, however, she pointed out that at the time of her abduction she was already wearied and almost broken with the frequent uproars and rebellions raised against her since she returned to Scotland. It is also clear that she was very ill in July 1567, when she was forced to abdicate. Although she was not in continuous ill-health or even in a permanent state of mental debility during the first part of 1567, the cumulative strain of threats to her rule should not be forgotten.

It must be pointed out that there are important gaps in Mary's accounts of the events. She did not provide a detailed refutation of her failure to find and prosecute the murderers of Darnley, despite the critical and adverse propaganda being mounted against her in both Scotland and other countries. It is not clear at what stage she began to have doubts about Bothwell's innocence, but from Nau's record she may have been uncertain over his actions at least by the time of Carberry. She also never gave details to support her accusations against Moray and his associates.

Perhaps her most important omission was that she never provided a detailed rebuttal of the Casket Letters. Unless she knew they were genuine, she must have been very curious to see them. She was, however, never shown them officially though it is probable that at some time she saw copies of at least some of them. It has been surmised that copies were passed to her about the time of the Conference at York but this cannot be substantiated.[6] In November 1571, she complained bitterly to the French Ambassador about the libellous contents of Buchanan's *Detection* after one of Elizabeth's servants had given her a copy.[7] It is probable that such an early edition of the *Detection* did not contain all of the Casket Letters.[8] Mary did not specifically mention them in her letter to the Ambassador. Nau's account provides no further information about Mary's reactions to the Casket Letters. He does not mention the Letters and gives no details of the proceedings at York and Westminster and Hampton Court. Although Mary firmly denied writing any letters relating to the murder of Darnley, there is no record that she specifically refuted the authenticity of the Stirling Letters, the Marriage Contracts or the Sonnets. That, however, cannot be accepted as proof of their authenticity.

Mary's silence over the details of the Casket Letters could be deemed to point to her guilt. On the other hand, she may have been maintaining the stance she took during the Westminster Conference to avoid conceding to Elizabeth the right of jurisdiction over her. Furthermore, if the Casket Letters were a mixture of forged, manipulated and authentic material, it would have been dangerous for Mary to concede that some of the material was genuine without running the risk that even a partial admission would be held to prove her guilt. By January 1569 she can have held little expectation of a fair hearing. Subsequently, even her life was in great jeopardy.

There is no indication of Mary's reaction to the discovery that Bothwell had kept some of her Letters and also Sonnets and Letters from another woman. She must have pondered what had been his reasons and motives. Presumably the discovery and publicity were further humiliations for her. Bothwell's retention of the various documents may have convinced her that he was basically disloyal to her and that there was no reason not to proceed with a divorce and another marriage.

All these omissions in Mary's defence may or may not point to her guilt or innocence. Sceptics may discount the sincerity and veracity of her own statements, but the evidence to support their aspersions is not there. In contrast the evidence produced by her opponents is riddled with lies and fabrications. The deeper their evidence is probed, the more it is found to be unrealistic and untenable. It is astonishing that so many historians have accepted so uncritically the evidence of Mary's foes but have given scant credit to her own statements.

There remains uncertainty over many of the events in 1567–68 for lack of relevant and reliable evidence, and any attempt at reconstruction depends at least partly on conjecture and theory. Some of the lies, myths and misconceptions can nevertheless now be cleared away, and a sound and substantial measure of historical revision substituted for them. Mary's version stands as a reasonable starting-point for any future account of her personal reign in Scotland.

Appendices

APPENDIX 1:
TEXTS OF THE EIGHT CASKET LETTERS

LETTER I – SCOTS TRANSLATION FROM LEKPREVIK'S *DETECTION*

1. It adpeiris, that with zour absence thair is alswa joynit forzetfulness, seand yat at zour departing ze promysit to mak me advertisement of zour newis from tyme to tyme. The waitting upon yame[1] zisterday causit me to be almaist in sic joy as I will be at zour returning, quhilk ze have delayit langer than zour promeis was.

2. As to me, howbeit I have na farther newis from zow according to my commission, I bring the man with me to Craigmillar upon Monounday, quhair he will be all Wednisday; and I will gang to Edinburgh to draw blude[2] of me, gif in the meane tyme I get na newis in ye contrarie fra zow.

3. He is mair gay than ever ze saw him; he puttis me in remembrance of all thingis yat may mak me beleve he luifis me. Summa,[3] ze will say yat he makis lufe to me; of ye quhilk I tak sa greit plesure, yat I enter never where he is, bot incontinent I tak ye seiknes of my sair syde, I am sa troubillit with it. Gif[4] Paris bringis me that quhilk I send him for, I traist it sall amend me.

4. I pray zow, advertise me of zour newis at lenth, and quhat I sall do in cace ze be not returnit quhen I am cum thair; for in cace ze wirk not wysely, I se yat the haill burding of this will fall upon my schoulderis. Provide for all thing, and discourse upon it first with zour self.

5. I send this be Betoun, quha gais to ane day of law[5] of the Laird of Balfouris. I will say na further, saifing that I pray zow to send me gude newis of zour voyage. From Glasgow this Setterday in the morning.

LETTER I – ENGLISH TRANSLATION AT THE PUBLIC RECORD OFFICE

1. It seemyth that with your absence forgetfulnes is joynid,

consydering that at your departure you promised me to sende me newes from you; nevertheles I can learn none.[1] And yet did I yesterday looke for that that shuld make me meryer then I shall be. I think you doo the lyke for your returne, prolonging it more than you have promised.

2. As for me, if I heare no other matter of you, according to my commission I bring the man Mondaye to Cregmiller, where he shall be upon Wednisdaye. And I [t]o go to Edinboroughe to be lett blud, if I have no word to the contrayry.

3. He is the meryest that ever you sawe, and doth remember unto me all that he can to make me beleve that he loovith me. To conclude: you wold saye that he makith love to me, wherein I take so muche plesour that I never com in there but my payne of my syde doth take me; I have it sore todaye. Yf Paris doth bring back unto me that for which I have sent, it shuld muche amend me.

4. I pray you send me word from you at large, and what I shall doo if you be not returnid when I shall be there; for if you be not wyse, I see assuredly all the wholle burden fallen upon my shoulders. Provide for all, and consider well.

5. First of all,[2] I send this present to Ledinton[3] to be delivered to you by Beton, who goith to one day a law of Lard Balfour. I will saye no more unto you, but that I pray God send me good newes of your voyage. From Glasco this Saterday morning.

Endorsed: 'Ane short lettre from Glasco to the Erle Bothwell. Prufes her disdayn against her husband.'

LETTER II – SCOTS TRANSLATION FROM LEKPREVIK'S *DETECTION*

1. Being departit from the place quhair I left my hart, it is esie to be judgeit quhat was my countenance seing that I was evin als mekle[1] as ane body without ane hart, quhilk was the occasioun that quhile dennertyme I held purpois[2] to na body: nor zit durst ony present thameselfis unto me, judging yat it was not gude sa to do.

2. Four myle or I come to the towne, ane gentilman of the Erle of Lennox come and maid his commendatiounis unto me; and excusit him that he come not to meit me, be ressoun he durst not interpryse the same, becaus of the rude wordis that I had spokin to Cuninghame;[3] and he desyrit that he suld

come[4] to the inquisitioun of ye mater yat I suspectit him of. This last speiking was of his awin heid, without ony commissioun. I answerit to him, that thair was na recept culd serve aganis feir; and that he wald not be affrayit, in cace he wer not culpabill; and that I answerit bot rudely to the doutis yat wer in his letteris. Summa, I maid him hald his toung. The rest were lang to wryte.

3. Schir James Hammiltoun met me, quha schawit, that the uther tyme quhen he[5] hard of my cumming, he departit away, and send Howstoun, to schaw him, that he wald never have belevit that he wald have persewit him, nor yit accompanyit him with the Hammiltounis. He answerit, that he was only cum bot to se me, and yat he wald nouther accompany Stewart nor Hammiltoun, bot be my commandement. He desyrit that he wald cum and speik with him. He refusit it.

4. The Laird of Lusse, Howstoun and Caldwellis sone, with XL hors or thairabout, come and met me. The Laird of Lusse said, he was chargeit to ane day of law be the Kingis father, quhilk suld be this day, aganis his awin handwrit, quhilk he hes; and zit notwithstanding, knawing of my cumming, it is delayit. He was inquyrit to cum to him, whilk he refusit, and sweiris that he will indure nathing of him. Never ane of that towne come to speik to me, quhilk causis me think that thay ar his; and nevertheless he speikis gude, at the leist his sone. I se na uther gentilman but thay of my company.[6]

5. The King send for Joachim zisternicht, and askit at him, quhy I ludgeit not besyde him, and that he wald ryse the soner gif that wer; and quhairfoir I come, gif it was for gude appointment? and gif ze wer thair in particular? and gif I had maid my estait, gif I had takin Paris and Gilbert to wryte to me?[7] and yat I wald send Joseph away. I am abaschit[8] quha hes schawin him sa far; zea, he spak evin of ye marriage of Bastiane. I inquyrit him of his letteris, quhairintil he plenzeit[9] of the crueltie of sum; answerit, that he was astonischit, and that he was sa glaid to se me, that he belevit to die for glaidnes. He fand greit fault that I was pensive.

6. I departit to supper. Yis beirer will tell zow of my arryving. He prayit me to returne, the quhilk I did. He declairit unto me his seiknes, and that he wald mak na testament, but only leif all thing to me; and that I was the caus of his maladie, becaus of the regrait that he had that I was sa strange unto him. And thus he said: Ze ask me quhat I mene be the crueltie contenit in my letter? It is of zow alone that will not accept

my offeris and repentance. I confes that I have failit, but not
into that quhilk I ever denyit[10] and siclyke hes failit to[11] sindrie
of zour subjectis, quhilk ze have forgevin. I am zoung. Ze
wil say that ze have forgevin me oft tymes, and zit yat I
returne to my faultis. May not ane man of my age, for lacke
of counsell, fall twyse or thryse, or in lacke[12] of his promeis,
and at last repent himself and be chastisit be experience. Gif
I may obtene pardoun, I protest I sall never mak fault agane.
And I craif na uther thing bot yat we may be at bed and
buird togidder as husband and wyfe; and gif ze wil not consent heirunto I sall never ryse out of yis bed. I pray zow, tel
me zour resolution. God knawis how I am punischit for
making my God of zow, and for having na uther thocht bot
on zow; and gif at ony time I offend zow, ze ar the caus,
becaus quhen ony offendis me, gif for my refuge I micht
playne unto zow, I wald speik it unto na uther body; bot
quhen I heir ony thing, not being familiar with zow, necessitie
constrainis me to keip it in my breist, and yat causes me to
tyne[13] my wit for verray anger.

7.   I answerit ay unto him, bot that wald be ovir lang to wryte at
       lenth. I askit quhy he wald pas away in ye Inglis schip. He
       denyis it, and sweirs thairunto; bot he grantis that he spak
       with the men. Efter this I inquirit him of the inquisitioun of
       Hiegaite. He denyit the same, quhill I schew him the verray
       wordis was spokin. At quhilk tyme he said that Mynto[14] had
       advertisit him, that it was said that sum of the counsell had
       brocht ane letter to me to be subscrivit to put him in presoun,
       and to slay him gif he maid resistence. And he askit the same
       at Mynto himself; quha answerit that he belevit ye same to
       be trew. The morne I will speik to him upon this point.[15] As
       to the rest of Willie Hiegaite's, he confessit it, bot it was the
       morne efter my cumming or he did it.[16]

8.   He wald verray fane that I suld ludge in his ludgeing. I refusit
       it, and said to him that he behovit to be purgeit, and that
       culd not be done heir. He said to me, I heir say ze have brocht
       ane lytter with zow; bot I had rather have passit[17] with zow. I
       trow he belevit that I wald have sent him away presoner. I
       answerit, that I wald tak him with me to Craigmillar, quhair
       the mediciner and I micht help him, and not be far from my
       sone. He answerit that he was reddy when I pleisit, sa I wald
       assure him of his requeist.

9.   He desyris na body to se him; he is angrie quhen I speik of
       Walcar, and sayis, that he sal pluk the eiris out of his heid,

and that he leis.[18] For I inquyrit him upon that, and yat he was angrie with sum of the Lordis, and wald threittin thame. He denyis that, and sayis he luifis[19] thame all, and prayis me to give traist to nathing aganis him.

10. As to me he wald rather give his lyfe or he did ony displesure to me. And efter yis he schew me of sa mony lytil flattereis, sa cauldly and sa wysely, that ze will abasche[20] thairat. I had almaist forzet that he said he could not dout of me in yis purpois of Hiegaite's; for he wald never belief yat I, quha was his proper flesche, wald do him ony evill; alsweill it was schawin that I refusit to subscrive ye same. Bot as to ony utheris that wald persew him, at leist he suld sell his lyfe deir aneuch; bot he suspectit na body, not yet wald not, but wald lufe all yat I lufit.

11. He wald not let me depart from him, bot desyrit yat I suld walk[21] with him. I mak it seme that I beleve that all is trew, and takis heid thairto, and excusit my self for this nicht that I culd not walk. He sayis, that he sleipis not weil. Ze saw him never better, nor speik mair humbler. And gif I had not ane prufe of his hart of waxe, and yat myne were not of any dyamont quhairintill na schot can mak brek, bot that quhilk cummis furth of your hand, I wald have almaist had pietie of him. But feir not, the place[22] sall hald unto the deith. Remember, in recompence thairof, that ze suffer not zouris to be wyn[23] be that fals race that will travell[24] na les with zow for the same.

12. I beleve they have bene at schuillis togidder. He hes ever the teir in his eye; he salutis every body, zea, unto the leist, and makis pieteous caressing unto thame to mak thame have pietie on him. This day his father bled at the mouth and nose; ges quhat presage[25] that is. I have not zit sene him, he keipis his chamber.[26] The King desyris that I suld give him meit with my awin handis, bot gif na mair traist quhair ze ar than I sall do heir.

13. This is my first jornay. I sall end ye same ye morne. I wryte all thingis, howbeit thay be of lytill wecht, to the end that ze may tak the best of all to judge upon. I am in doing of ane work heir that I hait greitly. Have ye not desyre to lauch to se me lie sa weill, at ye leist to dissembill sa weill, and to tell him treuth betwix handis.[27] He schawit me almaist all that is in the name of the Bischop and Sudderland, and zit I have never twichit[28] ane work of that ze schawit me, but allanerly[29] be force, flattering, and to pray him to assure himself of me.

167

And by pleinzing[30] on the Bischop I have drawin it all out of him. Ze have hard the rest.

14. We are couplit with two fals races; the devill sinder us, and God knit us togidder for ever for the maist faithfull coupill that ever He unitit. This is my faith, I will die in it.[31] Excuse I wryte evill, ze may ges ye half of it; bot I cannot mend it, becaus I am not weil at eis; and zit verray glaid to wryte unto zow quhen the rest are sleipand, sen I cannot sleip as they do, and as I wald desyre, that is, in your armes, my dear lufe, quhome I pray God to preserve from all evill, and send yow repois. I am gangand to seik myne til ye morne, quhen I sall end my Bybill;[32] bot I am faschit[33] that it stoppis me to wryte newis of myself unto zow, becaus it is sa lang. Advertise me quhat ye have deliberat to do in the mater ze knaw upon yis point, to ye end that we may understand utheris[34] weill, that nathing thairthrow be spilt.

15. I am irkit[35] and ganging to sleip, and zit I ceis not to scrible all this paper in sa mekle as restis thairof. Waryit mot this pockische man be[36] that causes me haif sa mekle pane, for without him I suld have ane far plesander subject to discourse upon. He is not over mekle deformit, zit he has ressavit verray mekle. He hes almaist slane me with his braith; it is worse then zour uncle's,[37] and zit I cum na neirer unto him, bot in ane chyre at the bed-feit, and he being at the uther end thairof.

16. The message of the father in the gait.[38]

The purpois[39] of Schir James Hammiltoun.

Of that the Laird of Lusse schawit me of the delay.

Of the demandis that he askit at Joachim.

Of my estait, of my company, of the occasioun of my cumming, and of Joseph.

Item. The purpois that he and I togidder. Of the desyre that he hes to pleis me, and of his repentance.

Of the interpretation of his letter.

Of Willie Hiegaite's mater[40] of his departing.

Of Monsiure de Levingstoun.

17. I had almaist forzet, that Monsiure de Levingstoun said in the Lady Reres eir at supper, that he wald drink to ye folk yat I wist of, gif I wald pledge thame. And efter supper he said to me, quhen I was lenand upon him warming me at the fyre, ze have fair going to se seik folk, zit ze cannot be sa welcum to thame as ze left sum body this day in regrait, that will never be blyth quhill he se zow agane. I askit at him,

quha that was. With that he thristit my body, and said, that sum of his folkis had sene zow in fascherie;[41] ze may ges at the rest.

18. I wrocht this day quhill[42] it was twa houris upon this bracelet, for to put ye key of it within the lock thairof, quhilk is couplit underneth with twa cordounis. I have had sa lytill tyme that it is evill maid; bot I sall mak ane fairer in the meane tyme.[43] Tak heid that nane that is heir se it, for all the warld will knaw it, becaus for haist it was made in yair presence.

19. I am now passand to my fascheous purpois.[44] Ze gar me dissemble sa far that I haif horring[45] thairat; and ye caus me do almaist the office of a traitores. Remember how gif it wer not to obey zow, I had rather be deid or I did it; my hart bleidis at it. Summa, he will not cum with me, except upon conditioun that I will promeis to him, that I sall be at bed and buird with him as of befoir, and that I sall leif him na ofter; And doing this upon my word, he will do all thingis that I pleis, and cum with me. Bot he has prayit me to remane upon him quhil uther morne.[46]

20. He spak verray braifly[47] at ye beginning, as yis beirer will schaw zow, upon the purpois of the Inglisman, and of his departing; Bot in ye end he returnit agane to his humilitie. He schawit, amangis uther purposis, yat he knew weill aneuch that my brother had schawin me yat thing, quhilk he had spokin in Striviling, of the quhilk he denyis ye ane half, and abone all, yat ever he come in his chalmer. For to mak him traist me it behovit me to fenze[48] in sum thingis with him: Thairfor, quhen he requeistit me to promeis unto him, that quhen he was haill we suld have baith ane bed; I said to him fenzeingly, and making me to beleve his promisis, that gif he changeit not purpois betwix yis and that tyme, I wald be content thairwith; bot in the meane tyme I bad him tak heid that he leit na body wit thairof, becaus, to speik amangis our selvis, the Lordis culd not be offendit, nor will evill thairfor: Bot they wald feir in respect of the boisting he maid of thame, that gif ever we aggreit togidder, he suld mak thame knaw the lytill compt thay tuke of him; and that he counsallit me not to purchas sum of thame by him. Thay for this caus wald be in jelosy, gif at anis, without thair knawledge, I suld brek the play set up in the contrair in thair presence. He said verray joyfully, and think zow they wil esteme zow the mair of that? Bot I am verray glaid that ze speik to me of the Lordis, for I beleve at this tyme ze desyre that we suld leif

togidder in quyetnes: For gif it wer utherwyse, greiter inconvenience micht come to us baith than we ar war of; bot now
I wil do quhatever ze will do, and will lufe all that ze lufe,
and desyris zow to make thame lufe in lyke maner. For sen
thay seik not my lyfe, I lufe thame all equallie.

21. Upon yis point this beirer will schaw zow mony smal thingis.
Becaus I have over mekle to wryte, and it is lait, I give traist
unto him upon zour word. Summa, he will ga upon my word
to all places. Allace! I never dissavit ony body: Bot I remit
me altogidder to zour will. Send me advertisement quhat I
sall do, and quhatsaever thing sall cum thairof, I sall obey
zow. Advise to with zourself, gif ze can find out ony mair
secreit inventioun by medicine; for he suld tak medicine and
the bath at Craigmillar. He may not cum furth of ye hous
this lang tyme.

22. Summa, be all that I can leirne, he is in greit suspicioun,
and zit notwithstanding, he gevis credite to my word; bot zit
not sa far that he will schaw ony thing to me bot nevertheles,
I sall draw it out of him, gif ze will that I avow all unto him.
Bot I will never rejoyce to dissaive ony body that traistis in
me: zit notwithstanding ze may command me in all thingis.
Have na evill opinioun of me for that caus, be ressoun ze are
the occasion of it zourself; becaus, for my awin particular
revenge, I wald not do it to him.

23. He gevis me sum chekis[49] of yat quhilk i feir, zea, evin in the
quick. He sayis this far, yat his faultis wer publeist, bot yair
is that committis faultis, that belevis they will never be spokin
of; and zit thay will speik of greit and small. As towart the
Lady Reres, he said, I pray God that scho may serve zow for
your honour; And said, it is thocht, and he belevis it to be
trew, that I have not the power of myself into myself, and
that becaus of the refuse I maid of his offeris. Summa, for
certanetie he suspectis of the thing ze knaw, and of his lyf.
Bot as to the last, how sone yat I spak twa or thre gude wordis
unto him, he rejoysis, and is out of dout.

24. I saw him not this evening for to end zour bracelet, to the
quhilk I can get na lokkis. It is ready to thame[50] and zit I feir
that it will bring sum malhure, and may be sene gif ze chance
to be hurt. Advertise me gif ze will have it, and gif ze will
have mair silver, and quhen I sall returne, and how far I mey
speik.

25. He inrages when he heiris of Lethingtoun, or of zow, or of
my brother. Of zour brother he speikis nathing. He speikis

of the Erle of Argyle. I am in feir quhen I heir him speik; for he assuris himself yat he hes not an evill opinioun of him. He speikis nathing of thame that is out[51] nouther gude nor evill, bot fleis that point.

26. His father keipis his chalmer,[52] I have not sene him. All the Hammiltounis ar heir, that accompanyis me verray honorabilly. All the freindis of the uther convoyis me quhen I gang to se him. He desyris me to cum and se him ryse the morne betyme. For to make schort, this beirer will tell zow the rest. Ane gif I leirne ony thing heir, I will make zow memoriall at evin. He will tell zow the occasioun of my remaning. Burne this letter, for it is ovir dangerous, and nathing weill said in it, for I am thinkand upon nathing bot fascherie. Gif ze be in Edinburgh at the ressait of it, send me word sone. Be not offendit, for I gif not ovir greit credite.[53]

27. Now seing to obey zow, my deir lufe, I spair nouther honour, conscience, hasard, nor greitnes quhatsumevir, tak it, I pray zow, in gude part, and not efter the interpretatioun of zour fals gude-brother, to quhome, I pray zow, gif na credite aganis the maist faithfull luifer that ever ze had, or ever sall have. Se not hir, quhais fenzeit teiris suld not be sa mekle praisit nor estemit, as the trew and faithful travellis[54] quhilk I sustene for to merite hir place. For obtening of the quhilk aganis my naturall, I betrayis thame that may impesche[55] me. God forgive me, and God give zow, my only lufe, the hap and prosperitie quhilk zour humble and faithful lufe desyris unto zow, quha hopis to be schortly ane uther thing to zow, for the reward of my irksum travellis.

28. It is lait. I desyre never to ceis fra wryting unto zow; zit now, efter the kissing of zour handis, I will end my letter. Excuse my evill wryting, and reid it twyseover. Excuse that thing that is scriblit, for I had na paper zisterday quhen I wrait that of ye memoriall. Remember upon zour lufe, and wryte unto hir, and that verray oft. Lufe me as I sall do zow.

    Remember zow of the purpois of the Lady Reres
    Of the Inglismen
    Of his Mother
    Of the Erle of Argyle
    Of the Erle Bothwell
    Of the Ludgeing in Edinburgh

LETTER II – ENGLISH TRANSLATION AT THE PUBLIC RECORD OFFICE

1. Being gon from the place where I had left my harte, it may be easily judged what my countenance was, consydering what the body may, without hart, which was cause that till dynner I had used lyttle talke, neyther wold any body advance him selfe therunto, thinking that it was not good so to doo.

2. Fowre myles from thence a gentleman of the Erle of Lennox cam to made his commendacions and excuses unto me, that he cam not to meete me, because he durst not enterprise so to doo, consydering the sharp wordes that I had spoken to Conyngham, and that he desyred that I wold com to the inquisition of the facte which I did suspecte him of. This last was of his own head without commission, and I tolde him that he had no receipte against feare, and that he had no feare, if he did not feele him selfe faulty, and that I had also sharply aunsweared to the doubtes that he made in his lettres, as though ther had bene a meaning to poursue him. To be short: I have made him hold his peace; for the rest, it weare to long to tell you.

3. Sir James Hamilton cam to meete me, who told me that at another tyme he went his waye when he hard of my comming; and that he sent unto him Houstoun, to tell him that he wold not have thought that he wold have followed and accompany him selfe with the Hamiltons. He aunsweared that he was not com but to see me, and that he wolde not follow Stuard nor Hamilton, but by my commandement. He prayed him to go speake to him: he refused it.

4. The Lard Lus, Houston, and the sonne of Caldwell, and about XL hors cam to meete me, and he told me that he was sent to one day a lau from the father, which shuld be this daye, against the signing of his own hand which he hathe; and that knowing of my comming he hath delayed it, and hath prayed him to go see him; which he hath refused, and swearith that he will suffer nothing at his handes. Not one of the towne is com to speake with me, which makith me to think that they be his, and then he speakith well of them, at leaste his sonne.

5. The King sent for Joachim,[1] and asked him why I did not lodge nighe to him? and that he wold ryse sooner, and why I cam, whither it wear for any good appoyntment that he cam, and whither I had not taken Paris and Guilbert to write, and

that I sent Joseph. I wonder who hath told him so muche, evin of the mariage of Bastian. This bearer shall tell you more upon that. I asked him of his lettres, and where he did complayne of the crueltye of som of them, he saide that he did dreme, and that he was so glad to see me that he thought he shuld dye. Indeede that he had found faulte with me ... ...²

6. I went my waye to supper, this berer shall tell you of my arryv ...³ praied me to come agayne, which I did, and he told me his grefe and that he wold make no testament but leave all unto me, and that I was cause of his sicknes for the sorrow he had that I was so strange unto him, 'And' (said he) 'you asked me what I ment in my lettre to speake of cruelty: it was of your cruelty who will not accepte my offres and repentance: I avowe that I have don amisse, but not that I have always disavowed: and so have many other of your subjectes don, and you have well perdonid them, I am yong. You will saye that you have also perdonid me many tymes, but that I returne to my faultes. May not a man of my age for want of counsell, fayle twise or thrise, and mysse of promes, and at the last repent and rebuke him selfe by his experience? Yf I may obtayn this perdon, I protest I will never make faulte agayne, and I aske nothing but that we may be at bed and at table togither as husband and wife. And if you will not, I will never rise from this bed. I pray you tell me your resolution heerof; God knowith that I am punished to have made my God of you, and had no other mynd but of you: and when I offende you som tyme, you are cause therof, for if I thought whan any body doth any wrong to [me]⁴ that I might for my refuge make my mone therof unto you, I wold open it to no other. But whan I heare any thing, being not familiar with you, I must keepe it in my mynde, and that troublith my wittes for anger'.⁵

7. I did still answear him, but that shall be to long. In the end I asked him why he wold go in the English shipp? He doth disavow it and swearith so, but confessith to have spoken to the men. Afterward I asked him of the inquisition of Hiegate? He denyed it till I tolde him the very woordes, and then he said that Minto sent him word that it was said that som of the counsayle had brought me a lettre to signe to putt him in prison, and to kill him if he did resiste, and that he asked this of Minto him selfe, who said unto him that he thought it was true. I will talke with him tomorrowe upon that poynte:

the rest as Wille Hiegate hath confessed, but it was the next daye that he cam hither.

8. In the end he desyred much that I shuld lodge in his lodging; I have refused it. I have told him that he must be pourged, and that could not be don heere. He said unto me, 'I have hard saye that you have brought the lytter, but I wold rather have gon with your selfe.' I told him that so I wolde myselfe bring him to Cragmillar, that the phisicians and I also might cure him without being farre from my sonne. He said that he was ready when I wolde, so as I wolde assure him of his requeste.

9. He hath no desyre to be seene, and waxeth angry whan I speake to him of Wallcar, and sayth that he will pluck his eares from his head, and that he lyeth: for I asked him before of that and what cause he had to complayne of ...[6] the Lordes, and to threaten them? He denyeth it, and sayth that he had allready prayed them to think no such matter of him.

10. As for myself: he wold rather lose his life than doo me the leaste displeasour. And then used so many kindes of flatteryes so coldly and so wysely as you wold marvayle at. I had forgotten that he sayde that he could not mistrust me for Hiegates wordes, for he could not beleve that his own flesh (which was my selfe) wold doo him any hurte (and in deede it was sayde that I refused to have him lett blud)[7] but for the others he wold at leaste sell his lyfe deere ynoughe: but that he did suspecte no body, nor wolde, but wolde love all that I did love.

11. He wold not lett me go, but wold have me to watche with him. I made as though I thought all to be true, and that I wold think upon it. And have excused my selfe from sytting up with him this night, for he sayth that he sleepith not. You never hard one speake better nor more humbly, and if I had not proofe of his hart to be as waxe and that myne weare not as a dyamant, no stroke but comming from your hand, could make me but to have pitie of him. But feare not, for the place shall contynue till death. Remember also in recompense therof not to suffer yours to won by that fals race that wold doo no lesse to your selfe.

12. I think they have bene at schoole togither, he hath allwais the teare in the eye. He saluteth every man evin to the meanest, and makith much of them, that they may take pitie of him. His father hath bled this daye at the nose and at the mouth: gesse what token that is! I have not seene him, he is

174

in his chambre. The King is so desyrous that I shuld give him meate with my own handes, but trust you no more there where you are than I doo here.

13. This is my first journay, I will end tomorrow. I write all, how little consequence so ever it be of, to the end that you may take of the wholle that that shall be best for *you to judge*.[8] I doo heere a work that I hate muche, but I had begon it this morning.[9] Had you not lyst to laughe, to see me so trymly make a lye, at the leaste, dissemble? and to mingle truthe therwith? He hath almost told me all on the bisshops behalfe and of Suderland,[10] without touching any word unto him of that which you had told me, but only by muche flattering him and pr[essing?] him to assure him selfe of me, and by my complayning of the r ...[11] en the wormes out of his nose.[12] You have hard the rest.

14. We are tyed to with two false races, the goodyeere[13] untye us from them. God forgive me, and God knytt us togither for ever, for the most faythfull couple that ever he did knytt together. This is my fayth, I will dye in it. Excuse it, yf I write yll, you must gesse the one halfe, I can not doo with all, for I am yll at ease, and glad to write unto you when other folkes be asleepe, seeing that I cannot doo as they doo, according to my desyre, that is betwene your armes, my deere lyfe, whom I besech God to preserve from all yll, and send you good rest as I go to seeke myne till tomorrow in the morning, that I will end my bible. But it greevith me that it shuld lett me from wryting unto you of newes of myselfe, so much I have to write.[14] Send me word what you have determinid heerupon, that we may know the one the others mynde for marryng of any thing.

15. I am weary and am asleepe, and yet I cannot forbeare scribling, as long as ther is any paper. Cursed be this pocky fellow that troublith me thus muche, for I had a pleasanter matter to discourse unto you, but for him. He is not muche the worse, but he is yll arayde.[15] I thought I shuld have bene kylled with his breth, for it is worse than your uncles breth, and yet I was sett no neerer to him than in a chayre by his bolster, and he lyeth at the furder syd of the bed.

16. The message of the father by the waye:- The talke of Sir James Hamilton of the ambassade – That the Lard a Luss hathe told me of the delaye. The questions that he asked of Jochim of my state, of my companye, and of the cause of my coming, and of Joseph. The talke that he and I have had, and

of his desyre to please me, of his repentance, and of th'interpretation of his lettre of Will Hiegates doinges and of his departure, and of the L. of Levinston.

17. I had forgotten of the L. of Levinston, that at supper he sayd softly to the Lady Rivees [Reres] that he dronk to the persons that I knew [if] I wold pledge them. And after supper he said softly ... .[16] I was leaning upon him and warming myselfe – 'You may well go and see sick folkes, yet can you not be so wellcom unto them, as you have this daye left som body in payne, who shall never be meary till he have seene you agayne.' I asked him who it was? he tooke me about the body, and said 'One of his folkes that hath left you this daye.' Gesse you the rest.[17]

18. This daye I have wrought till two of the clock upon this bracelet to putt the keye in the clyfte of it, which is tyed with two laces. I have had so lyttle tyme that it is very yll, but I will make a fayrer, and in the meane tyme take heed that none of those that be heere doo see it, for all the world wold know it, for I have made it in haste in theyr presence.

19. I go to my tedious talke; you make me dissemble so muche, that I am afrayde therof with horrour, and you make me almost to playe the parte of a traytour. Remembre that if it weare not for obeyeng you, I had rather be dead; my hart bleedith for yt. To be shorte: he will not com but with condition that I shall promise to be with him as heeretofore at bed and borde, and that I shall forsake him no more, and upon my worde he will doo whatsoever I will, and will com, but he hath prayed me to tarry till after tomorrow.

20. He hath spoken at the fyrst more stoutly, as this bearer shall tell you, upon the mater of his Englishmen, and of his departure; but in the end he commith to his gentlenes agayne. He hath told me among other tak, that he knew well that my brother had told me at Sterling that which he had said there, wherof he denyed the halfe, and specially that he was in his chambre. But now to make him trust me, I must fayne somthing unto him: and therfore when he desyred me to promise that when he shuld be wholle, we shuld make but one bed, I told him fayning to beleve his faire promesses ...[18] did not change his mynde betwene this tyme and that, I was contented, so as he wold saye nothing therof: for (to tell it betwene us two) the Lordis wisshed no yll to him, but did feare, leste (consydering the threateninges which he made in case we did agree togither) he wolde make them feele the

176

small accompte they have maid of him, and that he wold persuade me to poursue som of them; and for this respecte shuld be in jelousy if at *one instant*[19] without their knowledge, I did breake a game made to the contrary in their presence. And he said unto me very pleasant and meary, 'Think you that they doo the more esteeme you therfore? but I am glad that you talke to me of the lordis. I here that you desyre now that we shall lyve a happy lyfe, for if it weare otherwise, it could not be but greater inconvenience shuld happen to us both than you think: but I will doo now whatsoever you will have me doo, and will love all those that you shall love, so as you make them to love me allso. For so as they seeke not my lyfe, I love them all egally.'

21. Therupon I have willed this bearer to tell you many prety thinges, for I have to muche to write, and it is late, and I trust him upon your worde. To be short, he will goe any where upon my worde; alas! and I never deceavid any body, but I remitt myself wholly to your will: and send me word what I shall doe, and whatever happen to me, I will obey you. Think also yf you will not fynde som invention more secret by phisick, for he is to take phisick at Cragmillar, and the bathes also, and shall not com fourth of long tyme.

22. To be short, for that that I may learne, he hath great suspicion, and yet nevertheles trustith upon my worde, but not to tell me as yet anything. Howbeit if you will that I shall *avowe*[20] him, I will know all of him, but I shall never be willing to beguile one that puttith his trust in me. Nevertheles you may doo all, and doo not estyme me the lesse therfore, for you are the caus ther of; for, for my own revenge, I wold not doo it.

23. He givith me certain charges (and those strong) of that that I feare evin to saye, that his faultes be published, but there be that committ som secret faultes and feare not to have them spoken of so lowdely, and that ther is speeche of great and small. And evin touching the Lady Rires, he saide, 'God graunte that she serve you to your honour,' and that men may not think nor he neyther, that myne owne powre was not in my selfe, seing I did refuse his offres. To conclude, for a suerety he mistrustith us of that that you know, and for his lyfe. But in the end, after I had spoken two or three good wordes to him, he was very meary and glad.

24. I have not seene him this night, for ending your bracelet, but I can fynde no claspes for yt: it is ready therunto, and

177

yet I feare least it shuld bring you yll happ, or that it shuld be knowen if you were hurte. Send me worde whither you will have it, and more monney, and whan I shall returne, and how farre I may speake. Now as farre as I perceave, I may do much with you: gesse you whither I shall not be suspected.[21]

25. As for the rest: he is wood[22] when he hearith of Ledinton, and of you[23] and of your brother he sayth nothing, but of the Erle of Arguile he doth. I am afraide of him to heare him talke, at the leaste he assurith him selfe that he hath no yll opinion of him. He speakith nothing of those abrode, nether good nor yll, but avoydith speaking of them.

26. His father keepith his chamber; I have not seene him. All the Hamiltons be heere, who accompany me very honestly. All the frendes of the other doo com allwais when I goe to visitt him. He hath sent to me and prayeth me to see him ryse to morrow in the morning early. To be short, this bearer shall declare unto you the rest, and if I shall learne any thing, I will make every night a memoriall therof. He shall tell you the cause of my stay. Burne this lettre, for it is to dangerous, neyther is ther anything well said in it, for I think upon nothing but upon greefe if you be at Edinboroughe.

27. Now if to please you my deere lyfe, I spare nether honour, conscience, nor hazard, nor greatnes, take it in good parte, and not according to the interpretacion of your false brother in lawe, to whom I pray you give no credit, against the most faythfull lover that ever you had or shall have. See not also her whose faynid teares you ought not more to regarde than the true travails which I endure to deserve her place, for obtayning of which against my own nature, I doo betraye those that could lett me. God forgive me, and give you my only frend the good luck and prosperitie that your humble and faythfull lover doth wisshe unto you: who hopith shortly to be an other thing unto you, for the reward of my paynes.

28. I have not made one worde, and it is very late, althoughe I shuld never be weary in wryting to you, yet will I end, after kyssing of your handes. Excuse my evill wryting, and reade it over twise – excuse also that ...[24] for I had yesternight no paper, wher I tooke the paper of a memoria[ll]... . Remembre your frende and wryte unto her and often. Love me all[wais] ... .

Endorsed: 'The long lettre written from Glasco from the Queen of Scottes to the Erle Bothwell.' And (by Cecil): 'English.'

LETTER III – COPY OF THE ORIGINAL FRENCH AT THE PUBLIC RECORD OFFICE

Monsieur, si lenvy de votre absence celuy de vostre oubli la crainte du dangier, tant promis d'un chacun a vostre tant ayme personne peuvent me consoller, je vous en lesse a juger, veu le malheur que mon cruel sort et continuel malheur mavoient promis a la suite des infortunes et craintes tant recentes que passes de plus longue main les quelles vous scaves; mais pour tout cela je me[1] vous accuserai ni de peu de souvenance ni de peu de soigne, et moins encores de vostre promesse violee ou de la froideur de vos lettres mestant ja, tant randue vostre que ce quil vous pleust mest agreable et sont mes penses tant volonterement, aux vostres a subjectes que je veulx presupposer que tout ce que vient de vous procede non par aulcune des causes desusdictes, avis pour telles qui sont justes et raisonnables et telles qui je desir moymesme qui est lordre que maves promis de prendre final pour la seurete et honnorable service du seul soubtien de ma vie, pour qui seul je la veus conserver et sens lequel je ne desire que breve mort et pour vous tesmoigner combien humblement sous vous commandemens je me soubmets. Je vous ay envoie en signe dhomage par Paris, lornement du cheif conducteur des aultres membres inferant que vous investant de sa despoille de luy, qui est principal, le rest ne peult que vous estre subject et avesques le consentement du cueur au lieu du quel puis que le vous ay ja lesse. Je vous envoie un sepulcre de pierre dure peinct de noir seme de larmes et de ossements: la pierre je la compare a mon cueur qui comme luy est talle en un seur tombeau ou receptacle de voz commandements et sur tout de vostre nom et memoire qui y sont enclos, comme mes cheveulx en la bague pour jamais nen sortir que la mort ne vous permet fair trophee des mes os comme la bague en est remplie, en signe que vous aves fayt entiere conqueste de moy, de mon cueur et jusque a vous en lesser les os pour memoir de vostre victoire et de mon agreable perte, et volontiere pour estre mieux employe que je ne le merite. Lesmail denviron est noir, qui signifie la fermete de celle que le lenvoie. Les larmes sont sans nombre, ausi sont les craintes de vous desplair les pleurs de vostre absence et le desplaiser de ne pouvoir estre en effect exterieur vostre commes je suys sans faintise de cueur et desprit et a bon droit quant mes merites seront trop plus grands que de la plus perfayte que jamais feut et telle que je desire estre et mettray poine en condition de contrefair pour dignement estre emploiee soubs vostre domination.

179

Reseves[2] la donc mon seul bien en aussi bonne part comme avecques extreme joie jay fait vostre mariage qui jusques a celuy de nos corps en public ne sortira de mon sein, comme merque de tout ce que jay ou espere ni desire de felicite en ce monde or craignant mon cueur de vous ennuyer autant a lire que je me plaise descrir.

Je fineray apres vous avoir baise les mains[3] daussi grande affection que je prie Dieu (o le seul soubtien de ma vie) vous la donner longue et heureuse, et a moy vostre bonne grace comme le seul bien que je desire et a quoy je tends.

Jay dit a ce porteur ce que jay apris, sur le quel je me remets, sachant le credit que luy donnes comme fait celle qui vous veult estre pour jamais humble et obeisante loyalle femme et seulle amye qui pour jamais vous voue entierement le cueur le corps sans aucun changement, comme a celuy que je fait possesseur du cueur du quel vous pouves tenir seur jusques a la mort ne changera car mal ni bien onque ne estrangera.

Endorsed 'To pruif the affectioun'; and (by Cecil): 'French lettre.'

LETTER III – SCOTS TRANSLATION FROM LEKPREVIK'S *DETECTION*

My Lord, gif the displesure of zour absence, of zour forzetfulnes, ye feir of danger sa promisit be everie ane to zour sa luifit persone, may gif me consolatioun, I leif it to zow to juge, seing the unhap that my cruell lot and continuall misadventure hes hitherto promysit me, following ye misfortunes and feiris as weill of lait, as of ane lang tyme bypast, the quhilk ye do knaw. Bot for all that, I will in na wise accuse zow, nouther of zour lytill remembrance, nouther of zour lytill cair, and leist of all of zour promeis brokin, or of ye cauldnes of zour wryting, sen I am ellis sa far maid zouris, yat yat quhilk pleisis zow is acceptabill to me; and my thochtis ar as willingly subdewit unto zouris, that I suppois yat all that cummis of zow proceidis not be ony of the causis foirsaid, bot rather for sic[1] as be just and ressonabill, and sic as I desyre myself. Quhilk is the fynall order that ze promysit to tak for the suretie and honorabil service of ye only uphald of my lyfe. For quhilk alone I will preserve the same, and without the quhilk I desyre not bot suddane deith, and to testifie unto zow how lawly I submit me under zour com-mandementis, I have send zow, in signe of homage, be Paris, the ornament[2] of the heid, quhilk is the chief gude[3] of the uther memberis, inferring thairby that, be ye seising[4] of zow in the

180

possessioun of the spoile of that quhilk is principall, the remnant cannot be bot subject unto zow, and with consenting of the hart. In place thairof, sen I have ellis left it unto zow, I send unto zow ane sepulture of hard stane, collourit with blak, sawin with teiris and bones. The stane I compair to my hart, that as it is carvit in ane sure sepulture or harbor of zour commandementis, and abone all, of zour name and memorie that ar thairin inclosit, as is my heart[5] in this ring, never to cum furth, quhill deith grant unto yow to ane trophee of victorie of my banes, as the ring is fullit, in signe that yow haif maid ane full conqueis of me, of myne hart, and unto yat my banes be left unto yow in remembrance of your victorie and my acceptabill lufe and willing, for to be better bestowit than I merite. The ameling[6] that is about is blak, quhilk signifyis the steidfastness of hir that sendis the same. The teiris are without number, sa ar the dreddouris to displeis yow, the teiris of your absence, the disdane that I cannot be in outward effect youris, as I am without fenzeitnes of hart and spreit, and of gude ressoun, thocht my meritis wer mekle greiter than of the maist profite that ever was, and sic as I desyre to be, and sall tak pane in conditiounis to imitate, for to be bestowit worthylie under your regiment.

My only wealth ressaif thairfoir in als gude part ye same, as I have ressavit your marriage with extreme joy, the quhilk sall not part furth of my bosum, quhill yat marriage of our body is be maid in publict, as signe of all that I outher hope or desyris of blis in yis warld. Zit my hart feiring to displeis you as mekle in the reiding heirof, as I delite me in ye writing.

I will mak end, efter that I have kissit zour handis with als greit affectioun as, I pray God (O ye only uphald of my lyfe) to gif yow lang and blissit lyfe, and to me zour gude favour, as the only gude yat I desire, and to ye quhilk I pretend.

I have schawin unto this beirer that quhilk I have leirnit, to quhom I remit me, knawand the credite[7] that ze gaif him, as scho dois that will be for ever unto zow humbill and obedient lauchfull wife, that for ever dedicates unto zow hir hart, hir body, without ony change, as unto him that I have maid possessour of my hart, of quhilk ze may hald zow assurit, yat unto ye deith sall na wayis be changeit, for evill nor gude sall never mak me go from it.

LETTER IV – COPY OF THE ORIGINAL FRENCH VERSION AT HATFIELD

1.   J'ay veille plus tard la hault que je n'eusse fait si ce neust

este pour tirer ce que ce porteur vous dira que Je treuve la plus belle commoditie pour excuser vostre affaire que se pourroit presenter. Je luy ay promise de le luy mener demain si vous le trouves bon mettes y ordre.

2. Or monsieur j'ay ja rompu ma promesse Car vous ne mavies rien comande[1] vous envoier ni escrire si ne le fais pour vous offencer et si vous scavies la craint que j'en ay vous nauries tant des subçons contrairs que toutesfois je cheris comme procedant de la chose du mond que je desire et cherche le plus c'est votre bonne grace de laquelle mes deportemens m'asseureront et je n'en disesperay Jamais tant que selon vostre promesse vous m'en dischargeres vostre coeur aultrement je penseras que mon malheur et le bien composer de ceux qui n'ont la troisiesme partie de la fidelité ni voluntair obéissance que je vous porte auront gaigné sur moy l'avantage de la seconde amye de Jason. Non que je vous compare a un si malheureuse ni moy a une si impitoiable. Combien que vous men fassies un peu resentir en chose qui vous touschat ou[2] pour vous preserver et garder a celle a qui seulle vous aporteins si lon se peult appropier ce que lon acquiert par bien et loyalment voire uniquement aymer comme je fais et fairay toute ma vie pour pein ou mal qui m'en puisse avenir. En recompence de quoy et des tous les maulx dont vous maves este cause, souvenes vous du lieu icy pres.

3. Je ne demande que vous me tennes promesse de main mais que nous truvions[3] et que nadjousties foy au subçons quaures sans vous en certifier, et Je ne demande a Dieu si non que coignoissies tout ce que je ay au coeur qui est vostre et quil vous preserve de tout mal au moyns durant ma vié qui ne me sera chere qu'autant qu'elle et moy vous serons agreables. Je m'en vois coucher et vous donner le bon soir mandes moy de main comme vous seres porté a bon heur. Car j'enseray en pein.[4]

4. Et faites bon guet si l'oseau sortira de sa cagé ou sens son per[5] comme la tourtre demeurera seulle a se lamenter de l'absence pour court quelle soit. Ce que je ne puis faire ma lettre de bon coeur si ce nestoit que je ay peur que soyes endormy. Car je nay ose escrire devant Joseph et bastienne[6] et Joachim qui ne font que partir quand J'ay commence.

Endorsed by Cecil: 'french lre'; and, in a secretary's hand, 'Lettre concerning Halyruid house.'

182

LETTER IV – SCOTS TRANSLATION FROM LEKPREVIK'S *DETECTION*

1. I have walkit[1] laiter thair up then I wald have done, gif it had not bene to draw[2] sumthing out of him, quhilk this beirer will schaw zow; quhilk is the fairest commoditie[3] that can be offerit to excuse zout affairis. I have promysit to bring him to him the morne. Put ordour to it, gif ze find it gude.

2. Now, Schir, I have brokin my promeis; becaus ze commandit me nouther to wryte nor send unto zow. Zit I have not done this to offend zow, and gif ze knew the feir yat I have presently, ze wald not have sa mony contrary suspiciounis in your thocht; quhilk notwithstanding I treit and chereis, as proceeding from the thing in the warld that I maist desyre, and seikis fastest to haif, quhilk is zour gude grace; of the quhilk my behaviour sall assure me. As to me: I sall never dispair of it, and prayis zow, according to zour promeis, to discharge zour hart unto me, Utherwayis I will think that my malhure,and the gude handling of hir[4] that has not ye third part of the faithful nor willing obedience unto zow that I beir, hes wyn, aganis my will, yat advantage over me, quhilk the second lufe of Jason wan; not that I will compair zow unto ane sa unhappy as he was, nor zit myself to ane sa unpietifull ane woman as scho. Howbeit, ze caus me to be sumthing lyk unto hir in onything that tuichis zow, or that may preserve and keip zow unto hir, to quhome only ze appertene; gif it be sa that I may appropriate that quhilk is wyn thocht[5] faithfull, zea, only lufing of zow, as I do, and sall do all the dayis of my lyfe, for pane or evill that can cum thairof. In recompense of the quhilk, and of all the evillis quhilk ze have bene caus of to me, remember zow upon the place heir besyde.

3. I craif with that ze keip promeis to me[6] the morne; but that we may meit togidder, and that ye gif na faith to suspiciounis without the certanetie of thame. And I craif na uther thing at God, but that ze may knaw that thing that is in my hart quhilk is zouris; and that he may preserve zow from all evill, at the leist sa lang as I have lyfe, quhilk I repute not precious unto me, except in sa far as it and I baith ar aggreabill unto zow. I am going to bed, and will bid zow gude nicht. Advertise me tymely in the morning how ze have fairin; for I will be in pane unto I get worde.

4. Mak gude watch, gif the burd eschaip out of ye caige, or

without hir mate. As ye turtur I sall remane alone for to lament the absence, how schort yat sa ever it be. This letter will do with ane gude hart, that thing quhilk I cannot do myself, gif it be not that I have feir that ze ar in sleiping, I durst not wryte this befoir Joseph, Bastiane, and Joachim, that did bot depart even quhen I began to wryte.

LETTER IV – ENGLISH TRANSLATION AT HATFIELD

1. I have watched later ~~then~~ there above than I wold haue don, if it had not bene to draw out that that this bearer shall tell you, that I fynde the fayrest commoditie to excuse yor busynes that might be offred: I have promised to him to ~~p~~ bring him to morrowe. Yf you think it, give ordre therunto.

2. Now Sr I have <u>not yet</u> broken my promes wt you for you had not commaunded me ~~nothing and~~ to send you any thing or to write, and I doo it not, for offending of you, And if you knew the feare that I am in therof, you wold not have so many contrary suspicios, wch nevertheles I cherishe as proceeding from the thing of this worlde that I desyre and seeke the moste, that is yor favor <u>or good will</u>, of wch my behaviour shall assure me, And I will never dispayre therof as long as according to yor promes you shall discharge yor harte to me, Otherwise I wold think that my yll luck and the fayre behavior of those that have not the third parte of the faythfulnes and voluntary obedience that I beare unto you, shall have wonne the advantage over me ~~the advantage~~ of the second Loover of Jason. Not that I doo compare you to so wicked ~~a person~~ or myself to som greefe in a matter that toucheth you, and to preserve & keepe you to her to who alone you belong, if a body may clayme to him selfe that wch is won by ——[1] well, faythfully, yea entierly loving, as I doo, & will doo all my lyfe for payne or hurt what soever may happen to me therby. In recompence wherof, and of all the evils that you bene cause of to me, Remember the place ~~nighe~~ heereby.

3. I desyre not that you keepe promes wt me to morrowe, but that we may be togither, and that you give no Credit to the suspicions that you shall have, wt out being assured therof. And I aske no more of God but that you might know all that

I have in my harte, wch is yours, and that he preserve you fro all evill, at the least during my lyfe, wch shall not be deere unto me, but as long as yt & I shall please you. I go to bed, & give you good night. Send me word to morrow early in the morning how you have don for I shall think long.[2]

4. And watche well if the byrde shall fly out of his Cage or wt out his make,[3] as the turtle shall remayne alone to lament & morne for absence how short soever it be. That that I could not doo my lre shuld doo it wt a good will, yf it weare not that I feare to wake you, for I durst not write before Joseph & Bastian & Joachim, who weare but new gon from I begon.

    Endorsed by Cecil: 'Copy. English.'

    Endorsed in another hand 'lre concerning Holly Roode House.'

LETTER V – COPY OF THE ORIGINAL FRENCH VERSION IN THE PUBLIC RECORD OFFICE

Mon cueur helas fault il que la follie d'une famme dont vous connoisses asses l'ingratitude vers moy soit cause de vous donner displesir veu que je neusse sceu y remedier sans le scavoir; et despuis que men suis apersue Je ne vous lay peu dire pour scavoir comment mi gouvernerois car en cela ni aultre chose je ne veux entreprandre de rien fayre sans en scavoir votre volontay, laquelle je vous suplie me fayre entandre car je la suivray toute ma vie plus volontiers que vous ne me la declareres, et si vous ne me mandes ce soir ce que volles que jen faise je men deferay au hazard de la fayre entreprandre ce qui pourroit nuire a ce a quoy nous tandons tous deux et quant elle sera mariee je vous suplie donnes men une ou ien prandray[1] telles de quoy vous contanteres quant a leur condition may de leur langue ou fidelite vers vous ie ne vous en respondray. Je vous suplie qune opinion sur aultrui ne nuise en votre endroit a ma constance. Soupsonnes moi mays[2] quant je vous en veulx rendre hors de doubte et mes clersir ne le refeuses ma chere vie et permetes que je vous face preuve par mon obeisance de ma fidelite et constance et subjection volontaire, que je prands pour le plus agreeable bien que je scaurois rescevoir si vois le voulles accepter, et nen faytes la ceremonie car vois ne me scauriez davantage outrasger ou donner mortel ennui.[3]

LETTER V – SCOTS TRANSLATION FROM LEKPREVIK'S *DETECTION*

My hart, allace! must the foly of ane woman quhais unthank-fulness toward me ze do sufficiently knaw, be occasioun of displesure unto zow, considering yat I culd not have remeidit thairunto without knawing it? And sen that I persavit it, I culd not tell it zow, for that I knew not how to governe myself thairin: for nouther in that nor in any uther thing will I tak upon me to do ony thing without knawlege of zour will, quhilk I beseik zow let me understand; for I will follow it all my lyfe mair willingly than zow sall declair it to me; and gif ze do not send me word this nicht quhat ze will that I sall do, I will red myself of it, and hasard to caus it to be interprysit and takin in hand, quhilk micht be hurtfull to that quhairunto baith we do tend. And quhen scho sall be maryit, I beseik zow give me ane, or ellis I will tak sic as sall content zow for their conditiounis; bot as for thair toungis or faithfulness towart zow I will not answer. I beseik zow yat ane opinioun of uther persoun be not hurtfull in zour mynde to my constancie, Mistrust me; bot quhen I will put zow out of dout and cleir myselfe, refuse it not, my deir lufe, and suffer me to make zow some prufe be my obedience, my faithfulness, constancie, and voluntarie subjectioun, quhilk I tak for the pleasandest gude that I micht ressaif, gif ze will accept it; and mak na ceremonie at it, for ze culd do me na greiter outrage nor give mair mortall grief.

LETTER V – ENGLISH TRANSLATION AT THE PUBLIC RECORD OFFICE

My hart:[1] alas! must the folly of a woman whose unthankfulnes toward me you doo suffyciently knowe, be occasion of displesure unto you? Consydering that I could not have remedyed therunto withoute knowing it: and since that I perceavid it, I could not tell it you, for that I knew not how to gouverne my self therin. For nether in that nor in any other thing, will I take upon me to doo any thing without knowledge of your will: which I beseche you let me understande, for I will followe it all my lyfe more willingly than you shall declare it to me. And if you doo not send me worde this night what you will that I shall doo, I will rydde my selfe of it, and hasard to cause it to be entreprised and taken in hande, which might be hurtfull to that wherunto both we doo tende. And when she shall be maryed, I beseche you give me one, or els I will take suche as shall content you for their conditions; but as for their tongues [leur langue] or faythfulnes toward you, I will not answeare. I beseche you that an opinion of other person be not hurtfull in your mynd to my constancy. Mistrust me, but when I will putt you out of doubte and cleere my selfe, refuse it not my deere lyfe, and suffer me to make you som proofe by my obedience [of] my faythfulnes, constancy, and volontary subjection, which I take for the pleasantest good that I might receave, yf you will accepte it; and make no cerimony at it, for you could doo me no greater outrage, nor give me more mortall greefe.

Endorsed: 'Copia of a lettre from the Q. of Scottes to th'erle Bothwell' and 'Anentes the depesche of Margaret Carwood, quhilk was before her mariage. Prufes her affection.' and: 'Margaret Carwood was one speciall in truste with the S.Q. and moste previe to all her moste secret affayres.'

LETTER VI – COPY OF THE ORIGINAL FRENCH VERSION AT HATFIELD

Monsieur, helas pourquoy est vostre fiance mise en personne si indigne, pour subconner ce qui est entierement vostre.[1]

Vous m'avies promise que resouldries tout et que (me)[2] manderies tous les jours ce que j'aurais a faire. Vous nen aves rien fait. Je vous advertise bien de vous garder de vostre <u>faulx beau frere</u>.[3] Il est venu vers moy et sens me monstrer rien de vous me dist que vous luy mandies qu'il vous escrive ce qu'auries[4] a dire, et ou, et quant me troveres et ce que faires touchant luy et la dessubs m'a preschè que c'estoit une folle entreprinse, et qu'avecques mon honneur Je ne vous pourries Jamaiis espouser, veu qu'estant marié vous m'amenies et que ses gens ne l'endureroient pas et que les seigneurs se dediroient. Somme il est tout contrair. Je luy ay dist qu'estant venue si avant si vous ne vous en retiries de vous mesmes que persuasion ne la mort mesmes ne me fairoient faillir de a ma promesse. Quant au lieu vous estes trop negligent (pardonnes moy) de vous en remettre a moy. Choisisses le vous mesmes et me le mandes. Et cependant je suis malade je differaray Quant au propose cest trop tard. Il n'a pas tins a moy que n'ayes pense a heure. Et si vous pensee neussies non plus change de propos pensee[5] depuis mon absence que moy vous ne series a demander telle resolution. Or il ne manque rien de ma part et puis que vostre negligence vous met tous deux au danger d'un faux frere, s'il ne succede bien je ne me releveray Jamais. Je vous envoy ce porteur. Car Je ne m'ose me fier a vostre frere de ces lettres ni de la diligence, il vous dira en quelle estat Je suis, et Juges quelle amendemente[6] m'a porté ces incertains Nouvelles. Je voudrois estre morte. Car Je vois tout aller mal. Vous prometties bien autre chose de vostre providence Mais l'absence peult sur vous, qui aves deux cordes a vostre arc. Depesches la responce a fin que Je ne faille et ne vous[7] fies de ceste entreprinse[8] a vostre frere. Car il la dist, et si y est tout contrair.

Dieu vous doint le bon soir.

Endorsed by Cecil: 'frech'; and in another hand: 'frome Sterling affore the Rawissement – Pruifis hir Mak of Rawissing'.

LETTER VI – SCOTS TRANSLATION FROM LEKPREVIK'S *DETECTION*

Allace! my Lord, quhy is zour traist put in ane persoun sa unworthie, to mistraist that quhilk is haillely zouris? I am wod.[1] Ze have promysit me that ze wald send me word every day quhat I suld do. Ze haif done nathing yairof. I advertisit zow weill to tak heid of zour fals brother-in-law. He come to me, and without schawing me ony thing from zow, tald me that ze had willit him to wryte to zow that that I suld say, and quhair and quhen ze suld cum to me, and that that ze suld do tuiching him; and thairupon hes preichit unto me yat it was ane fulische interpryse, and that with myne honour I culd never marry zow, seing that being maryit ze did cary me away, and yat his folkis wald not suffer it, and that the Lordis wald unsay yameselvis, and wald deny that they had said. To be schort, he is all contrarie. I tald him that seing I was cum sa far, gif ze did not withdraw[2] zour self of zour self, that na perswasioun, nor deith itself suld mak me fail of my promeis. As tuiching the place ze are too negligent, pardoun me, to remit zour self thairof unto me. Cheis it zour self, and send me word of it. And in the meane tyme I am seik; I will differ[3] as tuiching the mater it is to lait. It was not lang of me yat ze have not thocht thairupon in time. And gif ze had not mair changeit zour mynd sen myne absence, then I have; ye suld not be now to ask sic resolving. Weill, thair wantis nathing of my part; and seing that zour negligence dois put us baith in the danger of ane fals brother, gif it succeidit not weill I wil never ryse agane.

I send this beirer unto zow, for I dar not traist zour brother with thir letteris, nor with the diligence.[4] He sall tell zow in quhat stait I am, and judge ze quhat amendment[5] yir new ceremonies have brocht unto me. I wald I wer deid, for I se all gais ill. Ze promysit uther maner of mater of zour foirseing, bot absence hes power over zow, quha haif twa stringis to zour bow. Dispatch the answer yat I faill not, and put na traist in your brother for this enterpryse, for he hes told it, and is also all aganis it. God give zow gude nicht.

LETTER VI – ENGLISH TRANSLATION AT HATFIELD

Alas, my Lorde, why is yor trust putt in a pson so unworthy to mistrust that wch is wholly yours! I am wood.[1] You had promised me that you wold resolve all, And that you wold send me worde every daye what I shuld doo. You have don nothing thereof. I advertised you well to take heede of yor falce brother in lawe. He cam to me and wtout shewing me any thing from you told me that you had willed him to write to you that that I m̄ should saye, and where and whan you should com to me, and that that you shuld doo touching him. And therupon hath preached unto me that it was a foolish enterprise and that wt myn honor I could nevr marry you seing that ye being maryed you did carry me away.[2] And that his folk wold not suffer yt. And that the Lords wold unsaye themselves and wold deny that they had said. To be shorte he is all contrary. I told him that seing I was com so farre, if you did not wtdrawe yorselfe of yorselfe that no psuasion nor death it selfe shuld make me fayle of my promesse. As touching the place you are to negligent (pdon me) to remitt yorself therof unto me. Choose it yorselfe and send me word of it. And in the mean tyme I am sicke. I will differ as touching the matter it is to late. It was not long of me that you have not thought therupon in tyme. And if you had not more changed yor mynde since myne absence than I have, you shuld not be now to aske such resolving. Well ther wantith nothing of my pte. And seeing that yor negligence doth putt us both in ye danger of a false brother, if it succeede not well, I will nevr rise agayne. I send this bearer unto you for I dare not trust yor brothr wt these lres nor wt the diligence. He shall tell you in what state I am, and judge you what amendment[3] these new ceremonies[4] have brought unto me. I wold I weare dead. For I see all goith yll. You promised other

189

manner of matter of your forseing, but absence hath powre ovr you, who ~~hath~~ have ij strings to yor bowe. Dispatche the aunsweare that I fail, ~~you~~ not. And put no trust in yor brothr for this enterprise For he hath told yt, and is also all against it. God give you good night.

Endorsed: 'Copie, from Sterling ~~after~~ afore[5] the ravissmt. Prufs her mask of Ravishing.'

LETTER VII – SCOTS TRANSLATION FROM LEKPREVIK'S *DETECTION*

1. Of the place and ye tyme I remit myself to zour brother and to zow. I will follow him, and will faill in nathing of my part. He findis mony difficulteis. I think he dois advertise zow thairof, and quhat he desyris for the handling of himself. As for the handling of myself, I hard it ains weill devysit.[1]

2. Me thinkis that zour services, and the lang amitie, having the gude will of ye Lordis, do weill deserve ane pardoun, gif abone the dewtie of ane subject yow advance yourself, not to constrane me, bot to asure yourself of sic place neir unto me, that uther admonitiounis or forane[2] perswasiounis may not let[3] me from consenting to that that ye hope your service sall mak yow ane day to attene. And to be schort, to mak yourself sure of the Lordis, and fre to mary; and that ye are constranit for your suretie, and to be abill to serve me faithfully, to use ane humbil requeist joynit to ane importune actioun.

3. And to be schort, excuse yourself, and perswade thame the maist ye can, yat ye are constranit to mak persute aganis zour enemies. Ze sall say aneuch, gif the mater or ground do lyke yow; and mony fair wordis to Lethingtoun. Gif ye lyke not the deid, send me word, and leif not the blame of all unto me.

LETTER VIII – SCOTS TRANSLATION FROM LEKPREVIK'S *DETECTION*

1. My Lord, sen my letter writtin, zour brother in law yat was, come to me verray sad, and hes askit me my counsel, quhat he suld do efter to morne[1] becaus thair be mony folkis heir, and amang utheris, the Erle of Sudderland,[2] quha wald rather

die, considdering the gude thay have sa laitlie ressavit of me, then suffer me to be caryit away, thay conducting me; and that he feirit thair suld sum troubil happin of it: Of the uther syde, that it suld be said that he wer unthankful to have betrayit me. I tald him, that he suld have resolvit with zow upon all that, and that he suld avoyde, gif he culd, thay that were maist mistraistit.

2. He hes resolvit to wryte thairof to zow be my opinioun; for he hes abaschit me to se him sa unresolvit at the neid. I assure myself he will play the part of an honest man: But I have thocht gude to advertise zow of the feir he hes yat he suld be chargeit and accusit of tressoun, to ye end yat, without mistraisting him, ze may be the mair circumspect, and that ze may have ye mair power. For we had zisterday mair than iii.c. hors of his and of Levingstoun's. For the honour of God, be accompanyit rather with mair then les; for that is the principal of my cair.

3. I go to write my dispatche, and pray God to send us ane happy enterview schortly. I wryte in haist, to the end ye may be advysit in tyme.

INITIAL LINES IN THE ORIGINAL FRENCH

The initial lines of each Casket Letter in what may be the Original French were printed before each Letter in early editions of George Buchanan's *Detection*. The versions shown below are from the Scots translation of the *Detection* published in 1572 by Lekprevik.

Letter I: Il semble qu'avecques vostre abscence soit joynt le oubly, ceu[1] qu'au partir vous me promistes de vous nouvelles. Et toutes foys je n'en puis apprendre, etc.

Letter II: Estant party du lieu ou je avois laissé mon coeur il se peult aysément juger quelle estoit ma contenance, veu ce qui peult un corps sans coeur, qui a esté cause que jusques à la disnée je n'ay pas tenu grand propos, aussi personne ne s'est voulu advancer jugeant bien qu'il n'y faisoit bon, etc.

Letter III: Monsieur, si l'ennuy de vostre absence, celuy de vostre oubly, la crainte du danger, tant prouvé[2] d'un chacun à vostre tant aymée personne, etc.

Letter IV: J'ay veillé plus tard la haut que je n'eusse fait, si ce n'eust esté pout tirer ce que ce porteur vous dira, que je trouve la plus belle commodité pour excuser vostre affaire qui ce purroit presenter, etc.

Letter V: Mon coeur, helas! fault il que la follie d'une femme, dont vous cognoissez assez l'ingratitude vers moy, soit cause de vous donner desplaisir, etc.

Letter VI: Monsieur, helas! pourquoy est vostre fiance mise en personne si indigne, pour soupconner ce qui est entierement vostre. J'enrage, vous m'aviez promis, etc.

Letter VII: Du lieu et l'heure je m'en rapporte à vostre frere et à vous. Je le suivray, et ne fauldray en rien de ma part. Il trouve beaucoup de difficultez, etc.

Letter VIII: Monsieur, depuis ma lettre escrite vostre beau frere qui fust, est venu à moy fort triste, et m'a demandé mon conseil de ce qu'il feroit apres demain, etc.[3]

APPENDIX 2:
TEXTS OF THE MARRIAGE CONTRACTS

(A) THE UNDATED
FRENCH CONTRACT[1]

Nous Marie par la grace de Dieu Royne descosse Douaryer de France etc. prometons fidellemant et de bonne foy et sans contraynte a Jacques Hepburn conte de Boduel, de navoir jamays autre espoulx et mary que lui, et de le prandre pour tel toute et quante fois quil men requirira, quoy que parante amye ou aultres y soient contrerayres: et puis que Dieu a pris mon feu mary Henry Stuart dit Darnelay, et que par se moien je suis libre, nestant soubs obeisance de pere ni de mere des mayntenant je protesteque, lui estant en mesme liberte, je seray prest et dacomplir les ceremonies requises au mariage, que je lui promets devant Dieu qua jenprante a tesmoignasge et la presante. Signee de may mayn ecrit ce. Marie R.[2]

(B) TRANSLATION OF THE
ABOVE CONTRACT

We, Mary, by the grace of God, Queen of Scotland, Dowager of France, etc., promise faithfully and in good faith and without constraint to James Hepburn, Earl of Bothwell, never to have any other spouse and husband than him, and to take him for such each and every time that he shall require it of me, although relative, friend or others be contrary to it; and since God has taken my late husband Henry Stuart called Darnley, and since for this reason I am free, not owing obedience to either father or mother at this present time, I protest that, he being in the same freedom, I shall be ready to perform the requisite ceremonies of marriage, which I promise him before God, whom I take as witness, and this present. Signed by my hand; written this. Marie R.

(C) THE CONTRACT OF 5 APRIL[1]

At Setoun, the V. day of Apryll, the zeir of God 1567, the richt excellent, richt heich and michtie Princes, Marie, be the grace of God, Quene of Scottis, consideddring the place and estait quhairin Almightie God hes constitute hir heichnes, and how, be the deceis of the King hir husband, hir Majestie is now destitute of ane Husband, leving solitaire in the stait of wedowheid: In the quhilk kynde of lyfe hir Majestie maist willingly wald continew, gif ye weill of hir realme and subjectis wald permit; bot on the uther part, consideddring the inconveniencis may follow, and the necessitie quhilk the realme hes, yat hir Majestie be couplit with ane husband, hir Heichness hes inclynit to mary. And seing quhat incommoditie may cum to this realme, in cace hir Majestie suld joyne in mariage with ony forane Prince of ane strange natioun, hir Heichnes hes thocht rather better to zeild unto ane of hir awin subjectis: Amangis quhome hir Majestie findis nane mair abill, nor indewit with better qualiteis, then the richt nobill, and hir deir cousing, James Erle Bothwell, &c. of quhais thankfull and trew service hir Heichnes, in all tymes bypast, hes had large prufe and infallibill experience. And seing not onely the same gude mynd constantly persevering in him, bot with that ane inward affection and hartly lufe towardis hir Majestie, hir Heichnes amangis the rest, hes maid hir chose of him: And thairof, in the presence of the eternall God, faithfully, and in the word of ane Prince, be thir presentis,[2] takis the said James Erle Bothwell as hir lawfull husband, and promittis and oblisis[3] hir Heichnes, that how sone ye proces of divorce, intentit betwix ye said Erle Bothwell and Dame Jane Gordoun, now his pretensit spous, beis endit be ye ordour of ye lawis, hir Majestie sall, God willing, thairefter schortly mary and tak the said Erle to hir husband, and compleit the band of matrimonie with him, in face of haly kirk, and sall never mary nane uther husband bot he only during his lyfetyme. And as hir Majestie, of hir gratious humanitie and proper motive, without deserving of the said Erle, hes thus inclynit hir favour and affection towardis him, he humblie and reverentlie acknawledging the same, according to his bound dewtie, and being als fre and abill to mak promeis of mariage, in respect of the said proces of divorce, intentit for divers ressonabill causis, and yat his said pretensit spous hes thairunto consentit, he presentlie takis hir Majestie as his lauchfull spous in the presence of God, and promittis and oblisis him, as he will answer to God, and upon his fidelitie and honour, that, in all diligence

194

possibill, he sall prosecute and set fordwart the said proces of divorce alreddy begunne and intentit betwix him and the said Dame Jane Gordoun his pretensit spous, unto the fynal end of ane decreit and declarator thairin. And incontinent thairefter, at hir Majesteis gude will and plesure, and quhen hir Heichnes thinkis convenient, sall compleit and solemnizat, in face of haly kirk, ye said band of matrimony with hir Majestie, and lufe, honour and serve hir Heichnes according to the place and honour that it hes pleisit hir Majestie to accept him unto, and never to have ony uther for his wyfe, during hir Majesteis lyfetime: In faith and witnessing quhairof, hir Heichnes and the said Erle hes subscrivit this present faithfull promeis with yair handis, as followis, day, zeir and place foirsaidis, befoir thir witnessis, George Erle of Huntly, and maister Thomas Hepburne Persoun of Auldhamstock, &c.

MARIE R.
JAMES ERLE BOTHWELL.

APPENDIX 3:
TEXTS OF THE SONNETS

THE SONNETS IN THEIR French version are printed from the earliest English version of Buchanan's *Detection*. It has been assumed that it was published late in 1571 in London. The spelling has not been modernised apart from introducing the letters v and j. In the French version a line is omitted in Sonnets 3 and 8, but these lines are shown in the Anglicised Scots translation of the Sonnets included in the same edition of the *Detection*. French translations of these lines are provided in brackets in those two Sonnets.

1. O Dieux ayez de moy compassion,
    Et m'enseignez quelle preuve certaine
    Je puis donner qui ne luy semble vaine
    De mon amour & ferme affection.
    Las[1] n'est il pas ja en possession
    Du corps, du coeur qui ne refuse paine
    Ny deshonneur, en la vie incertaine,
    Offense de parentz, ne pire affliction?
    Pour luy tous mes amis s'estime moins que rien,
    Et de mes ennemis je veux esperer bien.
    J'ay hazardé pour luy & nom & conscience:
    Je veux pour luy au monde renoncer:
    Je veux mourir pour luy avancer.
    Que reste il plus pour prouver ma constance?
2. Entre ses mains & en son plein pouvoir,
    Je metz mon filz, mon honneur, & ma vie,
    Mon pais, mes subjectz, mon ame assubiectie
    Est tout a luy, & n'ay autre voulloir
    Pour mon object, que sans le decevoir
    Suivre je veux, malgre toute l'envie
    Qu'issir[2] en peult, car je n'ay autre envie
    Que de ma foy, luy faire appercevoir
    Que pour tempeste ou bonnace qui face[3]
    Jamais ne veux changer demeure ou place.
    Brief je feray de ma foy telle preuve,

196

Qu'il cognoistra sans fainte ma constance,
Non par mes pleurs ou fainte obeyssance
Come autres ont fait, mais par divers espreuve.

3.   Elle pour son honneur vous doibt obeyssance
Moy vous obeyssant j'en puis recevoir blasme
N'estât, à mon regret, comme elle vostre femme.
Et si n'aura pourtant en ce point préeminence
Pour son profit elle use de constance.
Car ce n'est peu d'honneur d'estre de voz biens dame
Et moy pour vous aymer j'en puis recevoir blasme
Et ne luy veux ceder en toute l'observance:
Elle de vostre mal n' à l'apprehension
Moy je n'ay nul repos tant je crains l'apparence
Par l'advis des parentz, elle eut vostre accointance
Moy malgré tous les miens vous porte affection
(Et neanmoins, mon coeur, vous doubtez ma constance)
Et de sa loyauté prenez ferme asseurance.

4.   Par vous man coeur & par vostre alliance
Elle à remis sa maison en honneur
Elle à jouy par vous la grandeur
Dont tous les siens n'ayent nul asseurance
De vous, mon bien, elle à eu la constance,
Et à gaigné pour un temps vostre coeur,
Par vous elle à eu plaisir en bon heur,
Et pour vous a receu honneur et reverence,
Et n'a perdu sinon la jouyssance
D'un fascheux sot quelle aymoit cherement,[4]
Je ne la playns d'aymer donc ardamment,
Celuy qui n'a en sens, ny en vaillance,
En beauté, en bonté, ny en constance
Point de seçonde. Je vis en ceste foy.

5.   Quant vous l'amiez, elle usoit de froideur.
Sy vous souffriez pour s'amour passion
Qui vient d'aymer de trop d'affection,
Son doig[5] monstroit la tristesse de coeur
N'ayant plaisir de vostre grand ardeur.
En ses habitz monstroit sans fiction
Qu'elle n'avoit paour[6] qu'imperfection
Peust l'effacer hors de ce loyal coeur
De vostre mort je ne vis la peaur[7]
Que meritoit tel mary[8] & seigneur.
Somme, de vous elle à eu tout son bien
Et n'a prisé ny jamais estimé

197

    Un si grand heur[9] sinon puis qu'il n'est sien
    Et maintenant dit l'avoir tant aymé.

6.   Et maintenant elle commence à voir
    Qu'elle estoit bien de mauvais jugement
    De n'estimer l'amour d'un tel amant
    Et voudroit bien mon amy decevoir,
    Par les escriptz tout fardez de scavoir[10]
    Qui pourtant n'est en son esprit croissant
    Ains[11] emprunté de quelque autheur eluissant
    A faint tres bien un envoy[12] sans l'avoir
    Et toutesfois ses parolles fardez,
    Ses pleurs, ses plaincts remplis de fictions.
    Et ses hautz cris & lamentations
    Ont tant gaigné qui par vous sont gardez
    Ses lettres escriptes ausquelz vous donnez foy
    Et si l'aymez & croyez plus que moy.

7.   Vous la croyez las trop je l'apperçoy
    Et vous doutez de ma ferme constance,
    O mon seul bien & mon seul esperance,
    Et ne vous puis asseurer de ma foy.
    Vous m'estimez legier que le voy,[13]
    Et si n'avez en moy nul'asseurance,
    Et soupçonnez mon coeur sans apparence,
    Vous deffiant à trop grand tort de moy,
    Vous ignorez l'amour que je vous porte,
    Vous soupçonnez qu'autre amour me transporte,
    Vous estimez mes parolles du vent,
    Vous depeignez de cire mon las coeur
    Vous me pensez femme sans jugement,
    Et tout sela augmente mon ardeur.

8.   Mon amour croist & plus en plus croistra
    Tant que viuray, & tiendray à grandheur,
    Tant seulement d'avoir part en ce coeur
    Vers qui en fin mon amour paroistra
    Sy tres à clair que jamais n'en doutra,
    (Pour luy je lutterai contre malheur)
    Pour luy je veux recercher la grandeur,
    Et feray tant qu'en vray cognoistra,
    Que je n'ay bien, heur,[14] ne contentement,
    Qu'a l'obeyr & servir loyaument
    Pour luy jattendz toute bonne fortune,
    Pour luy je veux garder sainté & vie
    Pour luy tout vertu de suyvre[15] j'ay envie

Et sans changer me trouvera tout une.

9. Pur luy aussi je jette mainte larme.
    Premier quand il se fist de ce corps possesseur,
    Duquel alors il n'avoit pas le coeur;
    Puis me donna un autre dur alarme
    Quand il versa de son sang mainte dragme[16]
    Dont de grief il me vint lesser[17] doleur,
    Qui m'en pensa oster la vie, & frayeur
    De perdre las le seul rempar[18] qui m'arme.
    Pour luy depuis jay mesprisé l'honneur
    Ce qui nous peult seul pourvoir de bonheur.
    Pour luy j'ay hazarde grandeur & conscience.
    Pour luy tous mes parentz j'ay quité, & amis,
    Et tous autres respectz sont apart mis.
    Brief de vous seul je cerche l'alliance.

10. De vous, je dis seul soustein de ma vie
    Tant seulement je cerche m'asseurer,
    Et si ose de moy tant presumer
    De vous gaigner maugré toute l'envie.
    Car c'est le seul désir de vostre chere amie,
    De vous servir & loyaument aymer,
    Et tous malheurs moins que riens estimer,
    Et vostre volonté de la mien suivre
    Vous cognoistrez avecque obeyssance
    De mon loyal devoir n'omettant la sciance
    A quoy je estudiray pours tousiours vous complaire
    Sans aymer rien que vous, soubz la sujection.
    De qui je veux sans nulle fiction
    Vivre & mourir & à ce j'obtempere.

11. Mon coeur, mon sang, mon ame, e mon soucy,
    Las, vous m'avez promis qu'aurons ce plaisir
    De deviser avecques vous à loysir,
    Toute la nuict ou je languis icy
    Ayant le coeur d'extreme paour transy
    Pour voir absent le but de mon desir
    Crainte d'oublir un coup me vient à saisir:
    Et l'autre fois je crains que rendurcie
    Soit contre moy vostre amiable coeur
    Par quelque dit d'un meschant rapporteur.
    Un autre fois je crains quelque aventure
    Qui par chemin detourne mon amant,
    Par un fascheux & nouveau accident.
    Dieu detourne tout malheureux augure.

199

12. Ne vous voyant selon qu'avez promis
     J'ay mis la main au papier pour escrire
     D'un different que je voulu transcrire,
     Je ne scay pas quel sera vostre advis
     Mais je scay bien qui mieux aymer scaura
     Vous diriez bien que plus y gaignera.

TRANSLATION OF THE SONNETS

This is a relatively free version intended to convey their meaning rather than to provide a literal translation. The translation is kept as far as possible within each of the original lines to facilitate comparison. It is also not intended to be a poetical rendering of the Sonnets.

1. O gods, have compassion on me
    and show me what certain proof
    I can give, which does not seem hollow to him,
    of my love and constant affection.
    Alas! Is he not already in possession
    of my body and of my heart which shuns no pain
    nor dishonour, in this uncertain life,
    nor slight to relatives, nor worse affliction?
    For him I hold all my friends as less than nothing,
    and I will even wish well of my enemies;
    for him I have risked my reputation and conscience,
    for him I wish to renounce the world.
    I will die to set him forward.
    What else is there to prove my constancy?

2. In his hands and his full power
    I place my son, my honour and my life,
    my country, my subjects, my soul subjected
    all to him, and I have no other desire
    in mind than without deceiving him
    to follow him; and this I wish despite all the worries
    which can ensue, for I have no other desire
    than to make him perceive my faithfulness.
    Whatever may occur, for better or for worse,
    I will never wish to change my dwelling or place.
    In short, I shall give such proof of my devotion
    that he will realise my unfeigned fidelity,
    not by my tears or pretended obedience
    as others have done, but by various proofs.

3. She for her honour owes you obedience.
   In obeying you I can receive blame,
   not being, to my regret, as she is, your wife.
   Yet she shall not have precedence on this point.
   She makes use of constancy just for her advantage,
   for it is no small honour to be mistress of your possessions,
   and I for loving you can be censured
   but I will not give way to her on every point.
   She has no fear of any harm to you,
   but fearing even the semblance of danger I cannot relax.
   She made your acquaintance by the advice of her relations.
   I, despite all of mine, am fond of you,
   and nevertheless, my dear, you doubt my constancy
   and are firmly convinced of her loyalty.

4. By you, my dear, and by your marriage
   she has restored her family to honour.
   She has enjoyed through you the grandeur
   of which her own relations had no assurance.
   From you, my wealth, she has received faithfulness
   and has gained for a time your heart,
   and by you she has had pleasure and good fortune,
   and by you she has received honour and reverence,
   and has not sacrificed anything but the enjoyment
   of a tiresome fool whom she loved dearly.
   I do not complain of her loving so ardently
   the man who has not in good sense or valour,
   in beauty or kindness or constancy
   any equal. I live in that belief.

5. When you loved her, she was cold.
   Yet you suffered for her love the passion
   which comes from loving with too much fondness.
   Her mourning showed the sadness of her heart,
   not taking any pleasure from your great fervour.
   In her clothes she showed unfeignedly
   that she had no fear that her defects
   could remove her out of your loyal heart.
   I did not see in her the fear of your death
   of which such a husband and lord was worthy.
   In short, she has received all her wealth from you
   and has not weighed nor ever valued
   such great fortune since it is not hers,
   and now she says that she has loved you so much.

6. And now she begins to see

that her judgement has been very bad
in not appreciating the love of such a lover
and would fain deceive my dear
by letters disguised with learning
which nevertheless did not breed in her brain
but were borrowed from some scintillating author.
She has very cleverly pretended to have a longing for you
and always her made-up words,
her tears, her moans, full of dissimulation,
and her loud cries and lamentations
have been so successful that you keep
her letters and treat them as sincere,
and so you love her and believe her more than me.

7. You believe her, alas! I perceive it so well,
and you doubt my steadfast faithfulness,
O my only wealth and my only hope,
and I cannot convince you of my fidelity.
I see that you esteem me lightly,
and so you have no faith in me
and you suspect my heart for no apparent cause.
Your distrust hurts me very much.
You do not know the love which I have for you.
You suspect that another love enraptures me.
You value my words just as wind.
You describe my weary heart as made of wax.
You think of me as a woman without judgement,
and all that raises my passion.

8. My love increases and will grow more and more
as long as I live, and will keep its full measure
so much, just to have a share in that heart
where eventually my love will appear
so clearly that he will never doubt it.
For him I will struggle against misfortune
and for him I wish to seek for greatness
and will do so much that he will truly know
that I have no wealth nor happiness nor satisfaction
but in obeying and serving him loyally.
For him I expect all good fortune.
For him I wish to keep my health and life.
For him I wish to conform to every virtue,
and he will ever find me just the same.

9. I also shed many tears for him.
First when he made himself possessor of my body,

when he did not possess my heart.
Then he gave me more hard anguish
when he lost many drops of his blood
leaving me wounded with that suffering
which almost took away my life, and the fear
of losing, alas, the only rampart which defends me.
For him I have since despised honour,
which alone can bring us happiness.
For him I have risked character and conscience.
For him I have left all my kin and friends,
and all other forms of good repute have been put aside.
In short, I seek to marry only you.

10. I say to you, only supporter of my life
I only seek to assure myself,
and so I dare to presume so much
to win you in spite of all envy.
For it is the only desire of your dear love
to serve and love you loyally,
and to consider all misfortunes as less than nothing
and to follow your wishes as if they were mine.
You will know with what obedience,
not forgetting the knowledge of my loyal duty,
how I will study always to please you,
loving nothing but you, under the rule
of whom I wish, without any pretending,
to live and die with, and to this I comply.

11. My heart, my blood, my soul and my care.
Alas! You promised me that I should have the pleasure
of chatting with you at leisure.
All night when I pine here
with my heart chilled with great fear
for missing the mark of my desire,
fear of being forgotten grips me like a blow.
At other times I fear that
your loving heart is hardened against me
by some remark from a wicked gossip.
Another time I fear that some adventure
will turn aside my lover from his road,
some troublesome and fresh accident.
May God divert every unhappy omen.

12. Not seeing you as you had promised.
I have set about writing to you
about a discord which I wished to relate.

I do not know what will be your decision
but I know well who knows best how to love.
You may well say who will gain most from it.

Appendix 4:

Extracts from the Casket Letters sent to Queen Elizabeth from York in October 1568[1]

Elizabeth's Commissioners (Norfolk, Sussex and Sadler) enclosed with their letter of 11 October 1568 a paper noting 'the chief and special points of the said Letters'. The purpose was to show the love between Mary and Bothwell, her hatred for Darnley and her part in the conspiracy against him. The extracts when read at face-value certainly prove these points but, as explained in the commentaries on each Letter in Chapter 6, the passages quoted can be interpreted in alternative ways.

The passages were extracted from only Letters I, II and IV. Most of them come from Letter II. Unfortunately they do not help to clarify obscure passages in translations of those Letters, but the quotations from Letter II go far towards confirming that Letter II was in its final form by October 1568.

It should be noted that Elizabeth's Commissioners did not include all the passages in Letter II which appear to be especially incriminating such as paragraphs 11, 14 and 22. Furthermore, there are no extracts from Letters III, V, VI, VII or VIII. It is particularly interesting and significant that they did not include any passage referring to the alleged quarrel at Kirk o'Field between Darnley and Lord Robert. The inclusion of that passage would have clarified whether there was a suppressed Letter giving a full account of the episode or only the very vague and unconvincing allusion to it in paragraph 1 of Letter IV.

As the extracts follow closely and in most parts very accurately the Scots translation, the English Commissioners must have copied the passages rather than quoted them from memory.

A brief note of the chief and principall poincts of the Quene of Scottes Lettres written to Bothaill, which may tend to her condempnation, for her consent and procurement of the murder of her husband, as farre forthe as we coulde by the readinge gather.

First, the plaine and manifest wordes conteyned in the said lettres, declaringe the inordinat and filthie love betwene her and Bothaill.

Next, the like wordes plainely declaringe how she hated and abhorred her said husband.

Then for the declaration of the conspiracie, and her procurement and consent to the murder of her said husband, how she take her journey from Edenburghe to Glasco, to visite him beinge theare sicke, and purposely of intent to bringe him with her to Edenburghe.

She wrote to Bothaill from Glasco, how she flattered her said husband, to obtaine her purpose; and that the Earle of Lenox his father, that daye that she was devisinge to bringe his sonne to Edenburghe, did blede at the Noose and mowthe, willing the said Bothaill to ghesse what presage it was.[2]

She wrote also, that she was about a worke that she hated greatly, and that she lied and dissembled to get creadite with her husband, and to bringe her faschious purpose to passe, confessing herselfe therein to do the office of a traiteresse, which, weare it not to obey Bothaill, she had lever be dead then do it, for her harte did blede at it.[3]

Also she wrote that she had wonne her husband to goo with her to Edenburghe, and to do whatsoever she wolde have him to do, sayinge, Alas! she never deceaved anie before, remittinge herselfe altogether to the will and pleasure of Bothaill, wherein she wold obey him, whatsover come thereof; requyring him to advise with himself, if he coulde fynde owt anie other secreat invention by medicine, for her husband was to take medicine, and the Bath also at Cragmillar.[4]

She biddethe Bothaill to burn the lettre, for it was over dangerous to them, and nothinge well said in it, for that she was thinkinge upon nothinge but fascherie, requyringe him that, sithens to obey him, her dear love, she spared neither honour, conscience, hazard, nor greatnes whatsover, he woulde take it in good parte; and that he wold not see her, whose fained tears shoulde not be so muche praised, as the faithefull travailles which she susteyned to merite her place, for the obteyninge whereof against her nature, she betraied him that might impeche it, prayinge God to forgeave her, and to geave unto Bothaill, her only love, the happe and prousperitie which she his humble and faithfull love wishithe unto him; hoopinge shortely to be another thinge unto him, for the rewarde of her yrkesome troubles.[5]

Finally, she wrote to Bothaill, that according to her commission, she wolde bringe the man with her; prayinge him to worke wisely, or els the whole burden wolde lye on her shoulders;

and specially to make good watche, that the bird escaped not owt of the Cage.[6]

In addition to the extracts sent from York, the English records of the conferences contain a set of 'Notes drawin furth of the Quenis letters sent to the Erle Bothwell'.[7] The Notes contain extracts mainly from Letter II but also from Letters I and IV. They include some of the passages sent from York but are much fuller. These passages follow the Scots translations. There are many spelling variations and slight alterations, but there is nothing of major significance or substance. The most interesting variations are in the extracts from paragraph 3 of Letter I: 'he makis the court to me' instead of the Scots 'he makis lufe to me' and 'faschit' instead of the Scots 'troubillit'.

NOTES

A GUIDE TO THE NOTES

The following abbreviations are used:

Anderson   James Anderson, *Collections relating to the History of Mary Queen of Scots* (1727)

Arnot   Hugo Arnot, *Celebrated Criminal Trials in Scotland* (1785)

C.S.P.For.   Calendar of State Papers, Foreign Series

C.Scot.P.   Calendar of Scottish Papers

C.S.P.R.   Calendar of State Papers, Rome: vol. 1 (1558–71); vol. 2 (1572–78)

C.S.P.Sp.   Calendar of State Papers, Spanish

C.S.P.V.   Calendar of State Papers, Venetian

Davison   MH Armstrong Davison, *The Casket Letters* (1965)

Dickinson   WC Dickinson (ed.) John Knox's *History of the Reformation in Scotland* (1949)

Diurnal   *Diurnal of Remarkable Occurrents*, edited by T Thomson, Maitland Club (1833)

Gatherer   WA Gatherer (ed.) *The Tyrannous Reign of Mary Stewart by George Buchanan* (1958)

Goodall   W Goodall, *An examination of the letters of Mary Queen of Scots to Bothwell* (1754)

Gore-Browne   R Gore-Browne, *Lord Bothwell* (1937)

Herries   *Historical Memoirs of Lord Herries*, edited by Robert Pitcairn, Abbotsford Club (1836)

HMC   Historical Manuscripts Commission

Hosack   J Hosack, *Mary Queen of Scots and her Accusers* (2nd edition, 1870)

Keith   R Keith, *The History of the Affairs of Church and State in Scotland* (1734) Spottiswoode Society edition: vol. 1, 1844; vol. 2, 1845; vol. 3, 1850

Labanoff   Prince A Labanoff, *Lettres de Marie Stuart* (1844)

Laing   M Laing, *The History of Scotland* (1819)

Lang   Andrew Lang, *The Mystery of Mary Stuart* (1901)

Mahon (1923)   RH Mahon, *The Indictment of Mary Queen of Scots* (1923)
Mahon (1924)   RH Mahon, *Mary Queen of Scots: A study of the Lennox Narrative* (1924)
Mahon (1930)   RH Mahon, *The Tragedy of Kirk o' Field* (1930)
Melville   Sir James Melville, *Memoirs*, edited by T Thomson, Bannatyne Club (1827)
Nau   Claude Nau, *Memorials of Mary Stewart*, edited by J Stevenson (1883)
Pitcairn   R Pitcairn (ed.) *Ancient Criminal Trials in Scotland*, vol. 1, part 2, Maitland Club (1833)
Teulet (1852) A Teulet, *Papiers d'Etat relatifs à l'Histoire de l'Ecosse au 16e siècle*
Teulet (1862) A Teulet, *Relations politiques de la France et de l'Espagne avec l'Ecosse au 16e siècle* (1862)

1. Introduction

1 The original manuscript is held in the National Library of Scotland.
2 *Bannatyne Club* (1829) edited by H Cockburn and T Maitland.
3 Keith, vol. 3, page 304 for text. See also Gore-Browne (1937) page 454 on errors.
4 See edition edited by T Thomson.
5 Printed in *Fragments of Scottish History*, edited by JG Dalyell (1798). The location of the original manuscript is not known.
6 Goodall, vol. 2, page 249.
7 See edition edited by WC Dickinson (1949).
8 See WA Gatherer, *The Tyrannous Reign of Mary Stewart* (1958) and G Donaldson, *The First Trial of Mary Queen of Scots* (1969) for analyses of Buchanan's lack of veracity.
9 Printed in Mahon (1924) which provides a critical commentary on Lennox's lack of veracity.
10 Printed in Mahon (1923).
11 Printed in Donaldson (1969).
12 Printed in Gatherer (1958).
13 Edited by J Stevenson (1883).

2. Fact

1 Keith, vol. 3, pages 261–263; HMC, 6th Report, Appendix, page 641.
2 C.S.P.For. no. 885, but, according to Knox's Continuator, the Archbishop was persuaded to desist from exercising his jurisdiction. See Dickinson (1949) vol. II, page 201.
3 Mahon (1930) describes the site and shows models of how it would have looked before and after the explosion.

4 *Register of the Privy Seal of Scotland* no. 3123.

5 *Inventaires de la Royne d'Escosse, Bannatyne Club* (1863) ed. J Robertson, page 177: list of items which had been taken to Kirk o'Field and had been destroyed.

6 Keith, vol. I, page ci.

7 *Scottish Burgh Record Society*, vol. 4 (1875) pages 228 and 230. The Burgh Council authorised its Treasurer on 11 February 1567 to fill in the back door of the Provost's Lodging (presumably the New Lodging) with lime and sand. This indicates that the damage to that building was not disastrous. This is confirmed by the sketch of the scene sent to Sir William Cecil which marks the New Provost's Lodging as the house in which the King's corpse was placed after being found. On 7 May the Council authorised the rebuilding of the Town wall on the south side of the Provost of the Kirk o'Field's Lodging.

8 See article by HF Kerr in the *Proceedings of the Society of Antiquarians in Scotland*, vol. LXVI, page 140 on the distortions. The sketch-plan is in the PRO.

9 Melville (who was there) just stated 'between Linlithgow and Edinburgh'. Buchanan in his *History* said at the Bridge of Almond. The River Almond flows through Cramond. The *Diurnal* recorded between Kirkliston and Edinburgh at a place called the Briggis. Birrel stated that it was at the Bridge of Cramond. The Act of 15 December 1567 stated the Foulbriggs. For further discussion see R Chambers, *Domestic Annals of Scotland* (1858) vol. 1, page 41 note. He pointed to a 1543 reference to a place on the Almond Water called the Briggs. A Strickland, however, in her *Lives of the Queens of Scotland* (1854) vol. 5, pages 272–274, claimed that the name Foulbriggs came from the Foulburn in the area now called Fountainbridge, which is quite close to the Castle. Goodall, vol. 2, page 367, stated that Bothwell seized the Queen at the Foulbriggs about half a mile from the Castle.

10 Laing, vol. 2, page 109: letter of 17 June 1567 from James Beaton to be passed to his brother, the Archbishop of Glasgow in Paris.

11 Pitcairn (1833) pages 493–501.

12 Pitcairn (1833) pages 502–510.

13 Pitcairn (1833) pages 511–513.

14 See Arnot (1785) for the trials of Morton and Douglas.

15 Goodall, vol. 2, page 66.

16 G Donaldson, *Mary Queen of Scots* (1974) page 148, discusses the religious composition.

17 See C.Scot.P., pages 903, 906, 928 on the Eik.

18 Goodall, vol. 2, page 305.

3. Conjecture

1 C.S.P.V., no. 374.

2 Keith, vol. 1, page xcvi.

3 C.Scot.P., no. 832.

4 C.Scot.P., no. 850.

5 Labanoff, vol. 2, pages 219–222.

6 *Abbotsford Miscellany* (1837) vol. 1, *Boyd Papers*, page 23; *Register of the Privy Council of Scotland*, vol. 2, page 8.

7 C.S.P.R., vol. 1, no. 763. The approach to the Pope must throw doubt on the report a few weeks earlier on 19 January 1571 from Thomas Buchanan in Copenhagen to Cecil that Mary had sent certain writings to Bothwell desiring him to be of good comfort (C.S.P.For., no. 1512).

8 John Stuart, *A Lost Chapter in the History of Mary Queen of Scots Recovered* (1874) page 7, gives details of Mary's great interest in Lady Jane Gordon at the time of her wedding. See also the chapter on Jane Gordon in *Mary Stewart's People* (1987) by Margaret HB Sanderson.

9 John Stuart (1874) op. cit., pages 55–56 refer to Lady Jane's great prudence and good sense.

10 See *Register of the Privy Council of Scotland*, vol. xiv, pages xliv–xlv, cxii and 211 for Anna's passport in 1563; also C.S.P.For., no. 1034 for arrival of Bothwell in Scotland in 1561.

11 C.S.P.For., vol. 6, no. 839.

12 Davison, pages 228–229.

13 See sections on Letters III, IV, V and VI and the Sonnets in Chapter 8.

14 *Miscellany of the Scottish History Society* (1904), vol. 2, page 169. Some allusions to the French lady in twentieth-century books lack any further precise references to original sources and give conflicting dates about when she arrived in Scotland.

15 As mentioned in the *Lennox Narrative* and the statement of William Hiegait (see Chapter 4, page 67).

16 Keith, vol. 1, page xcvi.

17 Keith, vol. 2, page 480. See also JB Black, *The Age of Elizabeth* (1959) pages 96–98, 100.

18 C.Scot.P., no. 459.

19 See *Register of the Privy Seal of Scotland*, vol. V, part 2, no. 33 (Charter of 24 March 1567 confirming W Baillie's lands within the Barony of Glasgow and Sheriffdom of Lanark); G Brunton and D Haig, *Senators of the College of Justice* (1832) page 96, also on W Baillie; W Gemmell, *The Oldest House in Glasgow* (1910); R Renwick, *Glasgow Memorials* (1908), page 218 on Darnley's cottage.

20 John Leslie, *A defence of the honour of Mary Queen of Scotland* (1569).

21 Keith, vol. 1, page xcix.

22 See also C.S.P.R., vol. 2, no. 429 (concerning Mary's petition to divorce Darnley in 1575), which asserts that Darnley chose Kirk o'Field on the advice of some of the magnates in his suite.

23 Goodall, vol. 2, page 243.

24 See Philipson's article in the *Revue Historique*, vol. 36, page 38; A Fraser,

Mary Queen of Scots (1969 hardback edition) page 298; Mahon (1930) page 57; and for another view GM Thomson, *The Crime of Mary Stuart* (1967) pages 100–101.

25 C.S.P.Sp., vol. 1, no. 417.

26 Laing, vol. 2, page 97.

27 *Diurnal*, page 338.

28 C.S.P.For., no. 977.

29 *Maitland Club*, edited by Robert Adam (1834).

30 See the *Detection*, and also the *Hopetoun Manuscript*, printed in Donaldson (1969).

31 See Lennox's *First Narrative*, paragraphs IX and XVI and pages 126, 127 note, and 130 in Mahon (1924); Davison (1965) page 235.

32 C.S.P.R., vol. 2, no. 429.

33 C.S.P.For., no. 977.

34 Keith, vol. 1, page ci.

35 C.S.P.Sp., no. 417 – Guzman de Silva to Philip II dated 21 April 1567.

36 C.S.P.R., no. 439.

37 Davison, page 268.

38 Hay's deposition refers to a turnpike (Pitcairn, page 497).

39 C.S.P.V., no. 384. According to Birrel's *Diary*, Moretta departed from Edinburgh on 11 February.

40 Gore-Browne, pages 315–316.

41 Davison, pages 272–273.

42 C.S.P.For., no. 1199. Sir William Drury was the Deputy Governor of Berwick.

43 Arnot, page 18.

44 C.Scot. P., no. 473.

45 C.S.P.Sp., no. 431.

46 See Introduction 1, page 3, and Chapter 5, page 104.

47 See Chapter 6, page 133, and also Melville, page 174.

48 *Accounts of the Treasurer of Scotland* (1970), page xxxvii.

49 Lang (1901) page xv.

50 Anderson, vol. 2, pages 74–75.

51 *Register of the Privy Seal of Scotland* (1957), no. 3254.

52 C.Scot.P., no. 490.

53 C.Scot.P., no. 617; *Diurnal*, page 121.

54 Gore-Browne, page 443.

55 C.S.P.V., no. 384.

56 C.S.P.For., no. 1199.

57 C.S.P.R., no. 442; also Labanoff, vol. 7, page 105 for letter of the same date from the Papal Nuncio to the Grand Duke of Tuscany.

58 Keith, vol. 1, page ci. See G Donaldson, *The First Trial of Mary, Queen of Scots* (1969) page 173 on the funeral arrangements.

59 C.S.P.V., no. 384.

60 C.Scot.P., no. 471. Petcarne also lived in the Friars Wynd, but he neither

heard nor knew anything till about 4 hours … [words indecipherable] probably when a servant of Signor Francis came and cried on him to come to his master which he did and remained with him till about six hours. This probably refers to the Queen's Italian servant, Francisco de Busso, but the passage gives no further details and it is not clear what it was meant to purport. It is astounding that Petcarne was not wakened by the explosion as he lived close to Kirk o'Field.

61 Labanoff, vol. 7, pages 313–318.
62 *Maitland Club Miscellany*, vol. 3, part 1 (1842) page 185.
63 C.S.P.For., no. 1305.
64 *Diurnal*, page 106; C.S.P.V., no. 384.
65 Keith, vol. 2, pages 525–532.
66 Keith, vol. 2, page 538.
67 C.S.P.For., no. 1097 – letter from Sir John Forster at Alnwick to Cecil; *Acts of Parliaments of Scotland*, vol. 2.
68 C.Scot.P., no. 174 – Randolph to Cecil, 3 May 1565.
69 *Register of the Privy Council of Scotland*, vol. 1 (1877) page 504. See C Scot. P., no. 488 for record of the trial; also *State Trials* compiled by TB Howell (1816) vol. 1, page 902. The records of the trial, however, are not complete. The Justiciary Court records do not include the trial. *The Books of Adjournal for the Justiciary Court* (which provided the account printed in the C.Scot.P.) have disappeared for cases prior to 1576. There are no papers pertaining to the trial in the records held by the Duke of Argyll.
70 Pitcairn, page 512.
71 C.Scot.P., no. 492; Keith, vol. 2, page 563; Herries, page 88. It is possible that Aynesleyes was a mistake over the old Scots word 'anis' or 'annis' (both used in the plural). According to Dr Jamieson's *Scottish Dictionary*, this came from the Latin *asinus* and meant asses or foolish fellows – perhaps a suitable description of those attending the supper-party. Other contemporary references do not indicate that the party was held in a tavern.
72 C.Scot.P., no. 854; Goodall, vol. 2, page 141. For details of the Queen's Guard see C.S.P.For., no. 710, C.Scot.P., no. 1058 and the *Maitland Miscellany*, vol. 1, part 1 (1833) pages 27–36.
73 *Register of the Privy Council of Scotland*, vol. XIV (1898) page 273.
74 H.M.C., Cecil MSS., Addenda, part 13, page 73 gives details of a procuratory from Lady Jane Gordon appointing her proctors for a cause of divorce intended against Bothwell dated 20 March 1567.
75 C.S.P.Sp., no. 427. The Ambassador did not quote the source for his information.
76 Labanoff, vol. 7, page 317 (Letter to all Christian Princes – 'sua si troveva in grandissimo pericolo').
77 *Register of the Privy Council of Scotland*, vol. 1 (1877) page 340; Dickinson (1949) vol. 2, page 153; Melville page 135; but see also D Hay Fleming, *Mary Queen of Scots* (2nd edition, 1898) page 354 note 16.
78 C.Scot.P., no. 503.

79 C.S.P.Sp., no. 419.

80 C.S.P.R., vol. 2, no. 429. See also C.Scot.P., no. 490 on James Borthwick.

81 C.Scot.P., no. 501.

82 See *Diurnal* for 20 March and 8 May 1567.

83 C.S.P.R., vol. 2, no. 429.

84 *Register of the Privy Council for Scotland*, vol. 1 (1877) page 276; Keith, vol. 2, page 592.

85 C.S.P.For., no. 1173; Dickinson (1949) vol. 2, page 205; also C.S.P.Sp., no. 419.

86 It seems that the Nobility and Subjects of Aberdeen wrote on 27 April to the Queen offering their help. It is likely that Lethington took a copy of the letter which became part of the Lauderdale Papers. These were dispersed in the early nineteenth century. Some of them came into the possession of W Stevenson Fitch. A copy of the letter was printed at the back of Maitland's *Narrative* edited by Fitch and published in 1833. It is also shown in *The Memorials of Mary Stewart* edited by J Stevenson (1883) and FA Mumby's *The Fall of Mary Stuart* (1921). The National Library of Scotland now has the sixteenth-century copy of the letter (reference MS 3922 f.128) which had been in Fitch's collection of papers. It is not known what happened to the original letter or whether Mary received it or when Lethington had access to it. For further details on the history of the Aberdeen letter see the article on the Lauderdale Papers 1561–1570 by Dr Simon Adams in the *Scottish Historical Review* (1988).

87 Teulet (1862) vol. 2, page 297.

88 C.S.P.For., no. 1226.

89 See Chapter 2, note 10; and also C.S.P.For., no. 1289 and no. 1292, and references to the episode in Nau, the *Hopetoun Manuscript*, Knox's *Continuator* and Moray's *Diary* for further details and variations.

90 Teulet (1862) vol. 2, page 300.

91 C.Scot.P., no. 563. See also C.S.P.For., no. 1470 on Mary's danger at this time from her opponents.

92 For further discussion on Mary's pregnancy see AS MacNalty, *Mary Queen of Scots* (1960), page 220 and Sir John Dewhurst's article in the *Review of Scottish Culture* no. 3 (1987).

93 C.S.P.For., no. 1304.

4. Theory: Possible conspiracies

1 C.S.P.Sp., no. 408; see also Teulet (1862), vol. 5, page 20.

2 C.S.P.Sp., no. 417.

3 See Mahon (1930) page 278, Gore-Browne, page 296, and Davison, chapter 2.

4 *Scottish Historical Review*, vol. 34.

5 C.Scot.P., nos 407 and 464.

6 C.Scot.P., no. 389.

7 C.S.P.Sp., no. 390.
8 C.S.P.Sp., no. 403.
9 C.S.P.R., no. 406.
10 Nau, page cxlv.
11 C.S.P.R., no. 395. See also Keith, vol. 3, page 460 (letter of 20 October 1566 from Robert Melville in London to the Archbishop of Glasgow in Paris). Melville asserted that Darnley wanted Lethington (the Secretary), Bellenden (the Justice-Clerk) and MacGill (Clerk Register) to be put out of their offices, alleging they were guilty of Riccio's murder, but the Queen had found them not guilty.
12 C.S.P.R., no. 414.
13 Nau, Appendix 1, page 123.
14 Teulet (1862), vol. 2, page 289.
15 Keith, vol. 1, page xcix.
16 C.S.P.R., no. 381.
17 C.S.P.R., no. 395.
18 C.S P.R., no. 405.
19 C.S.P.R., no. 429.
20 C.Scot.P., no. 478.
21 C.S.P.R., no. 435.
22 C.S.P.R., no. 477. For a sympathetic interpretation of Lethington see William Blake, *William Maitland of Lethington* (1990).
23 Laing, vol. 2, page 366.
24 C.Scot.P., no. 947. (This includes Moray's reply.)
25 Goodall, vol. 2, page 354.
26 C.S.P.Sp., no. 402.
27 Laing, vol. 2, page 366.
28 *Maitland Club Miscellany*, vol. 4, part 1 (1847) page 120.
29 C.S.P.For., vol. 8, no. 1792.
30 C.S.P.For., vol. 9, no. 1334. There is also an interesting reference to 'the band in the green box' in C.Scot.P., no. 751 for 16 March 1581.
31 Laing, vol. 2, page 354.
32 C.Scot.P., no. 478. See also Herries, page 83 on Moray going to St Andrews.
33 C.S.P.For., no. 977.
34 C.S.P.R., no. 442.
35 C.Scot.P., no. 484.
36 Labanoff, vol. 7, page 105.
37 Labanoff, vol. 5, page 137.
38 C.Scot.P., no. 400.
39 C.S.P.For., no. 977, but consider also C.S.P.For., no. 1053 (despatch from Drury to Cecil dated 29 March 1567) about the powder being brought from Dunbar (where Bothwell was the Governor of the Castle) and John Hepburn's deposition (Pitcairn, page 498) which also said it was brought from Dunbar. Drury on 29 March made the cryptic statement that 'the men are well known who brought the powder from Dunbar', and he had spoken with those who had dealt with them.

40 C.S.P.For., no. 1116.
41 C.Scot.P., no. 544.
42 Keith, vol. 1, page ciii; see also *Revue Historique*, vol. 37, page 42.
43 J Stevenson, *Selections from Unpublished Manuscripts* (Maitland Club, 1837), page 173.
44 Labanoff, vol. 2, page 6.
45 *Cabala (Mysteries of State and Government)* 1663 and 1691 editions.
46 C.S.P.For., no. 996. In this context 'regiment' would mean 'control'.
47 C.S.P.For., no.1063. One of the suspected persons might have been Bastien who, according to a letter from Captain Cockburn in Dieppe to Cecil on 19 March 1567, had arrived there with his wife on 6 March (C.S.P.For., no. 1032). Bastien was the Queen's servant who was married on 9 February, but it is difficult to believe that he took part in the murder of Darnley later that night.
48 C.S.P.Sp., no. 396.
49 C.S.P.Sp., no. 408.
50 Keith, vol. 1, page xcvii.
51 Letter dated 27 February 1567 to the Constable of Montmorency, *Lettres de Catherine de Médicis, Collection de Documents Inédits*, published by H de la Ferrière-Percy, vol. III (1887) page 14.
52 J Stevenson, *Selections from Unpublished Manuscripts* (Maitland Club, 1837) page 165; C.S.P.For., no. 625.
53 Teulet (1862) vol. 5, pages 12–17.
54 C.S.P.For., no. 1502.
55 JB Black, *The Reign of Elizabeth* (1959) pages 92 and 93; and note 4 above.
56 C.S.P.For., no. 872.
57 Keith, vol. 2, page 702; C.S.P.For., no. 1526.
58 Scot. P., no. 477.

5. The Discovery and Disclosure of the Casket Letters

1 Dickinson (1949) vol. 2, page 212; Gatherer, page 147.
2 Published in TF Henderson, *The Casket Letters and Mary Queen of Scots* (1889).
3 C.Scot.P., no. 528. See also C.Scot.P., no 537 – letter from Queen Elizabeth to Mary Queen of Scots dated 30 June 1567. Elizabeth referred to Robert Melville as Mary's faithful servant who used much earnest speech on her behalf, but unfortunately she did not record the details.
4 C.S.P.Sp., no. 431.
5 See Mahon (1924) pages 143–144; Davison, page 74.
6 C.S.P.Sp., no. 432.
7 C.Scot.P., no. 554.
8 C.S.P.For., no. 1509.
9 C.S.P.Sp., no. 434.
10 *Acts of the Parliaments of Scotland* (ed. T Thomson) vol. III (1814).

11 C.Scot.P., no. 632.

12 C.S.P.Sp., no. 434.

13 For detailed analysis of the 'suppressed letter' see Lang (1901) pages 215–229 and Mahon (1924) pages 98 and 136–137.

14 C.Scot.P., no. 711 (Moray's enquiry); C.Scot.P., no. 721 (Cecil's notes dated 30 June 1568). Cecil considered that it would not be sufficient if the originals accorded with the copies, but that both parties must be heard.

15 C.Scot.P., no. 730.

16 Labanoff, vol. 2, page 193.

17 Melville, page 206.

18 *Register of the Privy Council of Scotland*, vol. 1 (1877) page 641.

19 C.Scot.P., no. 854.

20 See Appendix 4.

21 C.Scot.P., no. 854.

22 See Hosack, vol. 2, Preface, pages xi-xiii and page 497.

23 HMC, Cecil MSS, vol. 1, page 369.

24 See Donaldson (1969) for analysis of the *Book of Articles*.

25 C.Scot.P., no. 912.

26 C.Scot.P., no. 913.

27 C.Scot.P., no. 916.

28 See C.Scot.P., no. 854, page 526 for reference to the alleged warrant.

29 Peter D Anderson's *Robert Stewart, Earl of Orkney, Lord of Shetland* (1982) pages 45–49.

30 C.Scot.P., no. 916.

31 Goodall, vol. 2, page 256.

32 Goodall, vol. 2, pages 258–259.

33 C.Scot.P., no. 921.

34 Teulet (1852) vol. 2, page 237.

35 C.Scot.P., no. 839.

36 Haynes, *Collection of State Papers* (1740) page 52.

37 C.Scot.P., no. 908.

38 Keith, vol. 1, page cxv.

39 Goodall, vol. 2, pages 337–343.

40 C.Scot.P., no. 928.

41 Lang (1901) page 282 on those opposed to Cecil; and Hosack, vol. 1, pages 457–458 on Cecil's attitude.

42 *Register of the Privy Council of Scotland*, vol. XIV (1898) page 89. There is a gap in the *Register* after December 1569 until early September 1571. The reason for this is not known. It was filled to some extent by including in vol. XIV material from the Haddington MSS. Thomas Hamilton, the King's Advocate, was admitted to the Privy Council in 1596. He made and retained copies of certain earlier Privy Council records. In 1627 he became the Earl of Haddington.

43 *Surtees Society*, vol. XIV: 'The Correspondence of Robert Bowes' (1842). See Bowes' letters to Walsingham dated 8, 12, and 24 November and 2 December 1582.

44 *Register of the Great Seal of Scotland*, vol. IV (1866) edited by JM Thomson, no. 2640; *Register of the Privy Seal of Scotland*, vol. VII (1966) edited by G Donaldson, no. 891 for references to James Douglas' appointment at Pluscarden.

45 See Lang (1901) Chapter XVIII on the casket at Lennoxlove; also Davison, page 97.

46 See Introduction, page 3.

47 See Introduction, page 3.

48 This letter is in *The Compleat Ambassador*, compiled by Sir Dudley Digges (1665). Burghley sent a little Treatise 'newly printed in Latin, in commending or discommending the Queen of Scots' actions, to further her marriage with Bothwell'. He added that he had heard 'it is to be translated into English, with addition of many other supplements of like condition'. The reference to 'other supplements' implies that this edition contained more than the *Detection*. Burghley's letter obviously points to his complicity in the publications.

49 *George Buchanan – Glasgow Quatercentenary Studies* (1907) edited by G Neilson, pages 440–441.

50 McFarlane's *Buchanan* (1981) page 349; *Collection de Documents Inédits*, vol. IV (1891) published by H de la Ferrière-Percy, page 92, letter dated 22 March 1572 from Catherine de Medici to M de Thou, President of the Parlement of Paris, asking him to seize and burn secretly and without fuss copies of this book. It was falsely shown as having been published in Edinburgh.

51 See Mahon (1923) page 16; Donaldson (1969) page 220; and McFarlane (1981) pages 344–347 for further discussion on these points.

6. A Study of the Casket Letters

1 James Whitaker, *Mary Queen of Scots Vindicated* (1787) vol. 3, page 1.

2 C.Scot.P., pages 722–730. There is a copy of the Original French version of Letter V in the PRO in London (SP 53/2 no. 63) and the statement to the contrary at the top of page 730 in the Calendar of Scottish Papers is incorrect.

3 Lekprevik's edition is contained in Anderson, vol. 2.

4 See Appendix 1, page 191.

5 Goodall, vol. 2, page 360.

6 J Leslie, *A defence of the honour of Mary Queen of Scotland*. It is not known how and when he obtained this information, as at that time the Letters had not been published.

7 See Sir Edward Parry, *The Persecution of Mary Stewart* (1931) page 305.

8 C.Scot.P., no. 916.

9 See Letter II, English translation, note 22 and Letter VI, English translation, note 1 (Appendix 1).

10 See Letter I, English translation, note 1 and Letter IV, Scots translation, note 6 (Appendix 1).

11 For further comments on Mary's poetic ability see David Angus' article in

Review of Scottish Culture, no. 3 (1987). His view (based on her authentic work) was that she was a polished sonneteer. Robin Bell in 'Bittersweet Within My Heart' (1992) saw several similarities between the Sonnets and Mary's authentic poetry and regarded them essentially as genuine.

LETTER I

1 *Maitland Miscellany*, vol. 4, part 1 (1847) page 119.
2 See Mahon (1924) pages 112–113 on 'l'homme' in relation to Darnley and Prince James.
3 Gore-Browne, pages 281–283, suggested Saturday 30 November.
4 See C.S.P.For., no. 850, letter from Sir John Forster at Berwick to Cecil dated 11 December 1566: 'Bothwell is appointed to receive the ambassadors, and all things for the christening is [sic] at his appointment'.
5 Keith, vol. 1, page XCVI (Letter from du Croc to the Archbishop of Glasgow).
6 Mahon (1924) page 105. Davison also favoured this date.

LETTER II

1 See Lang (1901) page 299.
2 See Lang (1901) page 301.
3 *Register of the Privy Council of Scotland*, vol. 1 (1877) page 379.
4 Teulet (1862) vol. 2, page 268 shows a list compiled for payments from her income in 1567.
5 Labanoff, vol. 1, page 392; C.Scot.P., nos 465 and 466; C.S.P.For., nos 906, 931 and 977.
6 C.S.P.For., no. 1243.
7 C.S.P.For., no. 1226.
8 I am very grateful to Mr GR Dalgleish of the National Museums of Scotland and Dr RK Marshall for advice on this. See Dr Marshall's article on 'Mary Queen of Scots and Bothwell's bracelets' in the *Proceedings of the Society of Antiquaries of Scotland*, vol. 127 (1997) pages 889–898.
9 See Appendix 4.
10 C.Scot.P., no. 474.
11 Hamilton Papers, in *Maitland Club Miscellany*, vol. 4, part 1 (1847) page 119.
12 JB Black, *Andrew Lang and the Casket Letter Controversy* (1951) pages 27–28.
13 See Mahon (1924) page 136; Chauviré, *Revue Historique*, no. 174, page 458; W Fraser, *The Lennox*, vol. 1 (1874) page 469 on how Mary and Darnley may have conversed.

14 Lang's article on the Casket Letters in the *Encyclopaedia Britannica*, 11th edition (1910).

15 Davison, page 115, suggested Moray as the recipient; Gore-Browne, page 295, suggested that she wrote to Lethington. Either Moray or Lethington could subsequently have produced such a letter as the basis for Letter II.

Letter III

1 See section in Chapter 3 page 17, on Mary's relationship with Bothwell.

Letter IV

1 See Melville, page 174; also Chapter 3, page 44.
2 See Appendix 4.
3 *The Bannatyne Manuscript*, Part 5, page 706, compiled by George Bannatyne (1568) printed for the Hunterian Club (1879).
4 See A Fraser, *Mary Queen of Scots* (1969 hardback edition) page 400.
5 P Hume Brown (ed.) *Vernacular Writings of George Buchanan* (1892) page 39; Richard Bannatyne, *Memorials of Transactions in Scotland 1569–1573* (Bannatyne Club Edition, 1837) page 43.
6 C.Scot.P., no. 488.

Letter V

1 *Register of the Privy Seal of Scotland* (1957) vol. 5, page 270 for 8 February 1567, awarding Margaret Carwod a lifetime pension of 300 merks for her good, true and thankful service and describing her as a beloved familiar servant. *Accounts of the Treasurer of Scotland* (1970) vol. 12, page 41 for 10 February 1567 – gift of black velvet for her wedding; page 46 for 23 March 1567 – gift of fine cloth. See also J Robertson, *Inventaires de la Royne d'Escosse* (1863) Bannatyne Club, Preface, page lvii note. Margaret was one of the co-heiresses of Carwod or Carwood about $1^1/_2$ miles north of Biggar in Lanarkshire.
2 See Lang (1901) pages 329 and 390.

Letter VI

1 C.S.P.For., no. 1150.

2 See Davison, pages 187–188 for a detailed examination of this passage. He concluded that 'vous m'amenies' did really mean 'you brought me'.

3 See Lang (1901) page 330.

LETTER VII

1 Lang (1901) page 360.

2 Davison, pages 200–205.

3 A Postulate held high office without being confirmed in it. George Douglas was known as the Postulate of Arbroath Abbey. See John Dowden, *The Bishops of Scotland* (1912) pages 412–413.

4 C.S.P.For., nos 1792 and 2106.

5 D Hay Fleming, *Mary Queen of Scots* (2nd edition, 1898) pages 511–512 gives the inventory of what was sent to her on 5 May, and see also Fleming page 485.

6 On 3 March 1577, the Laird of Lochleven wrote a vitriolic letter to the Regent Morton rebuking him for his faults including his harlotry, ambition and avariciousness. In a reference to Queen Mary he said: 'there ran no vice in her, but that the same is largely in you, except that your grace condescended not to the destruction of your wife'. W Robertson, *The History of Scotland*, vol. 2 (1827) Appendix no. XL.

LETTER VIII

1 See Chapter 3, note 74. The Marriage Contract of 5 April stated that the process had already begun.

2 C.Scot.P., no. 503.

3 Davison, pages 192–197.

4 C.Scot.P., no. 541.

5 J Stevenson, *Selections from Unpublished Manuscripts* (Maitland Club, 1837) page 233.

THE MARRIAGE CONTRACTS

1 C.Scot.P., Appendix 2, page 730.

2 Mary referred to him as the King; an exception is in the Protestation sent to Huntly and Argyll, where he is referred to as 'Henry Stewart, her Majesty's husband'.

3 C.Scot.P., no. 912.

4 Davison, page 222.

5 C.Scot.P., no. 912.

6 C.Scot.P., no. 854.

THE SONNETS

1 Gore-Browne, page 105.
2 For references to William see the *Bannatyne Miscellany*, vol. 3 (1855) page 423 and *The Register of Privy Council of Scotland*, vol. 2, page 105.
2 HF Diggle, *The Casket Letters* (1960) pages 107–108.
4 Letter to Catherine de Medici dated 5 December 1571 in *Recueil des Dépêches etc des Ambassadeurs de France*, edited by C Purton Cooper (Bannatyne Club, 1840).

7. An Assessment of the Casket Letters

1 Melville, pages 182–183.

8. Mary's Own Version

1 James E Phillips, *Images of a Queen* (1964) pages 86–87.
2 Keith, vol. 1, page XCIX.
3 C.Scot.P., no. 702.
4 *Register of the Privy Council for Scotland*, vol. XIV (1898) page 273.
5 C.S.P.R., no. 763.
6 Lang (1901) in pages 247–250 discussed the allegation that during the Conference at York Lethington sent translated copies of the Casket Letters in Scots to Mary at Bolton, and the repudiation of this by Robert Melville. Lang asked whom do you believe?
7 Labanoff, vol. 4, page 3: Mary also requested that her defence be published in France.
8 It is not clear which edition of the *Detection* was passed to her, but probably it was the Latin version with only Letters I, II and IV. Mahon (1923) expressed his doubt that any of the Casket Letters were included in the version of the *Detection* passed to Mary and gave his reasons, but he admitted that an edition of the *Detection* without any of the Casket Letters could not be traced.

Appendix 1: Texts of the eight Casket Letters

Letter I – Scots translation from Lekprevik's *Detection*

1 'yame' means 'them'.
2 Possibly the translator mistook 'signer' for 'saigner', and the real meaning was that Mary would sign state papers in Edinburgh.
3 'Summa' would be 'En somme' in French, meaning 'in short' or 'the main point'.

4 'Gif' means 'if'.

5 'ane day of law' means 'a hearing in court'. It is not known where this was to take place, nor whether Beaton was John Beaton (the Master of the Queen's Household who died in 1570) or Archibald Beaton (the Queen's Usher). The Laird of Balfour (in Fife) was also a Beaton and should not be confused with James Balfour.

Letter I – English translation at the Public Record Office

1 English version correctly omits 'from time to time' (shown in Scots version) after 'newes from you', and adds 'nevertheles I can learn none'.

2 The Scots translation places the opening phrase at the end of the previous sentence.

3 Ledinton – a reference to Lethington.

Letter II – Scots translation from Lekprevik's *Detection*

1 'mekle' (muckle) means much, large.

2 'purpois': this word is shown several times in the Scots translation (eg paragraphs 16, 19, 20 and 28). It is presumably a translation of the French 'propos' which can mean purpose, subject, matter, talk etc. In this paragraph it seems to mean 'talk'. 'Zit' means 'yet'.

3 'Cuninghame' was probably Robert Cunningham, Lennox's supporter, who later appeared on his behalf at the trial of Bothwell, or possibly Alexander Cunningham, Earl of Glencairn, who was a leading opponent of Mary in 1567. 'The rude words' spoken to him probably means harsh or sharp words.

4 If the English translation is correct, 'he suld come' should be 'I suld come'.

5 The person who heard of the Queen's coming was presumably Lennox.

6 The sentence 'I se na uther gentilman but thay of my company' is omitted in the English.

7 In the Anglicised Scots translation included in early editions of the *Detection* there is a marginal note opposite the references to Paris and Gilbert: 'This berer will tell you somewhat upon this'. The phrase 'write to me' is meaningless. Probably it should have been 'write for her', referring just to Gilbert Curle as according to the declaration by Alexander Hay at the end of Paris' second deposition Paris seems to have been unable to read even French and could not have written letters for the Queen.

8 'I am abaschit' means 'I wonder'.

9 'plenzeit' means 'complained'.

10 'that quhilk I ever denyit' is possibly a reference to Darnley's participation in the murder of Riccio. If so, it reveals his lack of sincerity in January 1567.

11 Read 'too' for 'to'.

12 'lacke' means 'failure'.

13 'tyne' means 'lose'.

14 Minto was a friend of Lennox.
15 After the sentence ending 'upon this point' Andrew Lang (1901) page 301 suggested the insertion of paragraph 13 from 'This is my first jornay' to the sentence 'I am doing of ane work heir that I hait greitly' together with the words 'but I had begon it this morning' which appear only in the English translation. He suggested that this had occurred because she had written a list of headings before she began the Letter (see paragraph 16). The next morning she resumed writing but on the reverse side of the sheet with those headings. As a result her notes were incorporated into the Letter together with the opening lines of paragraph 13 written below the notes on the previous night, but Lang's reconstruction is not convincing.
16 Read 'before he did it' for 'or he did it'.
17 passit = travelled.
18 leis = lies.
19 luifis = loves.
20 abasche = marvel.
21 walk = watch.
22 'the place' can mean 'the fortress' in French and Scots.
23 wyn = won.
24 'travell' is probably a mistranslation from 'travailler' (to work).
25 'presage' may imply that Lennox was having 'cold feet' as the French idiom 'saigner du nez' means 'to be afraid'.
26 In paragraph 26 it is again stated that Darnley's father was staying in his room.
27 treuth betwix handis = between times.
28 twichit = touched.
29 allanerly = only.
30 pleinzing = complaining.
31 The first two sentences in this paragraph seem out of place here but would fit at the end of paragraph 11.
32 For 'Bybill' read 'letter' (French billet). Presumably the English translator copied this error in the Scots translation.
33 'faschit' means 'troubled, vexed, annoyed'.
34 'utheris' means 'each other'.
35 'irkit' means 'tired'. The translators into the Latin and subsequently the Published French versions made the error of reading 'irkit' as 'nakit'. Their readers must have been amazed at the implied state of the Queen.
36 'Waryit mot this pockische man be' means 'cursed may this pocked-marked man be', (referring to Darnley's disfigurement from small-pox).
37 Bothwell had no uncle. It may have been reference to his great-uncle the Bishop of Moray, who was not a saintly type, or perhaps this part of the Letter was addressed to someone other than Bothwell.
38 'gait' means 'way'.
39 'purpois': see note 2.
40 'mater' means 'business'. The reference to Hiegait seems to be separate from the phrase 'of his departing'.

41 'fascherie' means 'trouble', but here it seems to indicate 'disgruntlement'.

42 'quhill' means 'till'.

43 'in the meane tyme' is shown in the English translation at the start of the next clause.

44 'fascheous purpois' means 'troublesome matter'.

45 'gar' means 'force', and 'horring' means 'abhorrence'.

46 'quhil uther morne' means 'till to-morrow'.

47 'braifly' means 'bravely'.

48 'fenze' means 'feign'.

49 'chekis' means 'checks, reproofs, reproaches', but the meaning of the passage is obscure.

50 'thame' seems to be an error. The meaning is probably that it is 'ready otherwise' or 'ready for them'. The word 'thame' meaning 'them' also appears in paragraphs 9, 12, 17, 20 and 25.

51 Those who were 'out' were Morton and others who had taken part in the murder of Riccio and had fled to exile in England, but by this time they had returned to Scotland. A curious error.

52 'chalmer' means 'chamber'.

53 This sentence may have been the original end of the Letter. The subsequent passages were possibly the original conclusion of Letter V which ends abruptly. It is curious that the sentence was omitted in the English translation. It may refer to the degree of trust placed by Mary on the bearer of the Letter (see also paragraph 21).

54 'travellis' means 'toils' (from the French 'travail').

55 'impesche' means 'prevent' or 'hinder'.

Letter II – English translation at the Public Record Office

1 'Yesternight' omitted after 'Joachim'.

2 A blank left thus.

3 Worn off.

4 Worn off.

5 The translator substituted 'troublith my wittes for anger' instead of 'makith me out of my wytt.'

6 Word lost.

7 The translator mistook 'signer' for 'saigner'.

8 'your purpose' written on the margin.

9 The words 'but I had begon it this morning' are not shown in the Scots.

10 'Suderland' is presumably 'Sutherland'.

11 Several words torn off here.

12 After 'nose' the following is shown on the margin: 'I have disclosed all, I have knowen what I wold.' This, however, seems to conflict with the translation of the French idiom 'tirer les vers du nez de quelqu'un' meaning 'to worm secrets out of someone.' The literal translation of the phrase shows

that the English translator was working from the Original French. It is interesting but not conclusive evidence that Mary used this phrase in a letter she wrote to Bishop Leslie on 5 October 1568 (C.Scot.P., no. 837).

13 The English phrase 'goodyeere' at that time may have been used either to signify the expectation that things would become better or as an imprecation such as 'What the devil.' The latter usage would be in line with the Scots version. Perhaps the English translator was translating either the Original French or the Scots version into an idiomatic English phrase. As the Original French is not available, it is impossible to be sure of the precise translation. There remains, however, the question whether the Queen (or even the French lady) would have called on the devil to help her. The authenticity of the passage must be queried.

14 The translator originally put 'so long the same is' but substituted 'so much I have to write.'

15 'Arayde': the French 'recu' (from recevoir) was misread by the translator as 'vêtu' (from vêtir). See the Scots version for a clearer translation.

16 Words torn off.

17 The four words 'Gesse you the rest' may have been said by Livingstone, but the phrase 'Gesse you' also appears in paragraph 24.

18 Words torn off.

19 The words 'by and by' were written above 'at one instant'.

20 'avowe' is italicised. It is not clear what Mary was to disclose.

21 The sentence 'Now as farre … be suspected' is not shown in the Scots version. Cecil wrote in the margin: 'Jay bien la vogue avec vous.'

22 The words 'As for the rest' are not in the Scots version. 'Wood' is a mis-translation of the Scots word 'wod' meaning 'enraged'. The English translator made the same error in Letter VI, but it is curious that he made such an error in Letter II as the Scots version in Letter II did not use the Scots word 'wod'.

23 Some words were crossed out but an inserted word 'my' was not deleted. Compare with the Scots translation.

24 Several words torn off at the end of the Letter, but see the Scots trans-lation.

Letter III – Copy of the Original French at the Public Record Office

1 Read 'ne' for 'me'.
2 Reseves = receives.
3 There is a similar passage about kissing the recipient's hands in paragraph 28 of Letter II.

Letter III – Scots translation from Lekprevik's *Detection*

1 'sic' means 'such'.

2 The ornament of the head was presumably a lock of hair.

3 For 'gude' read 'guide'.

4 'seising' means 'placing'.

5 'heart' should be 'hair' or 'lock'.

6 'ameling' means 'enamelling'.

7 The reference to the 'credit' given to the bearer should be compared with a similar allusion in paragraph 21 of Letter II – see GM Thomson, *The Crime of Mary Stuart* (1967) page 164.

Letter IV – Copy of the Original French version at Hatfield

1 The word 'de' is added in the margin by another hand and would be inserted after 'comande'.

2 'ou' is a correction by another hand. The word for which it is substituted is illegible.

3 'truvions' originally written with 'm' and corrected to 'n' by another hand. One 'nous' has been omitted by the copyist. 'Nadjousties' is from 'ajoutir'. The translation of 'quaures' (that you may have) is omitted in the Scots version.

4 'Car j'enseray en pein' should probably be at the end of the preceding sentence.

5 'per' was originally 'pere'. The final 'e' is struck out by another hand.

6 'bastienne' should be 'Bastiane'.

Letter IV – Scots translation from Lekprevik's *Detection*

1 'walk' is Scots for 'watch'.

2 'tirer' should probably be translated not as 'to draw something out of him' but in the sense of 'tracer' (trace, outline) or 'écrire' (write) or 'dessiner' (draw, sketch) which were also meanings of 'tirer' at that time.

3 'the fairest commoditie' could be translated more appropriately as 'the most suitable way'. The English translator followed this error.

4 'ceux' was translated incorrectly as 'hir' instead of 'those'.

5 'thocht' should be 'throch' (through).

6 The English translation is more accurate but the real meaning of this passage is enigmatic.

Letter IV – English translation at Hatfield

1 Illegible word struck off.

2 'for I shall think long' could be translated as 'for I shall be anxious about you.'

3 'father' deleted and 'make' inserted by Cecil, but 'make' should be 'mate'.

Letter V – Copy of the Original French version in the Public Record Office

1 Version in TF Henderson, *The Casket Letters and Mary Queen of Scots* (1889) page 166, omits from 'men' to 'prandray'.
2 'Moys' is 'mais' (but).
3 As there is no proper ending to this Letter, it may have been continued in Letter II at paragraph 27.

Letter V – English translation at the Public Record Office

1 'Hart' is in another hand.

Letter VI – Copy of the Original French version at Hatfield

1 The words 'J'enrasge' inserted in margin by another hand. It would follow 'vostre'.
2 'me' interlined by another hand.
3 'E. of Huntlie' inserted in margin by another hand, referring to 'faulx beau frere'.
4 'auries' is 'aurais'.
5 Alteration by the copier of the Original.
6 The final 'e' of 'amendemente' is struck out.
7 'vous' inserted above the line by the copyist.
8 The 'n' in 'entreprise' is struck out.

Letter VI – Scots translation from Lekprevik's *Detection*

1 'wod' means 'wild'.
2 This could be translated as 'if you yourself did not back out of it'.
3 'differ' means 'defer'.
4 For 'the diligence' read 'haste'.
5 For 'amendment' read 'improvement'.

Letter VI – English translation at Hatfield

1 'wood' should be 'wild'. See also Letter II, English translation, note 22.
2 The correct translation of 'vous m'amenies' is 'you were bringing me'.
3 'amendment' would be more correctly shown as 'improvement'. In this context the French 'amendemente' means 'passage à un état meilleur'.
4 'ces incertains Nouvelles' should be translated as 'this uncertain news' instead of 'these new ceremonies'.
5 The deletion of 'after' and interlining of 'afore' is in Cecil's hand.

Letter VII – Scots translation from Lekprevik's *Detection*

1 Possibly the meaning is 'I understand it to be well devised', but the passage is not clear.
2 'forane' = 'foreign'.
3 'let' = 'hinder'.

Letter VIII – Scots translation from Lekprevik's *Detection*

1 The 1572 Scots translation printed the opening lines of the Letter in the Original French. This showed 'apres demain' for 'efter to morne'.
2 The forfeiture of the Earl of Sutherland for supporting the previous Earl of Huntly in the rebellion of 1562 had been formally rescinded by Act of Parliament on 19 April 1567, though Sutherland had returned to royal favour in 1566.

Initial lines in the Original French

1 'ceu' is corrected to 'veu' in other early editions of the *Detection* and in the Published French version, meaning 'seeing that'.
2 The copy of the Original French version at the PRO shows 'promis' instead of 'prouvé'.
3 It seems that Mary did not use accents in her letters. The accents shown in early editions of the *Detection* were added by a copyist or the printer.

Appendix 2: Texts of the Marriage Contracts

(A) The undated French Contract

1 C.Scot.P., vol. II, page 730.
2 Although the Contract was alleged to have been signed by the Queen, it was apparently undated.

(C) The Contract of 5 April

1 From Lekprevik's *Detection*.
2 'thir presentis' means 'these documents'.
3 'oblisis' means 'binds'.

Appendix 3: Texts of the Sonnets

1 'las' means 'alas'.

2 'issir' is now an old, rare verb equivalent in the sixteenth century to 'sortir' or 'provenir'.

3 'face' should presumably be 'fasse' (from the verb 'faire').

4 The reference to a tiresome fool may allude to Alexander Ogilvy, whom Lady Jane Gordon had wished to marry before her marriage to Bothwell. He eventually became her third husband.

5 'doig' should presumably be 'deuil' (mourning clothes) implying that Lady Jane was still wearing mourning for losing Ogilvy.

6 'paour' is 'peur' (fear).

7 'peaur' is also 'peur'.

8 'mary' is 'mari'.

9 'heur' is 'bonheur'.

10 Although there is no evidence to indicate that Lady Jane was a blue-stocking, she was at least able to write, unlike many of her contemporaries. See J Stuart, *A Lost Chapter in the History of Mary Queen of Scots Recovered* (1874) page 33.

11 'ains' is 'ainsi'.

12 'envoy' is 'envie' (longing, desire).

13 'que le voy' should probably be 'que je vois'.

14 'heur' is 'bonheur'.

15 'suyvre' is 'suivre'.

16 'mainte dragme' means 'many drops' (of blood).

17 'lesser' may be 'léser' (wound, injure etc).

18 'rempar' is 'rempart' (rampart).

Appendix 4: Extracts from the Casket Letters sent to Queen Elizabeth from York in October 1568

1 See Goodall, vol. 2, page 148.

2 From Letter II, paragraph 12.

3 From Letter II, paragraphs 13 and 19.

4 From Letter II, paragraphs 20 and 21. The full Scots and English translations, however, do not state she was remitting herself to 'the pleasure' of Bothwell. The Notes drawn from the Queen's Letters also add those two words.

5 From Letter II, paragraphs 26 and 27.

6 From Letter I, paragraphs 2 and 4, and Letter IV, paragraph 4.

7 Goodall, vol. 2, page 150.

INDEX